Global Food Security and Development Aid

T0291151

At the global level, international actors have repeatedly expressed their desire to end hunger and food insecurity. However, food insecurity has persisted. More analysis is hence needed on the link between continuously high levels of global food insecurity and the ever increasing flow of development aid.

Global Food Security and Development Aid investigates the impact that development aid has had on food security in developing countries and includes international case studies on Peru, Ethiopia, India and Vietnam. It examines the effect of development aid in general and the impact of aid divided into different categories based on donor, mechanism and sector to which it is provided. In each examined relationship between aid and food security, particular attention is paid to the potentially intervening role played by the quality of national and/or local governance. The book makes policy recommendations, most importantly that donors should take greater care in considering which types of aid are suitable to which specific countries, localities and development goals, and account for expected developments in the complex relationship between aid, food security and governance.

This book will be of considerable interest to students, researchers and policy-makers in the areas of development aid and food security.

Ivica Petrikova is Lecturer in International Relations and Development at the Royal Holloway, University of London, UK.

Routledge Explorations in Development Studies

This Development Studies series features innovative and original research at the regional and global scale.

It promotes interdisciplinary scholarly works drawing on a wide spectrum of subject areas, in particular politics, health, economics, rural and urban studies, sociology, environment, anthropology and conflict studies.

Topics of particular interest are globalization; emerging powers; children and youth; cities; education; media and communication; technology development; and climate change.

In terms of theory and method, rather than basing itself on any orthodoxy, the series draws broadly on the tool kit of the social sciences in general, emphasizing comparison, the analysis of the structure and processes, and the application of qualitative and quantitative methods.

The Domestic Politics of Foreign Aid
Erik Lundsgaarde

Social Protection in Developing Countries
Reforming Systems
Katja Bender, Markus Kaltenborn and Christian Pfleiderer

Formal Peace and Informal War
Security and Development in Congo
Zoë Marriage

Technology Development Assistance for Agriculture
Putting Research into Use in Low Income Countries
Norman Clark, Andy Frost, Ian Maudlin and Andrew Ward

Statelessness and Citizenship
Camps and the Creation of Political Space
Victoria Redclift

Governance for Pro-Poor Urban Development
Lessons from Ghana
Franklin Obeng-Odoom

Nationalism, Law and Statelessness
Grand Illusions in the Horn of Africa
John R. Campbell

Evaluation Methodologies for Aid in Conflict
Edited by Ole Winckler Andersen, Beate Bull and Megan Kennedy-Chouane

Digital Technologies for Democratic Governance in Latin America
Opportunities and Risks
Edited by Anita Breuer and Yanina Welp

Governance Reform in Africa
International and Domestic Pressures and Counter-Pressures
Jérôme Bachelard

Economic Development and Political Action in the Arab World
M. A. Mohamed Salih

Development and Welfare Policy in South Asia
Edited by Gabriele Koehler and Deepta Chopra

Confronting Land and Property Problems for Peace
Edited by Shinichi Takeuchi

Socio-Economic Insecurity in Emerging Economies
Building New Spaces
Edited by Khayaat Fakier and Ellen Ehmke

Foreign Aid and Emerging Powers
Asian Perspectives on Official Development Assistance
Iain Watson

The Political Ecology of Climate Change Adaptation
Livelihoods, Agrarian Change and the Conflicts of Development
Marcus Taylor

China's Foreign Relations and the Survival of Autocracies
Julia Bader

Democratic Accountability and Human Development
Regimes, Institutions and Resources
Kamran Ali Afzal and Mark Considine

Rural Livelihoods in China
Edited by Heather Xiaoquan Zhang

Global Food Security and Development Aid
Ivica Petrikova

Global Food Security and Development Aid

Ivica Petrikova

Routledge
Taylor & Francis Group

LONDON AND NEW YORK

First published 2017
by Routledge

2 Park Square, Milton Park, Abingdon, Oxfordshire OX14 4RN
711 Third Avenue, New York, NY 10017

Routledge is an imprint of the Taylor & Francis Group, an informa business

First issued in paperback 2018

British Library Cataloguing-in-Publication Data
A catalogue record for this book is available from the British Library

Library of Congress Cataloging-in-Publication Data
Names: Petrikova, Ivica, author.
Title: Global food security and development aid / Ivica Petrikova.
Description: New York, NY : Routledge, 2017. | Includes bibliographical
references.
Identifiers: LCCN 2016021684| ISBN 9781138683433 (hb) |
ISBN 9781315544496 (ebook)
Subjects: LCSH: Food security–Developing countries. | Hunger–
Developing countries–Prevention. | Economic assistance–Developing
countries. | Economic development–International cooperation.
Classification: LCC HD9000.6 .P487 2017 | DDC 338.191724–dc23
LC record available at https://lccn.loc.gov/2016021684

ISBN: 978-1-138-68343-3 (hbk)
ISBN: 978-1-138-61523-6 (pbk)

Typeset in Times
by Cenveo Publisher Services

Contents

List of tables, figures and boxes   vi
Acknowledgements   ix
List of abbreviations   x

Introduction   1

1 Development aid, governance and food security   7

2 Methodology, data and methods   44

3 Cross-country view   53

4 Peru, India, Ethiopia and Vietnam   79

5 Aid, governance and food security from the
   recipients' perspective   120

6 Up close and personal in Uttar Pradesh, India   149

7 Does *who* gives aid *where* and *how* affect food security?   176

Conclusion   202
Index   204

List of tables, figures and boxes

Tables

1.1	Factors with influence on food security	30
3.1	Summary statistics of all the variables utilised	57
3.2	The effect of aid on food security and the conditioning effect of governance (FE, 2SLS and GMM models)	61
3.3	Disaggregating the governance term	64
3.4	Sensitivity analysis: substituting WGI with *polity2*, ODA per GDP with net ODA per capita and including remittances and aid squared	66
3.5	The impact of *who* gives aid on recipients' food security	68
3.6	The impact of *how* aid is provided on recipients' food security	70
3.7	The impact of *where* aid is provided on recipients' food security	72
4.1	General trends in net aid provision between 1990 and 2010	90
4.2	Overview of economic and trade control variables	103
4.3	Overview of agricultural control variables	104
4.4	Overview of population and environmental control variables	106
5.1	Descriptive statistics of outcome indicators	123
5.2	Descriptive statistics of project types and governance	127
5.3	Descriptive statistics of control variables	128
5.4	The impact of project aid, conditioned on local governance, on recipients' food security	134
5.5	The impact of donor type, conditioned on local governance, on food security	136
5.6	The impact of credit vs non-credit aid, conditioned on local governance, on food security	138
5.7	The impact of food vs non-food aid, conditioned on local governance, on food security	140
5.8	The impact of aid to different sectors, conditioned on local governance, on food security	141
5.9	The impact of emergency, short- and long-term aid, conditioned on governance, on food security	143
6.1	Descriptive statistics of all variables used	158

6.2	The impact of aid on recipients' food security and the conditioning effect of governance	164
6.3	The impact of credit vs non-credit aid on recipients' food security	165
6.4	The heterogeneous impact of the various GDS components on food security	166
6.5	The heterogeneous impact of ration cards on food security	169
6.6	The impact of two/three aid initiatives combined on recipients' food security	170

Figures

1.1	Basic food security scheme	9
1.2	Aid categorisation displayed graphically	12
1.3	Theoretical conjectures vis-à-vis the effect of development aid on food security	19
1.4	Graphic summary of the expected effects of different types of aid on food security	29
2.1	Graphic depiction of the book's four different studies	45
3.1	Marginal effect of aid on undernourishment (90% c.i.)	62
3.2	Marginal effect of aid on stunting (90% c.i.)	63
4.1	The relationship between aid and food security (1990–2010)	80
4.2	The direct and indirect effects of aid on food security	82
4.3	Prevalence of undernourishment	84
4.4	Depth of hunger	84
4.5	The prevalence of underweight children	85
4.6	The prevalence of stunted children	85
4.7	Trends in aid per capita and per GDP receipts between 1990 and 2010	90
4.8	Trends in *who* provides aid	92
4.9	Trends in *how* aid is provided	93
4.10	Trends in *where* aid is provided (1): Sector distribution	95
4.11	Trends in *where* aid is provided (2): Division into 'short-term', 'long-term' and emergency	96
4.12	Trend in WGI scores between 1995 and 2010	101
4.13	Trend in political stability, regulatory quality and control of corruption	101
4.14	*Polity2* scores between 1990 and 2010	101
5.1	Visualising the significant impacts of aid projects on household food security	135
5.2	Visualising effects of *who* implements aid on household food security	137
5.3	Visualisation of select significant findings on credit vs non-credit aid	139
5.4	Visualising the positive effects of agricultural and social aid on food security	142

6.1   The envisioned effect of GDS agricultural intervention on
recipients' food security   152
6.2   The envisioned effect of GDS livestock intervention on
recipients' food security   153
6.3   The envisioned effect of GDS credit intervention on
recipients' food security   154
6.4   The envisioned effect of GDS WASH intervention on
recipients' food security   154
6.5   The envisioned effect of PDS cards on beneficiaries'
food security   155
6.6   Relationship between PDS participation and income per capita   160
6.7   Comparison of propensity scores between treated and
control matched households   163
7.1   Graphic summary of the discovered effects of different types
of aid on food security   184

Boxes

4.1   Aid, governance and food security in Ethiopia   108
4.2   Aid, governance and food security in Vietnam   109
4.3   Aid, governance and food security in India   111
4.4   Aid, governance and food security in Peru   112

Acknowledgements

I would like to express my most heartfelt gratitude to my PhD supervisors, Dr David Hudson and Dr Rodwan Abouharb. They took me on as a PhD student and believed in me from the beginning of my research career. They supported me along the way, David with praise and Rod with helpful comments. I also want to thank Dr Slava Mikhaylov and my fellow PhD students at University College London (UCL) for their constructive criticism. Further, I am grateful to UCL, not only for accepting me as a PhD student but also for supporting me financially for four years with its Graduate Research Scholarship, and to the London School of Hygiene and Tropical Medicine for granting me the Chadwick Travelling Fellowship, which allowed me to carry out field research in Nicaragua and India.

Related to that, I want to extend my gratitude to Raleigh International and the Grameen Development Services for granting me access to their projects in Nicaragua and in India, and to Mr Vatsalya Sharma for being a wonderful research assistant. This book has also benefited from constructive feedback from my PhD examiners, Professor Jane Harrigan and Dr Michael Seiferling, anonymous peer reviewers and the editor, Ms Kelly Watkins.

Last, but not least, I want to thank my family: my parents for watching my children so that I could write, my husband for emotional support and my children for being.

List of abbreviations

2SLS	Two-stage least squares
AAY	Antyodaya Anna Yojana
AP	Associated Press
APL	Above Poverty Line
ATET	Average treatment effect on the treated
AU	African Union
BMI	Body mass index
BPL	Below Poverty Line
CO_2	Carbon dioxide
CRS	Creditor Reporting System
CSO	Civil society organisation
DAC	Development Assistance Committee
DFID	Department for International Development
DFPD	Department of Food and Public Distribution
EPRDF	Ethiopian People's Revolutionary Democratic Front
EU	European Union
FAO	Food and Agriculture Organisation
FAOSTAT	Food and Agriculture Organisation Statistics
FCM	Federation of Canadian Municipalities
FE	Fixed effects
FIAN	Food First Information and Action Network
FPS	Fair price shop
G8	Group of Eight
GBP	Great British pound
GDP	Gross domestic product
GDS	Grameen Development Services
GMM	Generalised method of moments
GMO	Genetically modified organism
GO	Governmental organisation
H	Hypothesis
hh	Household
HDI	Human Development Index

HRW	Human Rights Watch
ICESCR	International Covenant on Economic, Social, and Cultural Rights
IFAD	International Fund for Agricultural Development
IFPRI	International Food Policy Research Institute
IIPS	International Institute for Population Sciences
IMF	International Monetary Fund
IPCC	Intergovernmental Panel on Climate Change
IYCN	Infant and young child nutrition
kCal	Kilocalorie
LDC	Least developed country
LSMS	Living Standard Measurement Study
MDG	Millennium Development Goal
NFSA	National Food Security Act
NGO	Non-governmental organisation
NHS	National health survey
NREGS	National Rural Employment Guarantee Scheme
NTP-PR	National Targeted Program for Poverty Reduction
NYT	*New York Times*
ODA	Official development assistance
OECD	Organisation for Economic Cooperation and Development
OLS	Ordinary least squares
OXFAM	Oxford Committee for Famine Relief
PBS	Promotion of Basic Services
PDS	Public Distribution System
PPP	Purchasing power parity
PPP	Public–private partnership
PRSP	Poverty Reduction Strategy Paper
PSCAP	Public Sector Capacity Building
PSM	Propensity score matching
PSNP	Productive Safety Net Programme
QWIDS	Query Wizard for International Development Statistics
SDG	Sustainable Development Goal
UCLG	United Cities and Local Governments
UN	United Nations
UNDHR	Universal Declaration of Human Rights
UNDP	United Nations Development Programme
UP	Uttar Pradesh
US	United States (of America)
USAID	United States Agency for International Development
USD	United States Dollar
USSR	Union of Soviet Socialist Republics
WASH	Water, sanitation and hygiene
WB	World Bank

WDI	World Development Indicators
WFP	World Food Programme
WGI	Worldwide governance indicators
WHO	World Health Organisation

Introduction

The haunting reality of global food insecurity

As of 2016, close to 800 million people in the world are undernourished (Food and Agriculture Organisation [FAO], 2015). That means that every eighth person in the world lacks access to sufficient daily caloric intake. While there has been a positive trend in diminishing world hunger throughout the past century, a few recent developments indicate that global food insecurity will remain an important item on the development agenda for many decades to come.

The food crisis of 2008, during which prices of staple foods dramatically spiked in a matter of months and drove millions of people to the brink of starvation, demonstrated many of these. First, while insufficient access to food has recently been the main culprit behind ongoing food insecurity, there are signs that global food availability might resurface as a crucial issue. Ever since the 1970s, global food production has exceeded the energy requirements of all the world inhabitants combined, even though this has not translated into sufficient food access for all. However, continuing population growth, changing consumption patterns, deteriorating environmental conditions and stagnating cereal yields are threatening to alter the situation.

The United Nations (UN) World Populations Prospects' 'medium-variant' population growth scenario predicts that the current world population of 7 billion will increase to 8 billion by 2030 and to more than 9.5 billion by 2050. Previously thought of as the peak, this number might climb further, to more than 12 billion by 2100 (Gerland *et al.*, 2014). Most of this population increase will occur in low-income countries; notably, the population of sub-Saharan Africa is projected to increase from the current 1 billion to 2.5 billion by 2050 (UN, 2013). According to the FAO, providing this augmented number of people with just sufficient daily energy, without taking into account the requirements of well-balanced diets, would necessitate raising global food production by 70 per cent by 2050 (FAO, 2009).

The changing patterns in food consumption in developing countries combined with the search for renewable energy sources might further hinder global food availability. As millions of people in China, India and other rapidly economically growing countries shift from low to middle incomes, their demand for protein-rich foods including meat and fish will grow. Consequently, yearly meat consumption is expected to rise by 2050 from the 32 kilograms per capita of today to more than 50 kilograms (Government Office for Science, 2011). These new consumption patterns will intensify pressure on both land and water resources while simultaneously augmenting agricultural CO_2 emissions. Shifting land from food to biofuel production may eventually achieve the opposite but it often threatens local food security and encourages deforestation, cultivation of fragile lands and other environmentally unsustainable practices (ibid.).

At the same time, however, the necessary rise in global food production must occur in a world with stagnating yields and deteriorating climate conditions. An influential study by Ray *et al.* (2012) concluded that in 24–39 per cent of crop-growing areas in the world, yields were either stagnant or actually collapsing. Climate change might slow down yield growth further as higher average temperatures, changing patterns of precipitation and a greater number of severe weather events are expected to reduce the yields of staple crops such as wheat, maize and rice by 2 per cent per decade (Intergovernmental Panel on Climate Change [IPCC], 2013).

Thus, in order to cope with food insecurity in the coming decades, people have to increase global food production while dealing with the challenges of climate change and the changing patterns in consumption and energy production. At the same time, sufficient food availability does not automatically translate into food security. After all, there has been enough food in the world *for everyone* for more than the past four decades and yet world hunger and undernourishment have persisted (Friedmann, 1982). This paradox is well exemplified by the increasing trend of 'land grabbing'.[1] This investment in agriculture by higher-income countries *might* bring about higher global food production, but it is not likely to improve local food security, as the land investment deals generally contain no clause that would require investors to create local employment opportunities or to distribute food back to the local populace even in the case of famines (Khan, 2008).

Can international initiatives help?

At the global level, international actors have repeatedly expressed their desire to end hunger and food insecurity. Among the most prominent of such pledges have been the first Millennium Development Goal (MDG) and the second Sustainable Development Goal (SDG), in which UN members pledged to first halve the proportion of people suffering from hunger by 2015 and second to eliminate hunger by 2030.[2] At almost every world food summit or G8 meeting, world leaders reiterate their commitment to these goals. For example, at the 2009 World Summit on Food Security in Rome participants adopted a declaration pledging 'renewed commitment to eradicate hunger from the face of the earth sustainably and at the earliest date' (FAO, 2009). In 2012, G8 and several African countries again restated their resolve to improve global food security and founded the New Alliance for Food Security and Nutrition.[3] These theoretical commitments have generally not translated into sustained global action. Even so, the MDG 1 goal of halving world hunger has been met in some developing regions, such as East Asia or Latin America, but particularly sub-Saharan Africa and South Asia have lagged significantly behind (FAO, 2015).

The problem rests partially in the lack of consensus on the most appropriate mechanism for addressing food insecurity. Some believe that food security can be best improved through increasing agricultural expenditures in developing countries, which would raise agricultural productivity and, in turn, farmers' income levels. Others emphasise the imperative to focus on improving social and economic infrastructure. Still others highlight the importance of social transfer programmes that would bring about a more equal distribution of food available at the national level. The one thing that most existing recommendations for improving food security have in common is the need for developing countries' governments to devote a larger portion of their budget to addressing the issue. In the context of one such initiative, the Maputo Declaration, 53 African countries committed to increasing their investment in agriculture to at least 10 per cent of their budgets by 2008 (African Union [AU], 2003). However, only eight countries complied with the pledge; the rest pleaded an inability to balance their budgets. A similar situation can be observed in other sectors that are crucial to the reduction of food insecurity, including transportation, education and health.

One potential way to fill these financial gaps is through development aid, expressly provided as a means of addressing global inequality and redistributing global wealth. Advanced economies have generally been very vocal about their willingness to help eradicate food insecurity using financial assistance. For example, at the 2008 summit in L'Aquila, Italy, the G8 countries promised 22 billion USD to food security efforts over the following three years. Only around half the promised funds were eventually disbursed as the US and EU struggled to shore up their economies instead (ONE, 2013). Nonetheless, despite the frequent noncompliance of donors with their promised aid targets, development assistance still constitutes a significant financial flow from the global North to the global South. While in large developing countries such as India or Indonesia it now denotes a marginal resource, in some countries it still constitutes an important source of income – in Ethiopia 20 per cent, in Sierra Leone 28 per cent and in Guinea-Bissau 37 per cent of GDP (Query Wizard for International Development Statistics [QWIDS] data for 2012).

Most aid is not allocated specifically to combat food insecurity. Nevertheless, the guarantee of freedom from hunger for all citizens constitutes one of the most basic social duties of the state. For example, the International Covenant on Economic, Social and Cultural Rights (ICESCR, 1966), to which most countries in the world are parties, recognises 'the fundamental right of everyone to be free from hunger' and binds parties to 'individual, and through international co-operation, measures, including specific programmes, which are needed' to address the issue (Art 11.2). Within this perspective, *all* development aid should, in theory, contribute to making its recipients better able to assure their domestic food security. Consequently, it is surprising that, unlike in the case of economic growth or poverty, there exist few studies evaluating the relationship between aid and food security, whether on the global, national or local levels.

Research question and plan of chapters

This book aims to contribute to filling this theoretical and empirical void and then to proceed beyond it. Aside from analysing whether aid flows overall affect food security, it examines whether some types of aid are more beneficial for food security than others and whether their impact is influenced by the quality of the recipients' governance. Development aid in general is aimed at bolstering recipients' economic and social development, including food security, but it is provided in a myriad of ways – by different actors, through different mechanisms, for different purposes and to countries with a diverse quality of institutions and policies. Yet research on aid's heterogeneity of impact has been relatively scarce.

In its quest to build more knowledge in these topics, the book proceeds as follows. Chapter 1 introduces the theoretical framework that provided the basis for my research, concisely discusses relevant existing literature and formulates the working hypotheses. Chapter 2 introduces the book's methodology. Chapter 3 examines the aid–food security relationship using cross-country quantitative data, while Chapter 4 does so qualitatively, on a case study of Peru, Ethiopia, India and Vietnam. Chapter 5, marking the switch from a macro to a micro perspective, examines household survey data from the same four countries. Chapter 6 takes us to Uttar Pradesh, India, and offers a close-up look at the issues in question, through data gathered from surveys and longer interviews. Chapter 7 summarises the main results and articulates several policy recommendations. Finally, the Conclusion expresses a few final observations.

Notes

1 'Land grabs' are large-scale land acquisitions; the buying or leasing of large pieces of land in developing countries, by domestic and transnational companies, governments and individuals.
2 http://www.un.org/millenniumgoals, http://www.un.org/sustainabledevelopment/sustainable-development-goals
3 https://www.whitehouse.gov/the-press-office/2012/05/18/fact-sheet-g-8-action-food-security-and-nutrition

References

AU (2003). *Maputo Declaration on Agriculture and Food Security*. Maputo: African Union.
FAO (2009). *How to Feed the World in 2050*. Available at: http://www.fao.org/fileadmin/templates/wsfs/docs/expert_paper/How_to_Feed_the_World_in_2050.pdf
FAO (2015). *The State of Food Insecurity in the World*. Available at: http://www.fao.org/3/a-i4646e.pdf
Friedmann, H. (1982). 'The political economy of food: the rise and fall of the post-war international food order', *American Journal of Sociology*, 88, pp. S248–S286.
Gerland, P., Raftery, A., Sevcikova, H., Li, N., Gu, D., Spoorenberg, T., Alkema, L., Fosdick, B., Chunn, J., Lalic, N., Bay, G., Buettner, T., Heilig, G., and Wilmoth, J. (2014). 'World population stabilization unlikely this century', *Science*, 346(6206), pp. 234–7.

Government Office for Science (2011). *The Future of Food and Farming: Challenges and Choices for Global Sustainability.* Available at: https://www.gov.uk/government/uploads/system/uploads/attachment_data/file/288329/11-546-future-of-food-and-farming-report.pdf

ICESCR (1966). Available at: https://www.law.georgetown.edu/rossrights/chapters/documents/originalICCPROP.pdf

IPCC (2013). *Food Security and Food Production Systems.* Available at: http://ipcc-wg2.gov/AR5/images/uploads/WGIIAR5-Chap7_FGDall.pdf

Khan, A. F. (2008, December 29). 'Corporate farming and food security', *Dawn.* Available at: http://www.dawn.com/news/829850/corporate-farming-and-food-security

ONE (2013). *A Growing Opportunity.* Available at: http://one-org.s3.amazonaws.com/us/wp-content/uploads/2013/03/Ag-fullreport-single-130326-small.pdf

Ray, D. K., Ramankutty, N., Mueller, N. D., West, P. C., and Foley, J. A. (2012). 'Recent patterns of crop yield growth and stagnation', *Nature Communications*, 3(1293), pp. 1–7.

UN (2013). *World Population Prospects: The 2012 Revision.* Available at: http://esa.un.org/wpp/Documentation/pdf/WPP2012_Volume-I_Comprehensive-Tables.pdf

1 Development aid, governance and food security

Introduction

This chapter lays the theoretical and conceptual groundwork for the book's empirical research. It starts out by defining the main concepts: food security, development aid and governance. Then it deliberates about how aid in general and in different forms might impact food security and what conditioning role the quality of institutions may play, in view of existing research. These deliberations give rise to several hypotheses. The chapter finishes with a discussion of factors other than aid and governance that influence food security.

Defining the main concepts

Food security

Food security is defined by the FAO and the World Health Organisation (WHO) as a state in which 'all people at all times have access to sufficient, safe, and nutritious food to maintain an active and healthy life'.[1] Conversely, food insecurity indicates the uncertainty of access to enough and appropriate foods (Barrett, 2002; also Pinstrup-Andersen, 2009). Food (in)security thus inherently embodies an *ex ante* condition, with states such as hunger, malnutrition and undernourishment related *ex post* concepts (ibid.). Maxwell (1996, p. 159) captures this notion by expanding the definition of food security to a condition, in which 'food systems operate in such a way as to remove the [people's] fear that there will not be enough to eat'. Food security, he stressed, 'will be achieved [only] when the poor and vulnerable ... have secure access to the food they want' (ibid.). As the definitions above suggest, food security thus consists of four pillars: food availability, food access, food utilisation and stability or reasonable certainty about the future (FAO, 2015).

The *food availability* condition is satisfied when enough food is physically available in a country/region and people can obtain it either through purchase or as a donation. Sufficient *access to food* refers to people's ability to obtain enough food for themselves through legal and conventional means, which include producing, buying and receiving a donation but exclude stealing or begging.

Food utilisation relates to the body's physical process of digesting food and utilising its energy and micronutrients in further functioning. Its fulfilment is affected by both the type of food consumed and the health of the body consuming it and thus can be jeopardised by a lack of ingested micronutrients, unhygienic conditions of the food consumed or poor health. While the three elements mentioned so far jointly bring about adequate nourishment, *'stability'* or *'reasonable future certainty'* about having access to enough food in the future needs to be fulfilled as well in order to ensure lasting food security. Factors that bolster this dimension on the country level include low climatic vulnerability and low price volatility; at the household/individual level it is stable employment and the ownership of physical assets, the availability of social safety nets and lenders, and access to social capital (strong family, friend and community networks). Figure 1.1 graphically summarises the four aspects of food security.

Causes of food insecurity

The proximate or first-order causes of food insecurity are deficiencies in the four essential aspects of food security described above: that is, a lack of sufficient national food availability, insufficient access to food by households and individuals, improper utilisation of available food resources to secure adequate nutrition and uncertainty/anxiety about access to enough appropriate food in the future.

The distal or second-order causes of food insecurity, underlying the first-order effects, are much more numerous and complex. While they vary between those relevant on the country and on the household level and are highly mutually interlinked, they can be roughly divided into economic, trade and social factors; agricultural factors; political and policy factors; and population and environmental factors (e.g. King and Murray, 2002; Smith *et al.*, 2000). The first category – economic, trade and social factors – includes countries' economic growth and GDP per capita, development and humanitarian aid, global and local food prices, share of food in imports and the existence of social safety nets and of functioning food transport and storage systems. All of these have a bearing on one or more aspects of food security. The relevant agricultural factors range from food production on domestic or overseas land through food aid shipments to land irrigation and affect primarily countries' food availability and stability. Relevant political and policy factors include the general quality of countries' and localities' institutions and policies and political stability, as well as more specific issues, such as food safety regulation and inspection, availability of public health care and the political will to address existing inequalities. Finally, population and environmental factors that affect food security comprise total population numbers, population density and dependency ratios, along with air and water pollution, the rate of ground water depletion and fertile soil erosion and the quality of available water, sanitation and hygiene services.

In fact, so many aspects of political, economic, social and cultural development *can* have an indirect effect on food security that it becomes increasingly difficult to pinpoint factors that do not influence food security in any way. Despite the overlapping and numerous nature of second-order influents, however, food

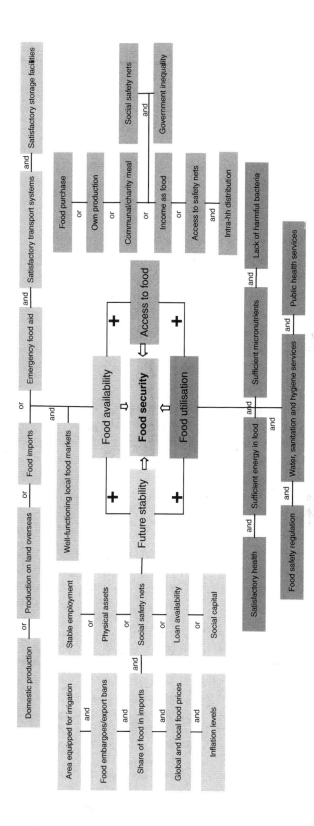

Figure 1.1 Basic food security scheme.

Source: Author's own deliberations

security constitutes a relatively easy-to-define concept, particularly in comparison with other popular development ones such as human security or sustainability (Paris, 2001). Consequently, while it may be difficult to always fully disentangle one determinant of food security from another, whether food security has been strengthened or weakened should not be equally contentious. This issue will be addressed further later in this chapter, as well as in Chapters 3 and 4.

Consequences of food insecurity

The consequences of food insecurity relate to people's coping strategies and depend on how serious the insecurity is. The first notable consequence is usually decline in the quality and the quantity of food consumption, accompanied by an increase in savings intended to help prevent hunger in the future (Merrigan and Normandin, 1996). The change in consumption patterns or fear thereof tend to inflict upon people negative physical, psychological and social effects, including feelings of exclusion, powerlessness, desperation, fear and stress, decline in productivity and concentration, and even increase in weight (Hamelin *et al.*, 1999; Olson, 1999; Reid, 2000).

If food insecurity persists or heightens to such a degree that simple curbing of consumption patterns no longer prevents undernourishment and hunger, food-insecure households turn to locally available means of credit and/or to selling assets. These survival strategies have significantly longer-lasting negative effects on the households' livelihoods and are not sustainable over the long term. Once they are no longer viable – because all potential lines of credit have been exhausted and all assets sold – some food-insecure people resort to an even more severe alternative, distress migration in search of sustenance (Barrett, 2002). This response is often the last one in a sequence of responses to food insecurity, as it commonly insinuates the loss of all the assets and employment left behind, and is followed only by death (Corbett, 1988).

Development aid

The term 'development aid', as used throughout this book, theoretically refers to all the financial flows from official development agencies and private charities in 'developed' countries to 'developing' ones that have the official goal of promoting economic and social development and whose grant element constitutes at least one fourth of the amount distributed (Organisation for Economic Cooperation and Development [OECD]). In reality, in the 'macro'-sections of the book, which examine the relationship between aid and food security on the country level, the measures of aid used capture primarily the flows of official development aid from Development Assistance Committee (DAC)[2] countries to the global South, given that the availability of data on aid provided by non-DAC donors and on private aid flows is very limited. However, the data include also information on humanitarian aid. This aid type is often analysed separately from development aid but it is included in the analysis here because 1) often it is very difficult to draw a separating line between a humanitarian and development action and 2) the OECD data on DAC aid includes humanitarian-assistance activities as well. In the 'micro' sections that consider the aid–food security relationship at the household/individual level, the measures of aid are further restricted, on the one hand, to aid provided by donors through programmes and projects. On the other hand, these measures include also data on non-DAC and on private aid, as the reporting is done by aid recipients rather than by donors.

As pointed out in the introduction, while it is useful to examine the effect of aid in general on food security because it has not been done to date, development aid constitutes such a varied financial and commodity flow that, in order to conduct meaningful and comprehensive analysis, it is imperative to analyse the effects of different types of aid on food security separately. Researchers thus far have not agreed on a unified systematic classification of aid;[3] therefore I have constructed my own, guided by three main dimensions: *who* gives aid, *how* it is given and *where* it goes. Figure 1.2 displays this classification, explained verbally below, graphically.

The first division, made according to the *donor's identity*, on the macro level is into official bilateral aid and multilateral aid (the category of 'private aid' was not included due to the unavailability of sufficient data). Official bilateral aid is further divided into aid provided by DAC versus by non-DAC members, although this division is difficult to assess accurately due to the limited reporting by non-DAC donors. On the micro level, the categorisation involves aid implemented by governmental versus by non-governmental agencies.[4]

The suggested divisions of aid according to the *giving mechanism* are into grants and concessional loans, into budget support as opposed to programme and project aid, into aid channelled through public–private partnerships as opposed to other channels, and into financial versus commodity aid (where food aid constitutes an absolute majority). Aid volatility is also added because, even though it is not a classification per se, it does characterise *how* aid is distributed. The classifications on the macro and micro level are similar with two exceptions: budget support is provided directly to the government budget and hence its effects on the micro level cannot be observed; and the macro division into loans and grants on the macro level is mirrored by the division of aid into credit and non-credit on the micro level.

In the last dimension of aid categorisation, according to *where* aid is implemented, a classification of aid into 'long-term', 'short-term' and humanitarian adopted from Clemens *et al.* (2004) is utilised, in order to examine whether short-term aid has a more discernibly positive impact on food security in the short run (normally three to five years) than long-term aid, as it does have on growth. Short-term aid encompasses activities that are likely to have a positive impact on countries' growth in that reasonably short time frame, such as budget support and programme/project aid for real-sector investment, transportation, communications, energy, banking, agriculture and industry. Long-term aid contains activities whose positive impact on growth is likely to become evident only later, such as technical cooperation, aid to research and development, investment in education,

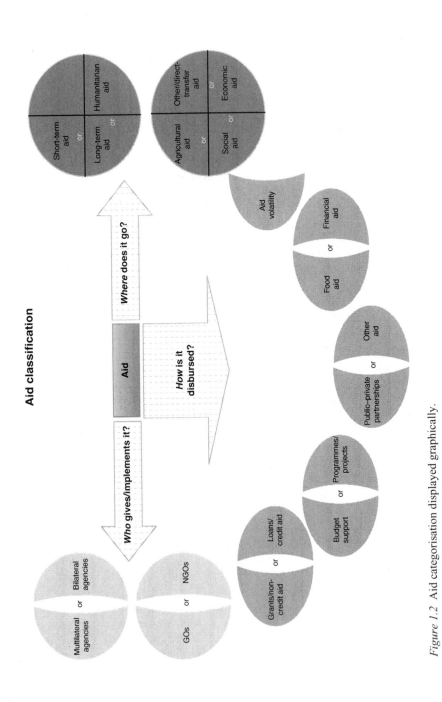

Figure 1.2 Aid categorisation displayed graphically.

Source: Author's own deliberations

health, population control and water sanitation. A second classification in this dimension is according to the sector where aid was invested – in agriculture, social infrastructure, economic infrastructure, or other sectors.[5] This categorisation seems particularly relevant when scrutinising the effect of aid on food security, since aid to agriculture has traditionally been regarded as the most directly supportive of food security, by both policy-makers (e.g. Maputo Declaration by AU, 2003; Mikhail *et al.*, 2013, from OXFAM) and researchers (e.g. Berti *et al.*, 2004; IYCN, 2011; Von Braun *et al.*, 1992).

Governance: the main intervening variable

The term 'governance' began gaining popularity in the 1950s but its definition remains vague and contested (e.g. Bovaird and Löffler, 2003; Grindle, 2004; Weiss, 2000). Some researchers believe that governance represents the process by which authority in a country is exercised, others understand it as the mechanisms and institutions that enable such process, while yet others include in the definition also the outcomes of the process – that is, policies (Abdellatif, 2003). As a brief illustration of the term's diverse understanding, the World Bank (WB, 1994) defines governance as 'the manner in which power is exercised in the management of a country's economic and social resources'. The United Nations Development Programme (UNDP, 1997) views governance as 'the exercise of economic, political, and administrative authority to manage a country's affairs at all levels'. The OECD (1995) sees governance as 'the use of political authority and exercise of control in a society in relation to the management of its resources for social and economic development', while according to the Department for International Development (DFID, 2001) governance relates to 'how institutions, rules, and systems of the state… operate at central and local level and how the state [interacts with] individual citizens, civil society, and the private sectors'.

Gisselquist (2012, p. 4) notes that the lowest common denominator of the definitions is that governance constitutes a process or mechanism through which power and/or authority is exercised to manage the collective affairs of a community. Whether governance relates to the institutions involved in the exercise or its outcomes remains more disputed. There is no agreement vis-à-vis the importance of politics in governance. The World Bank (WB) and the International Monetary Fund (IMF) have traditionally focused on the term's technical and administrative aspects while most researchers have posited that governance is inherently a political process (Dasandi *et al.*, 2015; Hudson and Leftwich, 2014; Weiss, 2000).

If agreeing on a definition of governance has been difficult, coming to an agreement about what constitutes 'good governance' has resembled attempting to 'nail a pudding on the wall' (Bovaird and Löffler, 2003, p. 316). The UN, for example, argues that governance is good when it promotes 'equity, participation, pluralism, transparency, accountability, and the rule of law, in a manner that is effective, efficient, and enduring'.[6] The UNDP equates good governance with democratic governance and defines as its main elements participation, consensus-orientation, strategic vision, responsiveness, effectiveness and efficiency, accountability, transparency, equity and the rule of law (UNDP, cited in Graham *et al.*, 2003). The OECD (2006) defines good governance as institutions and/or policies that are:

> participatory, consensus oriented, accountable, transparent, responsive, effective and efficient, equitable and inclusive and follow the rule of law. [Also, they] assure that corruption is minimised, the views of minorities are taken into account and that the voices of the most vulnerable in society are heard in decision-making.

The last definition is the one espoused most in this book, as it is reasonably but not overly nuanced. In addition, since this book uses the definition of and data on development aid from the OECD in the country-level studies, it seems fitting to follow the organisations' definition of good governance as well.

When confronted with the existing state of research on 'good governance', one inevitably comes to two conclusions. 'Good governance' is clearly something good, but what it is precisely depends on whom you ask. The ambiguity of the term likely underlies its popularity with development researchers and practitioners as it allows them to ascribe to the term their preferred meaning (Bovaird and Löffler, 2003). Second, and related to that, 'good governance' is inherently difficult to measure. That is not to say that people have not tried. The indicators proposed have been either rules-based or outcome-based (Kaufmann and Kraay, 2008). Rules-based indicators are generally believed to be more objective, as they measure whether countries have put in place specific institutions or policies. Their main downside is that the link between policies and outcomes is often complex, subject to lags and not very well-understood (ibid.). Hence, even countries with very good rules-based scores of governance can have weak governance outcomes in practice. Outcomes-based indicators, conversely, capture the view of institutional and policy quality either by experts or by local users, thus reflecting the actual quality of governance better than rules-based indicators. Their chief downside is the difficulty present in trying to link certain governance outcomes to specific institutions and policies (ibid.).

Addressing this topic, Thomas (2010, p. 51) opined that in view of the underdeveloped theory and fuzzy concept of governance, currently available data on the quality of governance were not just bad but wrong and the analysis of such data by researchers and policy-makers 'uninterpretable' and 'arbitrary'. Kaufmann *et al.* (2007, p. 23) retorted that not making use of any existing data on governance quality, however imperfect, would have been arbitrary in the extreme. Moreover, they argued – and I agree – that, 'endlessly waiting for the articulation of a complete, coherent, and consistent theory of governance before proceeding to measurement and action… while perhaps intellectually satisfying to a few, would be impractical to the point of irresponsibility' (ibid., p. 26).

Looking to the role of good governance, however specifically defined and measured, in aid effectiveness, some researchers have challenged its importance (Clemens *et al.*, 2004; Heady *et al.*, 2004; Morrissey, 2004). Nevertheless, my rational intuition suggests that, in theory, aid has the potential to be more successful at achieving its goals, including food security, when disbursed to countries with better-functioning institutions. A similar view can be extended with regard to the presence of democracy. In democracies, citizens generally have a more substantial voice in the administration of public affairs than in non-democracies and thus foreign aid receipts can be expected to be utilised more in favour of the public good.

Most of the reflections above have been related to national governance. Recently, however, researchers have begun to pay some attention to local govern-ance as well, noting its importance to desired development outcomes (e.g. Blair, 2000; Nijenhuis, 2002; Stoker, 2011). Local governance is described as the 'process through which local municipal decision-making is defined, incorporat-ing both local government, civil society, and the private sector' (Nijenhuis, 2002, p. 19). The definition of 'good local governance' does not stray too far from the definitions of national good governance either, being described as local institu-tions and policies that are 'participatory, transparent, accountable, and contribute to equity' (ibid.). Very little research to date has explored empirically the role of local governance in aid effectiveness; however, similar to the case of national-level governance, it seems intuitively logical that in regions and communities with better policies and institutions aid should have a chance to make more of a positive impact than elsewhere.

Relationship between food (in)security and development aid in general

Since the concept of food security encompasses the four different dimensions – food availability, access, utilisation and stability – a theoretical deliberation of the relationship between development aid and food security needs to evaluate the relationship between aid and each of the four components first. These deliberations are informed by a brief overview of existing findings. This section finishes with a summary of the evidence presented, pointing out gaps in existing research, and presents a hypothesis vis-à-vis the effect of aid on food security overall and the role played by recipients' governance in this relationship.

Effect on food availability

The first connection to consider is the one between aid and food availability. A country/region can obtain a satisfactory amount of food through domestic agricultural production, production of food on land purchased/leased abroad (e.g. 'grabbed land'), food imports or, in the worst-case scenario, the receipt of food aid (Figure 1.1). At first glance it can seem that any development aid should positively affect a country's food availability, as any financial inflow should enhance its ability to purchase food from abroad if it is not self-sufficient in food production. The relationship may not always be so clear-cut, however. Aid comes in a wide variety of forms and it is quite easy to imagine how, for instance, small development projects focusing on educational advancement might not increase a country's income and thus, in turn, its food availability at all, at least not in the short run. But, in theory, on the whole, aid's impact on food availability should be positive.

Literature evaluating the effect of development aid on food availability specifically does not, to my knowledge, exist. However, research on the effects of aid on economic growth, a second-order determinant most closely related to food availability,[7] is more than plentiful. Most researchers have discovered aid to have a statistically significant positive impact on growth (Burnside and Dollar, 2000, 2004; Hansen and Tarp, 2001; Lensink and White, 2001; Roodman, 2007). Meta-analyses challenged this finding (Doucouliagos and Paldam, 2008, 2011), highlighting that the positive results on the aid–growth relationship were fragile to changing samples and specifications, and were a result of publication bias, which facilitates the publication of significant results over non-significant ones. Nonetheless, even the most recent works on the aid–growth link have shown aid to have a positive effect on growth, most often through a positive impact on investment (e.g. Arndt *et al.*, 2015; Brückner, 2013; Galiani *et al.*, 2014).

Effect on access to food

Next comes the link between development aid and food access. Figure 1.1 suggested that there are many more paths to appropriate food access than to food availability. While most people access food by buying it or producing it themselves, they can also receive it from their families or neighbours as gifts, as income, as part of a social safety net or as a donation. Development aid can strengthen these entitlements in numerous ways. Agricultural development projects can provide farmers with tools to produce more food or raise incomes to purchase it; microfinance programmes can help people earn more money and thus buy more food; and budget-support grants can enable governments to launch school-feeding programmes. Nevertheless, as in the case of food availability, not all development aid is likely to increase people's food access in the short run – for example, an educational programme – and poor governance or faulty implementation can render ineffective even well-designed development projects that target specifically food security. Since better food access often results naturally from poverty reduction (a closely related second-order food-security factor), the bottom line in assessing the relationship between aid and food access is that if aid generally helps ameliorate poverty, it is likely to also improve people's access to food (Frongillo, 2003; Maxwell and Smith, 1992).

Literature on the effects of aid on poverty is also plentiful but when compared to the literature on the effects of aid on growth it is less unified in its results. One reason underlying this lack of agreement is the absence of a generally accepted poverty measure. Different researchers have operationalised poverty through a wide variety of variables, ranging from poverty rates through pro-poor expenditures and Human Development Index (HDI) scores to infant mortality and literacy rates (Agénor *et al.*, 2008; Gomanee *et al.*, 2003; Kosack, 2003; Masud and Yontcheva, 2005). It is not particularly surprising then that the results have also differed, with some researchers finding aid to reduce poverty while others concluding that aid had no measurable impact. The positive results have been, however, more numerous than the neutral ones, and particularly so on the household level.

Effect on food utilisation

Food utilisation is the most intimate and individual component of food security and hence its connection with development aid is harder to consider in theory than the previous two aspects. Appropriate food utilisation requires food that is sufficiently rich in energy and contains all the necessary micronutrients and no harmful bacteria (Figure 1.1). In addition, bad health can hinder food utilisation even if appropriate quantities and types of food are received. Thus, education (about hygiene and good nutrition), health (access to affordable health care and public health measures) and infrastructure (especially access to clean water and sanitation, to avoid the contamination of food with bacteria) appear to be the second-order food-security factors most closely linked to satisfactory food utilisation. While some development aid might influence these positively,[8] it is easy to imagine that in the short run many development projects and programmes will not improve food utilisation in any way, even if the country has good institutions and policies in place and aid projects/programmes are implemented exactly according to plan.

Literature specifically addressing the link between food utilisation and development aid does not exist. Furthermore, unlike in the two previous aspects of food security, there is no single variable whose increase can be approximated with a corresponding progress in food utilisation. Evidence regarding aid's effects on the sectors most closely positively linked with good food utilisation, including health, education, food safety regulation and water and sanitation sectors has been very mixed, too much so to draw any generalised conclusions (e.g. Dreher *et al.*, 2008; Heyneman, 1999; Kanbur *et al.*, 1999; Michaelowa and Weber, 2006).

Effect on 'reasonable future certainty'

Since the 'reasonable future certainty' or future stability aspect of food security is more psychological than the previous three, its relationship with development aid is the hardest to assess. As Figure 1.1 suggests, there are factors that strengthen a country's food stability, such as political stability, low exposure to climatic risks and relatively stable food prices, and factors that enhance an individual's or household's feelings of future food security, including stable employment, asset ownership, strong family ties, the existence of social safety nets and the accessibility of loans if needed. If development assistance brings about economic development, in the very long run it should bolster all the factors mentioned (except for family ties, perhaps). However, in the shorter run, this effect is not likely to be felt, in part thanks to the innately volatile nature of the assistance, which often decreases precisely when the need is most intense – such as during the global economic crisis of 2009/10 (QWIDS, 2015). Thus, the impact of aid on 'stability' or 'reasonable future certainty' might actually be even negative.

Equal to the previous cases, research addressing specifically the link between development aid and stability of food security does not exist. Regarding factors that can threaten future food-security stability on the country level, existing literature is somewhat conflicted vis-à-vis the intervening effects of aid. On one hand, aid has been shown to mitigate the negative impacts of external shocks, specifically drops in commodity prices (Collier and Goderis, 2009). On the other hand, rising food prices, which affect food stability negatively, have been found to have a negative impact on aid levels, since in a situation of higher prices and fixed aid budgets an allocated financial amount can purchase less food than previously (Rosen and Shapouri, 2008). On a more personal level, research established that in order to bolster feelings of security and psychological wellbeing, aid donors would need to adopt more complex and culturally sensitive approaches (Bigdon and Korf, 2002). These findings strengthen my original belief that aid is not likely to strengthen people's feelings of reasonable future certainty about food security overall and might even depress them, particularly in contexts with fragile institutions.

Effect of aid on food security and the conditioning role of governance

Figure 1.3 summarises the conjectures drawn up above with regard to the impact of aid on the four key dimensions within food security. According to these, we can expect aid to have a positive impact on food availability and on food access, with a less straightforward effect on food utilisation and a possibly negative effect on food stability. Hence, the impact of aid on food security overall can theoretically be expected to be mostly positive and, at the same time, positively conditioned on the quality of recipients' institutions and policies (that is, governance).[9]

The biggest shortcoming of the existing literature on the effects of aid on food security, obvious from the set-up of the discussion above, is the dearth of research addressing that specific relationship, particularly on the macro level. There are only a handful of studies on aid's impact on countries' food security. To mention the few, Bach and Matthews (1999) used computer simulations to estimate the effect of aid on food security and concluded that aid likely has a small but positive impact. Lips (2005), in suggesting that global food insecurity could be resolved through an annual $112 billion transfer from OECD to developing countries, implied a clear albeit not empirically established conviction that such transfer of funds would have a positive effect on food security. On the micro level, more researchers examined the link and often found it to be positive (Berti *et al.*, 2004; Hoque *et al.*, 1996; IYCN, 2011).

The literature on the links between aid and development outcomes other than food security, including growth and poverty reduction, to which I turned in an effort to formulate a hypothesis on the relationship between aid and food security in the absence of specific studies, has, however, also some important limitations. As the passages above made clear, there are conceptual problems with the terms examined, particularly with 'poverty' and 'poverty reduction'. There are also significant inconsistencies between the findings obtained through country-level versus household-level studies as well as through qualitative versus quantitative studies.

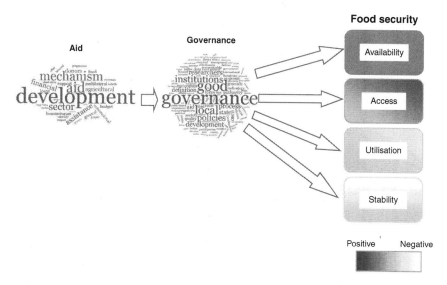

Figure 1.3 Theoretical conjectures vis-à-vis the effect of development aid on food security.

Source: Author's own deliberations

For example, researchers of the relationship between aid and economic growth highlighted several decades ago the existence of a 'macro–micro paradox', where aid appears to have a stronger positive impact when examined using household-level than country-level data case (Mosley, 1986; also McGillivray *et al.*, 2006).

This book does not propose to resolve these debates but it does aim to learn from them. Consequently, it conducts the analysis of the aid–food security relationship both on the macro (country) and on the micro (household) levels, using a combination of quantitative and qualitative methods. Moreover, in awareness of the complex nature of food security and the difficulty in its measurement, it uses multiple approximating variables so as to increase the external validity of results.

Turning attention now to the role of governance in aid effectiveness, my theoretical postulations indicated that in all four dimensions of food security (availability, access, utilisation and stability) countries and localities with better governance are likely to extract more benefits from the aid received than countries and localities with comparatively worse governance. Unsurprisingly, given the absence of literature analysing the relationship between aid and food security, empirical research has thus far not considered the conditioning role of governance in the aid–food security relationship specifically either. Nevertheless, most studies looking at the role of institutions and policies in other aid-effectiveness areas (economic growth, poverty reduction…) found it to be positive and significant. For example, the seminal article by Burnside and Dollar (2000)[10] concluded that aid's positive impact on growth was more pronounced in countries with sounder economic policies. In a similar vein, countries with higher quality or more democratic institutions were found to be more likely to distribute the aid received to intended beneficiaries (Jenkins and Scanlan, 2001; Kosack, 2003).

Some authors qualified or even challenged the positive relationship (Clemens *et al.*, 2004; Dalgaard and Hansen, 2001; Drèze, 2004; Morrissey, 2004). However, the majority of researchers and development practitioners believe that governance plays a positive role in aid effectiveness or, as Hudson (2015, p. 161) put it, 'the position that aid… work[s] if the [right] policies and institutions are in place is now the accepted wisdom'. Clearly, as the introductory section on governance showed, the debate remains complicated due to the question of what precisely constitutes governance and when it is 'good'. While not aspiring to settle the discussion, similar to the case of food security and its contested measurement this book uses two different governance measures to bolster the validity and applicability of its findings.

Keeping the caveats debated above in mind, on the basis of the theoretical postulations and existing research, my study starts with the following hypothesis:

> *Hypothesis 1: Development assistance in general has a small but significant positive impact on food security in developing countries, whether examined on the macro or micro level, and this effect is reinforced by the presence of good governance.*

Food security as a function of development aid

Before proceeding any further with the discussion, the treatment of development aid as an independent variable to food security in this book requires an explanation, or at least a disclaimer. It is not my intention to posit that development aid could ever fully resolve a country's food security. As the discussion in the previous pages has shown, food security is a complex phenomenon, which can only be satisfied through a combination of individual, household and country characteristics. Aid, as well planned and thought out as it may be, can consequently never be expected to align all the factors required for satisfactory food security on its own. It can, however, be plausibly seen as one of the factors that could either strengthen or weaken food security directly or indirectly via the second-order contributors debated above. Moreover, as Chapter 7 will discuss in greater depth, because development aid constitutes an indelible component of current global political economy and is unlikely to cease any time in the near future, it is important to understand what its effects on food security are on the country as well as on the household level.

Relationship between different types of development aid and food (in)security

Hence, it is useful to investigate what impact aid in general has on food security and how the relationship is influenced by recipients' governance. However, since aid is disbursed in a myriad of different modalities, in order to increase the value and usefulness of this study, it is crucial to consider the impact of the different types of aid on food security as well.

The categorisation of aid applied here (see Figure 1.2) encompasses three broad dimensions: *who* gives aid, *how* aid is given and *where* aid goes. As the previous section, this one discusses each aid categorisation's link with food security, first in theory and second in existing research, culminating in a hypothesis.

The impact of different types of donors on food security

There is an important difference to be made in this category between the identity of donors as observed on the macro and on the micro level. On the one hand, at the macro level, which works with country-level data, donor information refers to those countries and institutions that provided the aid in the first place. On the other hand, at the micro level, which works with data reported by households, information on donors refers to the agencies and institutions implementing the aid programmes and projects in question, without enquiring specifically about the original source of the programme/project financing. Keeping this distinction in mind, two different lines of consideration are followed.

At the macro level, aid according to *who* provides it is divided into bilateral and multilateral. Decisions about bilateral giving are made by single country governments while multilateral giving is agreed upon by many countries' governments jointly with the institutions' bureaucracies. Consequently, one can plausibly expect bilateral aid to be more inspired by geopolitical and strategic considerations. Old colonial and current linguistic ties are also likely to play a larger role among bilateral donors. Multilateral giving can be, conversely, expected to be distributed more on the basis of real development necessity and thus more effective at achieving its goals. Separately, within bilateral giving, DAC aid might be more effective than non-DAC aid, since it tends to be more transparent[11] and, unlike non-DAC aid, is bound by an agreed set of guidelines.

Looking at the existing literature, most researchers agree that multilateral aid is more efficient, cheaper and better coordinated than bilateral aid, which is, indeed, seen as more political, commercial and burdened with more 'strings attached' (Asher, 1962; Burnside and Dollar, 2000; Harrigan and Wang, 2011; Minch, 2005; Petrikova, 2016). Multilateral giving is hence largely believed to be more successful at achieving its official objectives, including the reduction of food insecurity.

At the micro level, the main considerations relate to the efficiency and effectiveness of project implementation. From this perspective, one can imagine that private – that is, non-governmental – institutions have a greater positive impact on food security as they tend to be smaller and less bureaucratic than official aid agencies and consequently face lower administrative costs. For the same reasons, NGOs may be more flexible in their ability to respond to changing situations on the ground even though possibly facing more problems with funding.

Ever since the 1990s, NGOs have, indeed, been praised for lower costs and higher efficiency in delivering aid when compared to official aid agencies (Hulme and Edwards, 1997; Lewis and Opoku-Mensah, 2006). More recent empirical studies have toned down the praise, suggesting that NGO aid does not differ from official multilateral and bilateral aid in its patterns of giving as much as originally believed

(Koch *et al.*, 2008; Nunnenkamp *et al.*, 2009) and might be only slightly more altruistic and efficient (Masud and Yontcheva, 2005; Petrikova, 2015). Nevertheless, many large multilateral and bilateral agencies implement a large portion of their aid through NGOs, still regarding them as more efficient and cost-effective.

On both the macro and the micro levels, the existing research findings thus approximately fall in line with my theoretical postulations. The corresponding hypotheses are consequently the following:

Hypothesis 2.1: Considered from the macro perspective, multilateral development aid is more effective than bilateral aid at bolstering food security. Aid provided by DAC donors is more beneficial than aid provided by non-DAC donors.

Hypothesis 2.2: Considered from the micro perspective, aid implemented by private (non-governmental) organisations is more effective at bolstering food security than aid implemented by official institutions, whether of the multilateral or bilateral type.

The impact of different types of aid mechanisms on food security

Grants versus loans/non-credit versus credit aid

The division of aid into grant and loan components can be applied both at the macro and micro levels of analysis, although with some differences. At the macro level, the classification refers to whether aid is provided to countries as grants or as loans offered at a concessional rate (the grant component has to be at least 25 per cent, otherwise the loan cannot be considered part of development aid). Compared to grants, loans require – at least in theory – greater activity and responsibility of the recipient government since they eventually need to be serviced, albeit at a lower than the market rate. Countries with better institutions and more responsible – for example, less corrupt – governments should consequently fare better with loans than countries with worse institutions and more corrupt governments. However, even countries with the best institutions experience recessions and therefore loans can lead even the best-meaning governments into unsustainable debt. Extending these observations to the effect of loans and grants on food security, loans can be expected to be less successful than grants, at least in the relatively short run normally observed by empirical studies, and particularly so in countries with relatively worse governance.

Existing literature generally confirms that grants deliver more benefits to the global poor at the same price as loans (Bulow and Rogoff, 2005; Lerrick and Meltzer, 2002). From a long-term perspective, however, grants have been accused of negatively affecting revenue collection and contributing to the creation of dependency mentality (Clements *et al.*, 2004; Odedokun, 2004). Thus, in line with the theoretical postulations, research concurs that grants are likely more beneficial to bolstering food security in the short run while in the long run the effect of loans may be equally good or even better in countries with better governance.

At the micro level, the classification also refers to whether aid provided to recipients needs to be repaid or not. While in the past credit-based aid programmes and projects were not too common, the success of microcredit institutions such as the Grameen Bank in Bangladesh inspired, from the 1990s onwards, an explosion of aid projects focused on microfinance. The considerations to make here are not dissimilar from those made at the macro level above; one can imagine that while microcredit aid might encourage aid recipients to work harder in order to be able to repay the loans, it can also easily lead to indebtedness, and hence non-credit aid is likely to be supportive of household food security in a more straightforward but perhaps also more 'addictive' manner. The quality of local governance probably also plays a positive role in this relationship, enabling microfinance institutions to work better in contexts with well-functioning institutions.

Existing research broadly supports these considerations. Seven recently conducted randomised-control studies of microfinance (Angelucci *et al.*, 2015; Attanasio *et al.*, 2015; Augsburg *et al.*, 2015; Banerjee *et al.*, 2015; Crépon *et al.*, 2015; Karlan and Zinman, 2011; and Tarozzi *et al.*, 2015 – summarised by the Poverty Action Lab[12]) have found all seven microfinance programmes to have no statistically significant impact on their participants' income and health or on female empowerment. The corresponding hypotheses are hence as follows:

Hypothesis 3.1: Considered from the macro perspective, grants are more directly supportive of food security than concessional loans while the effect of loans is more positively conditioned on good governance.

Hypothesis 3.2: Considered from the micro perspective, non-credit aid is more supportive of food security than credit aid, but credit aid is more positively conditioned on good governance.

General budget support versus programme/project aid

This division can only be examined at the macro level since by definition budget support is provided directly to recipient governments and hence its effect is impossible to measure using data reported by aid-receiving households. Unlike programme and project aid, general budget support requires a significantly larger involvement of the recipient government in its implementation, since the aid is infused into the government's budget un-earmarked, to be used for public spending according to the government's needs.[13] Therefore, similar to the case of loans, in order for this aid mechanism to be at all effective, the receiving government must be willing to use the aid for purposes that promote development rather than for own personal enrichment. The corresponding danger of aid programmes and projects is that since they are usually executed by donor agencies and their hired foreign or local staff, they can create an alternative administrative structure to the state one. In the long run, such a structure can undermine the country's quality of governance; however, in the shorter time frame this should not have a notably negative effect on countries' food security. Applying these reflections to the expected impact of aid on food security, one could expect programme and project aid to be on average more successful than budget support in enhancing food security, particularly in countries with relatively worse governance.[14]

Researchers indeed consider general, and to a lesser extent sectoral, budget support to be more fungible and hence to weaken local government capacity to a lesser extent than project assistance (Cordella and Dell'Arricia, 2007). These qualities render it, in their view, a more appropriate financing tool in countries with acceptable governance records and solid institutions (Devarajan and Swaroop, 2000). The fact that budget support does not suffer from the same 'myopic' vision focused on obtaining short-term results as project assistance further supports this argument (Crola, 2009). However, programme and project assistance allows donors to better ensure that the aid reaches its intended recipients, a particularly important characteristic in the effort to reduce food insecurity (Cordella and Dell'Arricia, 2007). In addition, the levels of programme and project aid are less volatile than budget supports, as they are usually disbursed on a multi-year basis (Eifert and Gelb, 2005). Thus, based on the existing research findings combined with the theoretical postulations, the corresponding hypothesis is the following:

Hypothesis 4: Project and programme aid are more successful at bolstering food security than general budget support unless the recipient possesses above-average governance records.

Aid channelled through public–private partnerships versus through other channels

Public–private partnerships (PPPs) became popular in development circles in the late 1990s. While no unified definition of the concept exists, the World Bank defines PPPs as 'long-term contract[s] between a private party and a government entity, for providing a public asset or service, in which the private party bears significant risk and management responsibility' (WB, 2015). PPPs have been described as capable of increasing both the efficiency and legitimacy of aid (Börzel and Risse, 2005). Further, the partnerships are seen as faster, cheaper and more financially sustainable than traditional modes of aid delivery, as well as capable of spurring private-sector development in recipient countries (Wallace, 2013). Others have, however, accused the PPPs of high establishing costs and of leaving out the poorest and most marginalised members of communities (ibid.). None of these claims stands on particularly strong empirical basis as little research thus far has analysed the effect of the partnerships on aid effectiveness. It is hence difficult to hypothesise about the impact of PPP- versus other mode-delivered aid on recipients' food security, other than to posit, similarly to the effect of aid in general, that governance is likely to enhance the effectiveness of PPP-delivered aid.

Hypothesis 5: Aid delivered via public–private partnerships does not differ in its effect on food security from the effect of aid delivered via other channels.

Financial versus commodity aid

The third classification within aid mechanisms is into commodity and financial aid. This classification can be applied both at the macro and at the micro level. As opposed to the divisions according to the donor's identity or into grant and loan components of aid, however, the effects of this division on the impact of aid on food security should not differ significantly whether measured on the macro or on the micro level.

Most aid flows are financial; however, some aid comes in the form of food (bulk of commodity aid) or other materials (e.g. unrefined oil, old clothes). Commodity aid is most often disbursed with the aim to fulfil a pressing need: food aid tends to be provided to famine areas where financial help could presumably not be as effective. Similarly, medicine supplies and old clothes are frequently sent to post-disaster areas, where they are believed to help more effectively than cash. While the cited reasons hold true in many emergencies, often there is a fine line between deciding to donate commodity instead of financial aid for purely altruistic reasons and doing so for more self-serving ones – since domestic producers of donated commodities stand to benefit from such aid provision (Lipsky and Thibodeau, 1988; Zerbe, 2004). Moreover, if the donated commodity is available also in the recipient locality, the free donations may displace local producers from the market. Keeping these considerations in mind, financial aid should have a more beneficial effect on food security than commodity aid, except for crises and emergencies.

The general consensus among aid researchers is similar; they see food aid as *potentially* more effective than monetary aid at bolstering food security, but only if it follows a set of rules that generally arise solely during humanitarian crises (Barrett, 2002; Uvin, 1992). In other situations, they regard monetary aid not only as more beneficial, but also food aid as possibly harmful, as it can inadvertently price out local food producers and hence provide a disincentive to local food production in the following years (Del Ninno *et al.*, 2007; Gelan, 2006). The suitable hypothesis in this aid classification is thus:

> *Hypothesis 6: Financial aid is generally more beneficial to food security than commodity (food) aid; the reverse is true only in humanitarian crises.*

Aid volatility

Aid volatility does not constitute a categorical division within aid as the previous three aid mechanisms discussed; nonetheless, it *is* an important characteristic of *how* aid is disbursed. While some developing countries receive steady annual inflows of aid, which increase proportionately to inflation rates and population growth, other countries face a much more volatile aid market, with high receipts one year and low receipts the next. This volatility translates also into the field where donor-run projects are set up and cancelled on an often very ad hoc basis. It is unquestionable that the impact of this precarious nature of aid on development as well as on all aspects of food security, and particularly on future certainty, is harmful, but the question remains regarding the extent of this negative effect.

Researchers have, indeed, found aid volatility to have a measurable negative effect on various development goals, resulting in a volatility of expenditures and instability of domestic policies (Bigsten and Tengstam, 2015; Bulíř and Hamann, 2008; Lensink and Morrissey, 2000; Rodrik, 1990). Aid volatility has also been shown to damage the macro effectiveness of aid and reduce the ability of the recipient countries' public sectors to implement coherent investment programmes and fiscal policies (Mosley and Suleiman, 2007). Thus, it seems clear that high levels of aid volatility have a negative effect on recipients' food security whether measured on the macro or micro levels, but an empirical analysis is needed to show how significant the negative effect is. Consequently, a simple hypothesis follows:

> *Hypothesis 7: Higher levels of aid volatility exacerbate food insecurity, both at the macro and the micro level.*

The impact of different aid targets on food security

Humanitarian aid versus short-term aid versus long-term aid

Since humanitarian aid is intended to only smooth short-term consumption, its long-term positive effects on development cannot be expected to be substantial. Regarding the short-term- and long-term-oriented aid, according to Clemens *et al.* (2004) both contribute to economic and social development, but while the impact of short-term aid (aid to productive sectors) can be observed in the short run (three to five years), the impact of long-term aid is likely to become apparent significantly later than the aid received and its impact might therefore be more difficult to separate from other factors influencing development at that point in time. Therefore, the authors hypothesised that only short-term aid would have a measurable effect on growth and subsequently confirmed this finding in their data analysis.

Applying this logic to food security, humanitarian aid usually cannot be expected to exert significant positive influence in the longer run, unless it helps prevent adverse coping strategies with long-term consequences. In some instances, the long-term effect of humanitarian aid – particularly of food aid – on food security may even be negative, as the donated free food might displace local food production. However, its immediate effect is likely to be at least somewhat positive. Both short-term and long-term aid should theoretically be able to contribute to an improved level of food security; however, according to Clemens *et al.*'s (2004) line of argument, as with growth, the impact of long-term aid on food security would appear only many years after the intervention and would be harder to discern at that point due to other affecting factors. The appropriate hypothesis hence is:

> *Hypothesis 8: Short-term aid has a more pronounced and discernible positive impact on food security than either humanitarian or long-term aid, both*

on the macro and micro levels (at least in the short term, conventionally measured in aid-effectiveness literature).

Aid to agriculture, economic infrastructure, social infrastructure and other sectors

The second division of aid according to *where* it flows, into that supporting agriculture, economic infrastructure, social infrastructure and other sectors, is the one where I expect the largest disparities in food-security impact. Since agricultural aid tends to focus on increasing agricultural productivity and production, it should generally have a long-lasting positive impact on food security, by boosting food availability and farmers' access to food, whether considered from a country-level or a household-level perspective. Improving economic and social infrastructure should, in most cases, also help improve access to food as well as food utilisation, through an increase in economic opportunities and the provision of better health and nutritional services. However, one can imagine situations in which such impacts are not achieved either because the aid programmes/projects are not implemented well or fail to empower the truly marginalised layers of the society. The effect of 'other' aid on food security is harder to analyse in theory, but unless it constitutes the bulk of all the aid received, its effects are not likely to be positive on the macro level. On the micro level, this type of aid is often constituted by direct transfers – whether of cash or of food – and the postulations about its effects on food security can be likened to those on the impact of food aid and of humanitarian assistance.

Looking to the existing literature, researchers also regard agricultural aid as the most crucial aid modality in bolstering food security. On the macro level, they see agricultural investment as directly supportive of agricultural and rural growth, which boosts poverty reduction and food security primarily in rural areas (Von Braun *et al.*, 1992). Agricultural growth is also regarded as being more effective at reducing poverty than economic growth in general (Christiaensen *et al.*, 2011; Ligon and Sadoulet, 2007). One potential downside might be that agricultural development assistance frequently fuels agricultural imports as well, as rising incomes lead to changing dietary preferences often satisfied only through imports (Pinstrup-Andersen and Cohen, 1998; Haque, 1999). That effect should not, however, harm recipients' food security in the short run.

On the micro level, the existing findings have been a little more nuanced. A major conclusion shared by many authors has been that while agricultural interventions generally increase crop production and sense of food security, nutritional outcomes such as children's height-for-age or weight-for-age scores are affected only occasionally (Berti *et al.*, 2004; IYCN, 2011). Other researchers have warned that agricultural projects often fail to reach the poorest, most marginalised farmers (Fiallos and Cantero, 2008). On the basis of these findings, authors of the IYCN meta-analysis recommended that agricultural knowledge-transfer projects aim at increasing the production of foods directly consumed by poor households, include explicit nutrition counselling and introduce micronutrient rich plant varieties (IYCN, 2011).

Research has thus far not evaluated the specific impact of aid to economic or social infrastructure on food security on the macro level; the results with regard to the impact of this type of aid on other outcomes have, however, been mixed (e.g. Dreher *et al.*, 2008; Williamson, 2008). Similarly, on the micro level social-infrastructure and economic-infrastructure projects have been examined quite frequently with regard to their impact on income generation or consumption, but rarely with a view to participants' food security specifically. One of the few empirical studies to link social-infrastructure projects with nutritional outcomes, Bhutta *et al.* (2008) analysed the effect of nutritional counselling on children's health and found that both the promotion of breast feeding and education about complementary infant feeding had a positive impact on children's height-for-age scores. Conversely, Hoque *et al.* (1996) examined the impact of a hygiene-education project in Bangladesh and discovered no difference between the treatment and control group in terms of sanitation knowledge five years after the project's implementation.

As a subset of economic-infrastructure projects, the previously discussed microfinance initiatives have likely no positive effect on recipients' food security. Evidence on the effect of other types of economic projects has been more varied. Vocational-training and income-generating projects were mostly found to be beneficial for participants, but particularly in the short term and if they focused on the strengthening of several types of capital (e.g. social, human) (Gibson, 1993; Oxenham, 2002).

Finally, no empirical research has linked 'aid to other sectors' with food security specifically, either on the macro or on the micro level. However, if one considers 'other' aid on the micro level to be constituted primarily by direct transfers of cash and/or food, then research linking it with food security of recipients does exist, but again is not unified in its conclusions. The views on the impact of food transfers on longer-term food security have been discussed here already; direct transfers of cash are generally considered to be more useful, but concerns have been raised that the money provided is often not used to increase dietary intake and hence does not consistently lead to better nutritional outcomes. Furthermore, rising food prices can rapidly reduce the real value of cash transfers (Bailey and Hedlund, 2012; Chen *et al.*, 2009).

On the basis of the theoretical deliberations and existing research, the final hypothesis is hence:

> *Hypothesis 9: Aid to agriculture has a more pronounced and discernible positive impact on food security than aid to social and economic infrastructure or aid to any other sector, both on the macro and on the micro levels.*

Figure 1.4 concisely summarises the hypotheses put forward above in a graphic manner.

	Hypothesised effects		Impact on food security — Levels		Testability (Levels I, II, III and IV)
			Macro	Micro	
	Aid in general		↑ G	↑ G	I, II, III, IV
***Who* gives/ implements aid?**	Multilateral agencies		↑ G		I, II
	Bilateral donors	DAC	↑ G		
		Non-DAC	? G		
	Governmental organisations (GOs)			↑ G	III, IV
	Non-governmental organisations (NGOs)			↑ G	
***How* is aid disbursed?**	Concessional loans/credit aid		↑ G	↑ G	I, II, III, IV
	Grants/non-credit aid		↑ G	↑ G	
	General budget support		↑ G		I, II
	Programme aid		↑ G		
	Project aid		↑ G		
	Public–private partnerships		↑ G	↑ G	I, II
	Other aid		↑ G	↑ G	
	Commodity/food aid		↑ G	↑ G	I, II, III
	Financial aid		↑ G	↑ G	
	Aid volatility		↓	↓	I, II, IV
***Where* does aid go?**	Humanitarian aid		↑ G	↑ G	I, II, III
	Short-term aid		↑ G	↑ G	
	Long-term aid		? G	? G	
	Agriculture		↑ G	↑ G	I, II, III, IV
	Social infrastructure		↑ G	↑ G	
	Economic infrastructure		↑ G	↑ G	
	Other sectors/direct transfers		? G	↑ G	

↑ positive effect, ↓ negative effect, ? mixed effect, − no effect; · most, · less, · least; G -positively conditioned on governance

Figure 1.4 Graphic summary of the expected effects of different types of aid on food security.

The role of other factors

Before proceeding to a discussion of the specific methods used to examine the relationships outlined in the hypotheses, factors other than aid that impact countries' and people's food security deserve a brief discussion. These include the most important second-order/distal food-security influents briefly mentioned above and divided into population and environmental factors;

Table 1.1 Factors with influence on food security

	Macro (country) level	Micro (household/individual) level
Population and environmental factors	Population (number, density...) Conflict Disaster Environmental pollution	Gender Age Health Family structure (e.g. female-headed hh) Education Disaster (flood, drought...)
Economic, trade and social factors	GDP (PPP) per capita Remittances, FDI... Debt repayments Trade openness Global and local food prices	Household income/wealth Family employment Government assistance (safety nets) Remittances Infrastructure availability Local food prices
Agricultural factors	Food production levels Cereal yields	Cereal yields
Political and policy factors	Governance quality Democracy, human rights	Local governance quality Social ties

Source: Author's own deliberations

economic, trade and social factors; agricultural factors; and political and policy factors.

They are listed in Table 1.1 and divided into country level and individual/ household level, depending on where their impact can best be observed and measured. Their enumeration is relatively inclusive but given the conceptual complexity of food security, for brevity's sake some variables that affect food security only marginally have been left out. For each of the variables listed, a short discussion of its anticipated impact on food security based on the existing research findings follows.

The enumerated factors are treated as independent of aid for the purposes of this discussion, but, as must have become clear from the discussion of the different aspects of food security, most of them can be influenced by aid as well. In that manner, they channel an additional indirect effect of aid on food security. This will be addressed in greater detail in Chapter 4.

Country-level variables

Population and environmental factors

Population and related concepts (population growth, population density, urbanisation) are largely accepted as partial determinants of food security at the national level. Larger population sizes are generally associated with lower food-insecurity levels, although the underlying mechanism is not clear (Petrikova and Chadha, 2013). High population growth and population density are even more significantly linked to adverse food security outcomes, while a larger portion of urban population generally has the opposite effect (Leisinger, 2000; Leisinger *et al.*, 2002).

Conflicts exert a negative bearing on all aspects of food security. Regarding food availability, agricultural production tends to fall by 1.5 per cent per year in periods of conflict (Kang and Meernik, 2005; Teodosijevic, 2003). Although international or national food aid often steps in, the average per capita daily intake of people decreases by 7 per cent (ibid.). The immediate reasons for this decline include the destruction of rural infrastructure, loss of livestock, deforestation, the use of land-mines and people's displacement. Moreover, hunger is sometimes used as a weapon (Messer, 1990; Duffield, 2007).

Natural disasters usually lead to massive loss of crops and destruction of stored foods, hence reducing national food availability (Carter *et al.*, 2007). Their negative impact tends to be particularly harmful in countries with rain-fed farming and in economies that are highly dependent on agriculture. Disasters also negatively influence people's food access, as poor people have generally fewer means to cope with the resultant increase in food prices (ibid.).

Economic, trade and social factors

At the country level, higher levels and rates of economic growth (GDP) translate into greater ability to purchase food in international markets and thus augment national food stocks. However, neither a high average GDP per capita nor its increase *automatically* boost national food security in all cases, as they might not elevate incomes and food access among the poorest levels of society, who generally suffer from food insecurity the most (Timmer, 2000). Aside from aid, levels of national income can be bolstered via other external financial flows, including remittances and foreign direct investment (FDI). These should, in theory, reduce country-level food insecurity, but, as Mihalache-O'Keef and Li (2011) demonstrate, it is not always the case. Debt repayments constitute another related concept to GDP, which – if high – can have dampening effects on countries' food security.

The dispute vis-à-vis the effects of trade barriers and trade openness on food security has been a highly charged one among development researchers for decades. According to the classic Ricardian comparative-advantage trade model, all countries benefit from trade. The positive relationship between trade and growth has been empirically confirmed by many economists, including Dollar and Kraay (2002) and Berg and Krueger (2003). However, some researchers challenged the assumptions on which the Ricardian model is based as unrealistic (Lipsey and Lancaster, 1956; Sawada, 2009). Thus, while the dismantlement of trade barriers and opening up to trade indisputably affect countries' economic growth and, in turn, their food security, the direction of the impact might vary according to the type of trade and other accompanying policies.

Vis-à-vis food prices, the literature has identified two important facts regarding their impact on food security. First, a rise in food prices tends to negatively affect food security the most in net food-importing countries where citizens' non-food expenditures are not large enough to accommodate this price augmentation

(Fafchamps, 1992). Second, the rise or fall in international food prices does not automatically translate into a rise/fall in local prices (FAO, 2011). Thus, a rise in food prices is likely to exacerbate food security, but this link is more direct in the case of local prices in net food-importing countries and contingent on countries' average income levels.

Agricultural factors

The question how much food countries ought to produce domestically is again quite controversial. On one side of the argument are the 'Malthusians', who worry about *global* food availability and urge all countries to raise food production levels (Cohen, 1995; Del Ninno *et al.*, 2007). On the other side are the 'techno-ecologists', who see as the main root of global food insecurity flawed redistribution, not insufficient production, and therefore encourage countries to liberalise trade and thereby gain foreign currency to purchase sufficient food for everyone (Bongaarts, 1996; Tweeten and McClelland, 1997). Given the large array of different arguments on this topic, it is hard to determine whether the effect of higher domestic food production on national food security is positive or neutral; most likely, the relationship varies by case.

Higher cereal yields are widely believed to increase countries' food availability and, in turn, their overall food security (Rosegrant and Cline, 2003).

Political and policy factors

As discussed already, governance, regime type and human-rights records constitute important conditioning factors in the aid–food security relationship, with the hypothesised potential to reinforce the positive effect of aid on food security. As such, these variables are not treated as simple control variables but ones that interact with aid in its influence on food security. However, on their own these indicators are also widely regarded as affecting food security positively if good and negatively if bad (Azmat and Coghill, 2005; Sahley *et al.*, 2005).

Individual/household-level variables

Population and environmental factors

The composition and demographic characteristics of households have been found to affect people's food security to a significant degree. High dependency ratios – more children or retired people per working-age adult – complicate the achievement of food access for all household members; however, this relationship does not hold for larger household sizes in general (Chazee, 2004). Furthermore, female-headed households tend to suffer from more food-access problems, but their difficulties are less pronounced with household head's higher age and education (IFAD, 1998). In addition, individual food security can be threatened by discriminatory intra-household relationships even in households with sufficient food access for all members. Behrman (1988) finds that parents in South Asia favour sons in food allocation over daughters, with the pattern more salient in the 'lean season'. Other authors have observed similar practices in other developing countries, in relation to daughters as well as adult women and the elderly (Maxwell, 1996). People's general health status also has a significant impact on their food security, as unhealthy individuals might not be able to achieve food security even if receiving a calorically sufficient and nutritional balanced diet (Strauss and Thomas, 2008).

Other influential factors in this category are the region where people live – whether urban or rural – and of what race/caste/ethnic origin they are. Regarding the rural–urban divide, people living in urban areas have traditionally been more food secure than rural inhabitants, contributing to increasing rates of urbanisation across the world. Nevertheless, as cities in developing countries have grown, the divide has become less notable and research on the effects of the most recent economic crisis suggested that the urban and rural poor were equally vulnerable to food insecurity (Garrett and Ruel, 1999; Haddad *et al.*, 1999; Ruel *et al.*, 2010). People of minority race and ethnic origins and in South Asia also people from the lowest castes have generally suffered from higher rates of poverty and food insecurity than others (e.g. Alkon and Agyeman, 2010; Mehta and Shah, 2003).

Just as conflicts and disasters negatively affect food security on the country level, they do so also on the local level. Furthermore, individual/household food security tends to be threatened by other household crises and shocks, including the death and serious illness of income providers, loss of employment, death of livestock or the loss of dwelling (Littrell *et al.*, 2011; Petrikova and Chadha, 2013).

Economic, trade and social factors

Many researchers have treated poverty rates as virtually identical with food security (Frongillo, 2003; Maxwell and Smith, 1992). However, while the relationship between poverty, food insecurity and negative nutritional outcomes, indeed, tends to hold for adult people, it is not always the case with infants and young children (Bhattacharya *et al.*, 2004). Thus, whereas it is safe to assume a strong positive relationship between poverty (low household income and/or low wealth index) and deficient food access, a complete identification of poverty with food insecurity as a whole should be avoided.

Similar to global food prices, the effects of higher local food prices on food security can be positive or negative, depending on whether a household is a net food consumer or a net food producer or both (Swinnen and Squicciarini, 2012).

Vis-à-vis employment and other income-generating opportunities, according to Von Braun (1995) they have a high chance of improving both national and local food security. This is especially true if labour markets operate freely and poor people can migrate throughout the country in search of work (not the case in China: Ling and Zhongyi, 1995). It can obviously be difficult for poor countries to significantly increase the number of formal work positions, and particularly so in rural areas; however, even food-for-work programmes have proven successful in strengthening participants' food access (Ahmed *et al.*, 1995).

Social safety nets constitute another effective economic mechanism that states can use to bolster citizens' food security. Their role is two-fold. Primarily, they can help individuals, families and communities that have been struck by crises respond to them without having to resort to severe coping measures, such as selling-off means of production or migrating in distress (Adato and Feldman, 2001). Second, they can also assist people who suffer from chronic food insecurity, by helping some poor people escape the cycle of chronic food insecurity and poverty (Devereux, 2002). Remittances could in theory function in a similar way to government safety nets. However, research has shown the funds to reduce household worries about food, but not always to actually increase consumption (Babatunde and Qaim, 2010; Abadi *et al.*, 2013).

Finally, good-quality local infrastructure, particularly the availability of easily accessible and well-equipped health centres and hospitals, can have a highly positive effect on people's food security (Strauss and Thomas, 2008).

Agricultural factors

Similar to the country level, higher cereal yields on the household level are associated with strengthened food security (Godfray *et al.*, 2010). However, a few caveats need to be mentioned here, most importantly that if the increase in cereal yield occurs due to new seed varieties that need chemical fertiliser or other inputs to grow, local food security will be strengthened overall only if small farmers' access to the inputs is facilitated as well (e.g. Spenser, 2012).

Political and policy factors

While existing research has not yet linked food security with the quality of local governance per se, similar to the country level one can anticipate the quality of local institutions and policies to play an important conditioning role in the relationship between aid and food security. On its own, it can also have a direct positive link with food security as regions with better-running services can generally respond more effectively to food crises and distribute government aid more effectively (Blair, 2000; Nijenhuis, 2002).

Another crucial factor is the strength of social ties, or social capital, whose importance in ensuring short-term household food security development researchers recognised only recently. Even in societies where the central government structures break down, as they did in Somalia, strong social ties within communities can act as a powerful type of informal insurance: if one household loses its access to food, another household or the community steps in to provide (Petrikova and Chadha, 2013; Pingali *et al.*, 2005).

Conclusion

This chapter has set up the theoretical and literature framework in which the empirical research of this book is grounded and against which it measures its findings. The brief overview of existing relevant literature has identified a lack of research specifically linking aid, both generally and in its various modalities, with food security, particularly on the country level. In an effort to enhance the relevance and applicability of the ensuing findings, I have strived to learn from the shortcomings of the existent aid-effectiveness literature and examine the relationships under consideration using a multitude of observational lenses (both macro and micro), of research methods (both quantitative and qualitative), as well as of food-security, aid and governance measures.

The next chapter discusses in relatively broad terms the book's methodology and tools used to gather and analyse data. Specific analytical methods are described in more detail in each empirical chapter separately, as they differ from one part of the study to another.

Notes

1 http://www.who.int/trade/glossary/story028/en/
2 Development Assistance Committee is a forum for selected OECD member states to discuss issues surrounding aid disbursement.
3 Most of the classifications utilised in the system of aid categorisation have, however, been used by researchers in the past.
4 Again, initially I divided the government-implemented aid further into bilateral and multilateral, but ended up excluding the division due to the unavailability of sufficiently detailed aid data.
5 On the country level, 'other' aid comprises primarily budget support and aid to industry, construction, trade and tourism; on the household level, 'other' aid often consists primarily of direct food and cash transfers.
6 http://www.un.org/en/globalissues/governance/
7 If a country's national income is rising, so is likely its ability to purchase more food from abroad if needed.
8 Moreover, if aid were to really bring about economic and social development, in the very long run it should always contribute to the improvement of all the three sectors mentioned.
9 Both aid and governance have been depicted in Figure 1.3 as word-clouds of terms and definitions commonly associated with the two concepts, in order to illustrate their heterogeneity and to figuratively open their 'black box'.
10 The article by Burnside and Dollar (2000) generated a heated academic polemic, with many researchers including Daalgard and Hansen (2001), Easterly (2003), Hansen and Tarp (2001) and Lensink and White (2001) finding Burnside and Dollar's results fragile to changing time frames and specifications. The specific choice of Burnside and Dollar's 'good' economic policies as low inflation, budget balance and trade liberalisation was also questioned, particularly for its clear neo-liberal bias.
11 DAC donors have to report data on their aid disbursements to the DAC database.
12 http://www.povertyactionlab.org/publication/where-credit-is-due
13 Many donors, however, place certain stipulations or conditions on the provision of budget support; for example, the promulgation of a Poverty Reduction Strategy Paper (PRSP).
14 If budget support were, indeed, provided only to countries with higher quality of governance as some donors have promised, the conditioning of this instrument would unlikely appear significant in the results. Nevertheless, there are many indications that donors often do not follow through with their rhetorical commitments (Eifert and Gelb, 2005).

References

Abadi, N., Techane, A., Tesfay, G., Maxwel, D., and Vaitla, B. (2013). *The Impact of Remittances on Household Food Security: A Micro Perspective from Tigray, Ethiopia*. Available at: https://editorialexpress.com/cgi-bin/conference/download.cgi?db_name=CSAE2014&paper_id=258

Abdellatif, A. (2003). 'Good governance and its relationship to democracy and economic development', in *Global Forum III on Fighting Corruption and Safeguarding Integrity*. Seoul: UNDCP.

Adato, M., and Feldman, S. (2001). 'Safety nets', in M. Agnes, R. Quisumbing and R. Suseela (eds), *Empowering Women to Achieve Food Security*. Washington, DC: IFPRI.

Agénor, P., Bayraktar, N., and El Aynaoui, K. (2008). 'Roads out of poverty? Assessing the links between aid, public investment, growth, and poverty reduction', *Journal of Development Economics*, 86(2), pp. 277–95.

Ahmed, A., Zohir, S., Kumar, S., and Haider Chowdhury, O. (1995). 'Bangladesh's food-for-work program and alternatives to improve food security', in J. Von Braun (ed.), *Employment for Poverty Reduction and Food Security*. Washington, DC: IFPRI.

Alkon, A. H., and Agyeman, J. (2011). *Cultivating Food Justice: Race, Class, and Sustainability*. Boston, MA: MIT Press.

Angelucci, M., Karlan, D., and Zinman, J. (2015). 'Win some lose some? Evidence from a randomized microcredit program placement experiment by Compartamos Banco', *American Economic Journal: Applied Economics*, 7(1), pp. 151–82.

Arndt, C., Jones, S., and Tarp, F. (2015). 'Assessing foreign aid's long run contribution to growth and development', *World Development*, 69, pp. 6–18.

Asher, R. (1962). 'Multilateral versus bilateral aid: an old controversy revisited', *International Organization*, 16(4), pp. 697–719.

Attanasio, O., Augsburg, B., De Haas, R., Fitzsimons, E., and Harmgart, H. (2015). 'The impacts of microfinance: evidence from joint-liability lending in Mongolia', *American Economic Journal: Applied Economics*, 7(1), pp. 90–122.

AU (2003). *Maputo Declaration on Agriculture and Food Security*. Maputo: African Union.

Augsburg, B., De Haas, R., Harmgart, H., and Meghir, C. (2015). 'The impacts of microcredit: evidence from Bosnia and Herzegovina', *American Economic Journal: Applied Economics*, 7(1), pp. 183–203.

Azmat, F., and Coghill, K. (2005). 'Good governance and market-based reforms: a study of Bangladesh', *International Review of Administrative Sciences*, 71(4), pp. 625–38.

Babatunde, R., and Qaim, M. (2010). 'Impact of off-farm income on food security and nutrition in Nigeria', *Food Policy*, 35(4), pp. 303–11.

Bach, C., and Matthews, A. (1999). 'Development aid and food security', in *Second Annual Conference on Global Economic Analysis*. Denmark: Gl Avernaes, pp. 20–2.

Bailey, S., and Hedlund, K. (2012). 'The impact of cash transfers on nutrition in emergency and transitional contexts: a review of the evidence', *HPG Synthesis Paper*. London: ODI.

Banerjee, A., Duflo, E., Glennerster, R., and Kinnan, C. (2015). 'The miracle of microfinance? Evidence from a randomized evaluation', *American Economic Journal: Applied Economics*, 7(1), pp. 22–53.

Barrett, C. (2002). 'Food security and food assistance programs', in *Handbook of Agricultural Economics*. Amsterdam: Elsevier, pp. 1–95.

Behrman, J. (1988). 'Intra-household allocation of nutrients in rural India: are boys favoured? Do parents exhibit inequality aversion?', *Oxford Economic Papers*, 40(1), pp. 32–54.

Berg, A., and Krueger, A. (2003). *Trade, Growth, and Poverty: A Selective Survey.* Washington, DC: IMF.

Berti, P., Krasevec, J., and FitzGerald, S. (2004). 'A review of the effectiveness of agriculture interventions in improving nutrition outcomes', *Public Health Nutrition*, 7(5), pp. 599–609.

Bhattacharya, J., Currie, J., and Haider, S. (2004). 'Poverty, food insecurity, and nutritional outcomes in children and adults', *Journal of Health Economics*, 23(4), pp. 839–62.

Bhutta Z., Ahmed T., Black R., Cousens S., Dewey K., Giugliani E., Haider B., Kirkwood B., Morris S., Sachdev H., and Shekar, M. (2008). 'What works? Interventions for maternal and child undernutrition and survival', *The Lancet*, 371(9610), pp. 417–40.

Bigdon, C., and Korf, B. (2002). 'The role of development aid in conflict transformation: facilitating empowerment processes and community building', in A. Austin, M. Fischer and N. Ropers (eds), *Berghof Handbook for Conflict Transformation*. Berlin, Germany: VS Verlag für Sozialwissenschaften, pp. 341–70.

Bigsten, A., and Tengstam, S. (2015). 'International coordination and the effectiveness of aid', *World Development*, 69, pp. 75–85.

Blair, H. (2000). 'Participation and accountability at the periphery: democratic local governance in six countries', *World Development*, 28(1), pp. 21–39.

Bongaarts, J. (1996). 'Population pressure and the food supply system in the developing world', *Population and Development Review*, 22(3), pp. 483–503.

Börzel, T., and Risse, T. (2005). 'Public–private partnerships: effective and legitimate tools of international governance', in E. Grande and L. Pauly (eds), *Complex Sovereignty: Reconstructing Political Authority in the Twenty First Century*. Toronto: University of Toronto Press, pp. 195–216.

Bovaird, T., and Löffler, E. (2003). 'Evaluating the quality of public governance: indicators, models and methodologies', *International Review of Administrative Sciences*, 69(3), pp. 313–28.

Brückner, M. (2013). 'On the simultaneity problem in the aid and growth debate', *Journal of Applied Econometrics*, 28(1), pp. 126–50.

Bulí , A., and Hamann, A. (2008). 'Volatility of development aid: from the frying pan into the fire?', *World Development*, 36(10), pp. 2048–66.

Bulow, J., and Rogoff, K. (2005). 'Grants versus loans for development banks', *American Economic Review*, 95(2), pp. 393–7.

Burnside, C. and Dollar, D. (2000). 'Aid, policies, and growth', *American Economic Review*, 90(4), pp. 847–68.

Burnside, C., and Dollar, D. (2004). 'Aid, policies and growth: revisiting the evidence', *World Bank Policy Research Working Paper*, 3251. Washington, DC: The World Bank Group.

Carter, M., Little, P., Mogues, T., and Negatu, W. (2007). 'Poverty traps and natural disasters in Ethiopia and Honduras', *World Development*, 35(5), pp. 835–56.

Chazee, L. (2004). 'New directions for agriculture in reducing poverty', *DFID Report.* London: DFID.

Chen, S., Mu, R., and Ravallion, M. (2009). 'Are there lasting impacts of aid to poor areas?', *Journal of Public Economics*, 93(3), pp. 512–28.

Christiaensen, L., Demery, L., and Kuhl, J. (2011). 'The (evolving) role of agriculture in poverty reduction: an empirical perspective', *Journal of Development Economics*, 96(2), pp. 239–54.

Clemens, M., Radelet, S., and Bhavnani, R. (2004). 'Counting chickens when they hatch: the short-term effect of aid on growth', *Center for Global Development Working Paper*, 44. New York: Center for Global Development.

Clements, B., Gupta, S., Pivovarsky, A., and Tiongson, E. (2004). 'Grants versus loans: why a shift of development aid from loans to grants should be accompanied by institutional strengthening in developing countries', *Finance and Development*, 41(3), pp. 46–9.

Cohen, J. (1995). *How Many People Can the Earth Support?* New York: W. W. Norton.

Collier, P., and Goderis, B. (2009). 'Structural policies for shock-prone developing countries', *Oxford Economic Papers*, 61(4), pp. 703–26.

Corbett, J. (1988). 'Famine and household coping strategies', *World Development*, 16(9), pp. 1099–112.

Cordella, T., and Dell'Ariccia, G. (2007). 'Budget support versus project aid: a theoretical appraisal', *Economic Journal*, 117(523), pp. 1260–79.

Crépon, B., Devoto, F., Duflo, E., and Parienté, W. (2015). 'Estimating the impact of microcredit on those who take it up: evidence from a randomised experiment in Morocco', *American Economic Journal: Applied Economics*, 7(1), pp. 123–50.

Crola, J. (2009). 'Aid for agriculture: turning promises into reality on the ground', *Oxfam Policy and Practice: Agriculture, Food, and Land*, 9(6), pp. 17–67.

Dalgaard, C., and Hansen, H. (2001). 'On aid, growth and good policies', *Journal of Development Studies*, 37(6), pp. 17–41.

Dasandi, N., Hudson, D., and Pegram, T. (2015). 'Post-2015 development agenda setting in focus: governance and institutions', in J. Waage and C. Yap (eds), *Thinking beyond Sectors for Sustainable Development*. London: Ubiquity Press.

Del Ninno, C., Dorosh, P. A., and Subbarao, K. (2007). 'Food aid, domestic policy, and food security: contrasting experiences from South Asia and sub-Saharan Africa', *Food Policy*, 32(4), pp. 413–35.

Devarajan, S., and Swaroop, V. (2000). 'The implications of foreign aid fungibility for development assistance', *The World Bank: Structure and Policies*, pp. 196–209.

Devereux, S. (2002). 'Can social safety nets reduce chronic poverty?', *Development Policy Review*, 20(5), pp. 657–75.

DFID (2001). *Making Government Work for Poor People*. London: DFID.

Dollar, D., and Kraay, A. (2002). 'Growth is good for the poor', *Journal of Economic Growth*, 7(3), pp. 195–225.

Doucouliagos, H., and Paldam, M. (2008). 'Aid effectiveness on growth: a meta study', *European Journal of Political Economy*, 24(1), pp. 1–24.

Doucouliagos, H., and Paldam, M. (2011). 'The ineffectiveness of development aid on growth: an update', *European Journal of Political Economy*, 27(2), pp. 399–404.

Dreher, A., Nunnenkamp, P., and Thiele, R. (2008). 'Does aid for education educate children? Evidence from panel data', *World Bank Economic Review*, 22(2), pp. 291–314.

Drèze, J. (2004). 'Democracy and right to food', *Economic and Political Weekly*, 39(17), pp. 1723–31.

Duffield, M. (2007). *Development, Security, and Unending War: Governing the World of Peoples*. Cambridge: Polity.

Easterly, W. (2003). 'Can foreign aid buy growth?', *Journal of Economic Perspectives*, 17(3), pp. 23–48.

Eifert, B., and Gelb, A. (2005). 'Improving the dynamics of aid: towards more predictable budget support', *World Bank Policy Research Working Paper*, 3732. Washington, DC: The World Bank Group.

Fafchamps, M. (1992). 'Cash crop production, food price volatility, and rural market integration in the third world', *American Journal of Agricultural Economics*, 74(1), pp. 90–9.

FAO (2011). *The State of Food Insecurity in the World*. Available at: http://www.fao.org/docrep/013/i1683e/i1683e.pdf

FAO (2015). *The State of Food Insecurity in the World*. Available at: http://www.fao.org/3/a-i4646e.pdf

Fiallos, E., and Ruiz Cantero, M. (2008). '¿A quién benefician los programas de salud dirigidos a los más pobres? Éxitos y fracasos'. Available at: http://rua.ua.es/dspace/bitstream/10045/8344/3/beneficios_programas_salud_pobres.pdf

Frongillo, E. A. (2003). 'Understanding obesity and program participation in the context of poverty and food insecurity', *Journal of Nutrition*, 133(7), pp. 2117–18.

Galiani, S., Knack, S., Xu, L., and Zou, B. (2014). 'The effect of aid on growth: evidence from a quasi-experiment', *SSRN*, 2400752.

Garrett, J., and Ruel, M. (1999). 'Are determinants of rural and urban food security and nutritional status different? Some insights from Mozambique', *World Development*, 27(11), pp. 1955–75.

Gelan, A. (2006). 'Cash or food aid? A general equilibrium analysis for Ethiopia', *Development Policy Review*, 24(5), pp. 601–24.

Gibson, A. (1993). 'NGOs and income-generation projects: lessons from the Joint Funding Scheme', *Development in Practice*, 3(3), pp. 184–95.

Gisselquist, R. (2012). 'Good governance as a concept, and why this matters for development policy', *WIDER Working Paper*, 30.

Godfray, H., Beddington, J., Crute, I., Haddad, L., Lawrence, D., Muir, J., Pretty, J., Robinson, S., Thomas, S., and Toulmin, C. (2010). 'Food security: the challenge of feeding 9 billion people', *Science*, 327(5967), pp. 812–18.

Gomanee, K., Morrissey, O., Mosley, P., and Verschoor, A. (2005). 'Aid, government expenditure, and aggregate welfare', *World Development*, 33(3), pp. 355–70.

Graham, J., Amos, B., and Plumptre, T. (2003). 'Principles for good governance in the 21st century', *Institute on Governance Policy Brief*, 15. Ottawa: Institute on Governance.

Grindle, M. (2004). 'Good enough governance: poverty reduction and reform in developing countries', *Governance*, 17(4), pp. 525–48.

Haddad, L., Ruel, M., and Garrett, J. (1999). 'Are urban poverty and undernutrition growing? Some newly assembled evidence', *World Development*, 27(11), pp. 1891–904.

Hamelin, A., Habicht, J., and Beaudry, M. (1999). 'Food insecurity: consequences for the household and broader social implications', *Journal of Nutrition*, 129(2), pp. 525S–528S.

Hansen, H., and Tarp, F. (2001). 'Aid and growth regressions', *Journal of Development Economics*, 64(2), pp. 545–70.

Haque, M. (1999). 'The fate of sustainable development under neo-liberal regimes in developing countries', *International Political Science Review*, 20(2), pp. 197–218.

Harrigan, J., and Wang, C. (2011). 'A new approach to the allocation of aid among developing countries: is the USA different from the rest?' *World Development*, 39(8), pp. 1281–93.

Heady, D., Rao, P., and Duhs, A. (2004). 'All the conditions of effective foreign aid', *Centre for Efficiency and Productivity Analysis Working Paper*, 8. Brisbane: Centre for Efficiency and Productivity Analysis.

Heyneman, S. (1999). 'The sad story of UNESCO's education statistics', *International Journal of Educational Development*, 19(1), pp. 65–74.

Hoque, B., Juncker, T., Sack, R., Ali, M., and Aziz, K. (1996). 'Sustainability of a water, sanitation, and hygiene education project in rural Bangladesh: a 5-year follow-up', *Bulletin of the World Health Organization*, 74(4), pp. 431–7.

Hudson, D. (2015). *Global Finance and Development*. London: Routledge.

Hudson, D., and Leftwich, A. (2014). 'From political economy to political analysis', *Developmental Leadership Program Research Paper*, 25. Birmingham Developmental Leadership Program.

Hulme, D., and Edwards, M. (1997). *Too Close for Comfort? NGOs, States, and Donors*. London: St Martin's Press.

IFAD (1998). *Rural Women in IFAD's Projects: The Key to Poverty Alleviation*. Available at: http://www.ifad.org/pub/other/!brocsch.pdf

IYCN (2011). *Nutrition and Food Security Impacts of Agriculture Projects*. Washington, DC: Infant and Young Child Nutrition Project.

Jenkins, J., and Scanlan, S. (2001). 'Food security in less developed countries, 1970 to 1990', *American Sociological Review*, 66(5), pp. 718–44.

Kanbur, R. (2006). 'The economics of international aid', *Handbook of the Economics of Giving, Altruism, and Reciprocity*, 2, pp. 1559–88.

Kang, S., and Meernik, J. (2005). 'Civil war destruction and the prospects for economic growth', *Journal of Politics*, 67(1), pp. 88–109.

Karlan, D., and Zinman, J. (2011). 'Microcredit in theory and practice: using randomised credit scoring for impact evaluation', *Science*, 332(6035), pp. 1278–84.

Kaufmann, D., Kraay, A., and Mastruzzi, M. (2007). 'Worldwide governance indicators project: answering the critics', *World Bank Policy Research Working Paper*, 4149. Washington: The World Bank Group.

Kaufmann, D., and Kraay, A. (2008). 'Governance indicators: where are we, where should we be going?', *World Bank Research Observer*, 23(1), pp. 1–30.

King, G., and Murray, C. (2002). 'Rethinking human security', *Political Science Quarterly*, 116(4), pp. 585–610.

Koch, D., Dreher, A., Nunnenkamp, P., and Thiele, R. (2008). 'Keeping a low profile: what determines the allocation of aid by non-governmental organizations?', *World Development*, 37(5), pp. 902–18.

Kosack, S. (2003). 'Effective aid: how democracy allows development aid to improve the quality of life', *World Development*, 31(1), pp. 1–22.

Leisinger, K. (2000). 'Yes: stop blocking progress', *Foreign Policy*, 119, pp. 113–22.

Leisinger, K., Schmitt, K., and Pandya-Lorch, R. (2002). *Six Billion and Counting: Population Growth and Food Security in the 21st century*. Washington, DC: IFPRI.

Lensink, R., and Morrissey, O. (2000). 'Aid instability as a measure of uncertainty and the positive impact of aid on growth', *Journal of Development Studies*, 36(3), pp. 31–49.

Lensink, R., and White, H. (2001). 'Aid allocation, poverty reduction and the Assessing Aid report', *Journal of International Development*, 12(3), pp. 399–412.

Lerrick, A., and Meltzer, A. (2002). 'Grants: a better way to deliver aid', *Quarterly International Economics Report*. Pittsburgh: Carnegie Mellon.

Lewis, D., and Opoku-Mensah, P. (2006). 'Moving forward research agendas on international NGOs: theory, agency, and context', *Journal of International Development*, 18(5), pp. 665–75.

Ligon, E., and Sadoulet, E. (2007). 'Estimating the effects of aggregate agricultural growth on the distribution of expenditures', *SSRN*, 1769944.

Ling, Z., and Zhongyi, J. (1995). 'Yigong-Daizhen in China: a new experience with labour- intensive public works in poor areas', in J. Von Braun (ed.), *Employment for Poverty Reduction and Food Security*. Washington, DC: IFPRI.

Lips, M. (2005). 'Sufficient nourishment worldwide via transfer payments', *Food Policy*, 30(1), pp. 81–96.

Lipsey, R., and Lancaster, K. (1956). 'The general theory of second best', *Review of Economic Studies*, 24(1), pp. 11–32.

Lipsky, M., and Thibodeau, M. (1988). 'Feeding the hungry with surplus commodities', *Political Science Quarterly*, 103(2), pp. 223–44.

Littrell, M., Boris, N., Brown, L., Hill, M., and Macintyre, K. (2011). 'The influence of orphan care and other household shocks on health status over time: a longitudinal study of children's caregivers in rural Malawi', *AIDS Care*, 23(12), pp. 1551–61.

Masud, N., and Yontcheva, B. (2005). 'Does foreign aid reduce poverty? Empirical evidence from nongovernmental and bilateral aid', *IMF Working Paper*. Washington, DC: IMF.

Maxwell, S. (1996). 'Food security: a post-modern perspective', *Food Policy*, 21(2), pp. 155–70.

Maxwell, S., and Smith, M. (1992). 'Household food security: a conceptual review', in S. Maxwell and T. R. Frankenberger (eds), *Household Food Security: Concepts, Indicators, Measurements*. New York: IFAD and UNICEF.

McGillivray, M., Feeny, S., Hermes, N., and Lensink, R. (2006). 'Controversies over the impact of development aid: it works; it doesn't; it can, but that depends...', *Journal of International Development*, 18(7), pp. 1031–50.

Mehta, A., and Shah, A. (2003). 'Chronic poverty in India: incidence, causes and policies', *World Development*, 31(3), pp. 491–511.

Merrigan, P., and Normandin, M. (1996). 'Precautionary saving motives: an assessment from UK time series of cross-sections', *Economic Journal*, 106(438), pp. 1193–208.

Messer, E. (1990). 'ood wars: hunger as a weapon in 1989', in R. Chen (ed.), *The Hunger Report 1989*. Providence: World Hunger Program, Brown University.

Michaelowa, K., and Weber, A. (2006). 'Aid effectiveness in the education sector: a dynamic panel analysis', *Frontiers of Economics and Globalization*, 1, pp. 357–85.

Mihalache-O'Keef, A., and Li, Q. (2011). 'Modernisation vs dependency revisited: effects of Foreign Direct Investment on food security in less developed countries', *International Studies Quarterly*, 55(1), pp. 71–93.

Mikhail, M., Hickson, C., and Willoughby, R. (2013). 'Donor in the dark: putting a spotlight on UK aid to small-scale farmers', *Oxford Committee for Famine Relief (OXFAM), Concern Worldwide, and Self Africa Help Research Paper*. Oxford: OXFAM.

Minch, K. (2005). 'Bilateral vs multilateral aid', *IDEA Working Paper*. Stockholm: International Institute for Democracy and Electoral Assistance.

Morrissey, O. (2004) 'Conditionality and aid effectiveness re-evaluated', *World Economy*, 27(2), pp. 153–71.

Mosley, P. (1986). 'Aid-effectiveness: the micro-macro paradox', *IDS Bulletin*, 17(2), pp. 22–7.

Nijenhuis, G. (2002). *Decentralisation and Popular Participation in Bolivia: The Link Between Local Governance and Local Development*. Utrecht, the Netherlands: KNAG/UU.

Nunnenkamp, P., Weingarth, J., and Weisser, J. (2009). 'Is NGO aid not so different after all? Comparing the allocation of Swiss aid by private and official donors', *European Journal of Political Economy*, 25(4), pp. 422–38.

Odedokun, M. (2004). 'Multilateral and bilateral loans versus grants: issues and evidence', *World Economy*, 27(2), pp. 239–63.

OECD (1995). *Participatory Development and Good Governance*. Paris: OECD.

OECD (2006). *DAC Guidelines and Reference Series Applying Strategic Environmental Assessment: Good Practice Guidance for Development Co-operation*. Paris: OECD.

Olson, C. (1999). 'Nutrition and health outcomes associated with food insecurity and hunger', *Journal of Nutrition*, 129(2), pp. 521S–524S.

Oxenham, J. (2002). *Skills and Literacy Training for Better Livelihoods: A Review of Approaches and Experiences*. Washington, DC: The World Bank Group.

Paris, R. (2001). 'Human security paradigm shift or hot air?', *International Security*, 26(2), pp. 87–102.

Petrikova, I. (2015). 'NGO effectiveness: evidence from the field of child labour in El Salvador', *Forum for Development Studies*, 42(2), pp. 225–44.

Petrikova, I. (2016). 'Promoting "good behaviour" through aid: do "new" donors differ from the "old" ones?', *Journal of International Relations and Development*, 19(1), pp. 153–92.

Petrikova, I., and Chadha, D. (2013). 'The role of social capital in risk-sharing: lessons from Andhra Pradesh', *Journal of South Asian Development*, 8(3), pp. 359–83.

Pingali, P., Alinovi, L., and Sutton, J. (2005). 'Food security in complex emergencies: enhancing food system resilience', *Disasters*, 29(s1), pp. S5–S24.

Pinstrup-Andersen, P. (2009). 'Food security: definition and measurement', *Food Security*, 1(1), pp. 5–7.

Pinstrup-Andersen, P., and M. Cohen. (1998). *Aid to Developing-Country Agriculture: Investing in Poverty Reduction and New Export Opportunities*. Washington, DC: IFPRI.

Reid, L. (2000). 'The consequences of food insecurity for child well-being: an analysis of children's school achievement, psychological well-being, and health', *Joint Centre for Poverty Research Working Paper*, 137. Chicago: Joint Centre for Poverty Research.

Rodrik, D. (1990). 'How should structural adjustment programs be designed?', *World Development*, 18(7), pp. 933–47.

Roodman, D. (2007). 'The anarchy of numbers: aid, development, and cross-country empirics', *World Bank Economic Review*, 21(2), pp. 255–77.

Rosegrant, M., and Cline, S. (2003). 'Global food security: challenges and policies', *Science*, 302(5652), pp. 1917–19.

Rosen, S., and Shapouri, S. (2008). 'Rising food prices intensify food insecurity in developing countries', *Amber Waves*, 6(1), pp. 16–21.

Ruel, M. (2003). 'Is dietary diversity an indicator of food security or dietary quality? A review of measurement issues and research needs', *Food Nutrition Bulletin*, 24(2), pp. 231–2.

Ruel, M. T., Garrett, J. L., Hawkes, C., and Cohen, M. J. (2010). 'The food, fuel, and financial crises affect the urban and rural poor disproportionately: a review of the evidence', *Journal of Nutrition*, 140(1), pp. 170S–176S.

Sahley, C, Groelsema, B., Marchione, T., and Nelson, D. (2005). *The Governance Dimensions of Food Security in Malawi, Vol. 20*. Washington, DC: USAID.

Sawada, Y. (2009). 'The immiserizing growth: an empirical evaluation', *Applied Economics*, 41(13), pp. 1613–20.

Smith, L., El Obeid, A., and Jensen, H. (2000). 'The geography and causes of food insecurity in developing countries', *Agricultural Economics*, 22(2), pp. 199–215.

Spenser, D. (2012). 'Issues in food security and cash crop production in Sierra Leone', *Enterprise Development Services for the World Bank*. Available at: http://www.eds-sl.com/docs/IssuesInFoodSecurityInSierraLeone.pdf

Stoker, G. (2011). 'Was local governance such a good idea? A global comparative perspective', *Public Administration*, 89(1), pp. 15–31.

Strauss, J., and Thomas, D. (2008). 'Health over the life course', *Handbook of Development Economics*, 4(5), pp. 3375–474.

Swinnen, J., and Squicciarini, P. (2012). 'Mixed messages on prices and food security', *Science*, 335(6067), pp. 405–6.

Tarozzi, A., Desai, J., and Johnson, K. (2015). 'The impacts of microcredit: evidence from Ethiopia', *American Economic Journal: Applied Economics*, 7(1), pp. 54–89.

Teodosijevic, S. (2003). 'Armed conflicts and food security', *FAO Working Paper*, 3(11). Rome: FAO.

Thomas, M. A. (2010). 'What do the worldwide governance indicators measure?', *European Journal of Development Research*, 22(1), pp. 31–54.

Timmer, C. (2000). 'The macro dimensions of food security: economic growth, equitable distribution, and food price stability', *Food Policy*, 25(3), pp. 283–95.

Tweeten, L., and McClelland, D. (1997). *Promoting Third-World Development and Food Security*. Westport: Praeger.

UNDP (1997). *Governance for Sustainable Human Development*. New York: UNDP.

Uvin, P. (1992). 'Regime, surplus, and self-interest: the international politics of food aid', *International Studies Quarterly*, 36(3), pp. 293–312.

Von Braun, J. (ed.). (1995). *Employment for Poverty Reduction and Food Security*. Washington, DC: IFPRI.

Von Braun, J., Bouis, H., Pandya-Lorch, R., and Kumar, S. (1992). *Improving Food Security of the Poor: Concept, Policy, and Programs*. Washington, DC: International Food Policy Research Institute.

Wallace, B. (2013). 'Public–private partnerships in international development: are we asking the right questions', *CAFOD Discussion Paper*. Available at: http://cafod.org.uk/content/download/9569/77021/file/PPP-interactive.pdf

WB (1994). *Governance, The World Bank's Experience*. Washington, DC: The World Bank Group.

WB (2015). *What Are Public–Private Partnerships?* Available at: http://ppp.worldbank.org/public-private-partnership/overview/what-are-public-private-partnerships

Weiss, T. (2000). 'Governance, good governance and global governance: conceptual and actual challenges', *Third World Quarterly*, 21(5), pp. 795–814.

Williamson, C. (2008). 'Foreign aid and human development: the impact of foreign aid to the health sector', *Southern Economic Journal*, 75(1), pp. 188–207.

Zerbe, N. (2004). 'Feeding the famine? American food aid and the GMO debate in Southern Africa', *Food Policy*, 29(6), pp. 593–608.

2 Methodology, data and methods

Introduction

This chapter offers an introductory overview of the methodology and methods underpinning the research presented in this book. First, it briefly introduces a map of empirical research discussed in the following chapters. Second, it talks about the book's methodological approach, with a specific focus on the advantages of the utilised mixed methods. Finally, it discusses the different data sources utilised.

A map to the empirical research ahead

This book examines the relationship between aid and food security through four different studies (graphically depicted by Figure 2.1).

First, in order to identify global patterns in the links between different aid modalities, recipient countries' food-security levels and quality of governance, Chapter 3 conducts a quantitative cross-country study of all developing (low- and middle-income) countries[1] from 1990–2010. The lower time boundary was set because data on food security prior to 1990 were collected differently from the way they are nowadays, hindering comparability; 2010 was chosen as the upper cut-off year as later data were not available at the time of analysis.

Second, so as to gain a closer look at the country-level relationships between aid, food security and governance, I carry out a case study of four developing countries. First, that study tests – when possible – whether the conclusions reached in part one hold also when using a case-study approach with qualitative data, specifically examining Peru, Ethiopia, India and Vietnam. In addition, the qualitative analysis in Chapter 4 explores and illuminates the processes and causal mechanisms underlying the aid–food security relationships in detail. The four countries were chosen mainly with a view to the availability of appropriate data, which has introduced a limitation into the study. Both the case selection and accompanying limitation are discussed at greater length in Chapter 4.

Third, to examine the aid–food security–governance link from the perspective of aid recipients, Chapter 5 carries out a quantitative analysis of household- and individual-level survey data. This study marks the beginning of the book's

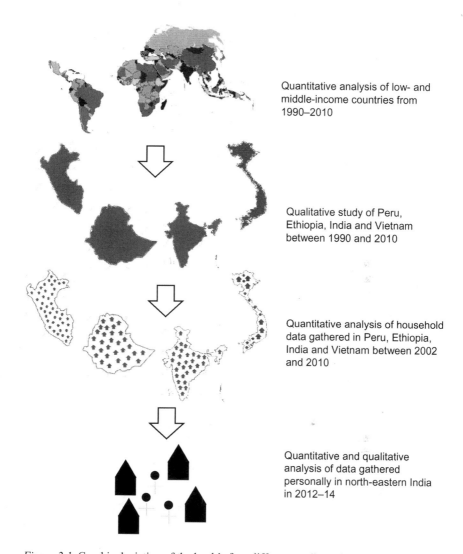

Quantitative analysis of low- and middle-income countries from 1990–2010

Qualitative study of Peru, Ethiopia, India and Vietnam between 1990 and 2010

Quantitative analysis of household data gathered in Peru, Ethiopia, India and Vietnam between 2002 and 2010

Quantitative and qualitative analysis of data gathered personally in north-eastern India in 2012–14

Figure 2.1 Graphic depiction of the book's four different studies.

Source: Author's own image

micro-level analysis. Using information collected by the Young Lives initiative from the same four countries as those examined in the preceding study, I study the effects of development projects on recipients' food security along with the intervening impact of local governance.

Finally, in Chapter 6 I tighten the observatory lens even further and inspect the process through which specific aid interventions influence household and individual food security through an analysis of personally collected information. I gathered the requisite data from surveys and longer interviews administered in a cluster of villages in northern India.

Methodological approach and related choices about methods

From a methodological standpoint, this book follows a post-positivist research paradigm. It embraces some of the key tenets of logical realism, including onto-logical realism and the possibility and desirability of objective truth. However, it considers the objective truth as a goal towards which one can strive but is unlikely to ever reach. Other areas where post-positivism diverges from positivism are acknowledgement that there is no neutral knowledge, recognition that dualistic, black-and-white view of the world is reductionist and emphasis on the ethical aspects of research (Halperin and Heath, 2012).

Adherence to the post-positivist paradigm has motivated the adoption of a multi-level, mixed-methods approach. There are at least two reasons that have influenced my decision to use a multi-level model. First, by investigating the impact of aid on food security from both a macro and a micro perspective, I can find out whether there are different factors driving the effectiveness of aid on the country level as compared to the project level. In this way, my research is able to offer insights into the aforementioned macro–micro paradox of aid effectiveness. Second, by inspecting both perspectives, the book can speak with authority on both global-level patterns and local-level specificities within the aid–food security relationship. Klein and Kozlowski (2000, p. 211) support this tactic, characteris-ing multi-level approach to research as 'complex, rigorous, and able to capture much of the nested complexity of real... life'.

The factors underlying the decision to use mixed methods in the book are also several. Mixed-methods research is 'the type of research in which a researcher... combines elements of qualitative and quantitative research approaches... for the broad purposes of breadth and depth of understanding and corroboration' (Johnson *et al.*, 2007, p. 123). There are many advantages to combining qualitative and quantitative approaches (see e.g. Creswell *et al.*, 2011; Greene, 2008; Yin, 2006). First, the utilisation of quantitative along with qualitative methods allows for the triangulation of data sources, which enhances the external validity of findings. Second, quantitative and qualitative methods compensate for each other's weaknesses and build on each other's strengths. Third, the combination of methods allows for expansion, facilitating construction of a larger and simultaneously more detailed picture of the aid–food security–governance relationship.

Mixed-methods research is not without its shortcomings, naturally. The chief one, as explained by Jick (1979), is the difficulty of replicating the results of such research, particularly of its qualitative parts, which reduces studies' reliability. However, as discussed in more detail further in this chapter, the consequently strengthened validity of the results obtained outweighs this drawback.

Availability of data on food security, development aid and governance

Data in the cross-country studies

On the global level, the best data sources on food security are provided by the Food and Agriculture Organisation (FAO) and the World Health Organisation (WHO). While both organisations have been criticised for the methodology of their data collection, their data sources cover the majority of developing countries for at least some years between 1990 and 2010 and both have gradually improved in data reliability (FAO, 2011). Two measures from each organisation are used: the *prevalence of undernourishment* and *depth of hunger* from the FAO; and the *proportion of stunted children under five* and the *proportion of underweight children under five* from the WHO.[2] All four indicators have been routinely used by researchers as approximates for country levels of food security, even though none of them captures the concept in its full complexity.

The FAO's measures of undernourishment prevalence and depth of hunger speak best about countries' ability to ensure sufficient food availability and access to food for its citizens. Out of the two, the depth of hunger focuses more on the severity of food insecurity while the prevalence of undernourishment on the pervasiveness of food insecurity; both, however, include only the more severe food-insecurity cases, where people have been negatively affected not only by uncertainty about future food access or the lack of nutritious food but also by actual caloric deficiency. The WHO food security measures, the proportion of under-five children that are stunted and that are underweight, better encapsulate the overall nutritional state of the population, as being underweight or stunted can be a result not only of faulty food availability or access, but also of deficient food utilisation. Nevertheless, they still do not reflect the cases of food insecurity characterised primarily by inadequate food stability and, by concentrating only on children younger than five years old, they do not portray countries' full state of food insecurity either.

Conversely, data availability on development aid is better on the global level than on any other. The QWIDS and CRS databases operated by the OECD contain good-quality longitudinal data on development aid committed as well as disbursed, divisible by the type of donor, by the aid mechanism utilised and by the sector to which the aid was provided (among other classifications). The main downside is that it is primarily the DAC members of the OECD who submit all their aid data to the databases and, to a lesser extent, other OECD members. Non-OECD donors are not equally open about their aid provision patterns and while their proportional global contribution to aid was very small until the late 1990s, as of late it has been increasing in importance, particularly with the economic rise of China (e.g. Hudson, 2015; Petrikova, 2016).

Governance data are again more problematic. As discussed in Chapter 1, researchers disagree about what governance is and when it can be considered good, which has, however, not prevented various attempts at quantification of 'good governance'. As my primary measure of governance, I use the worldwide governance indicators (WGI) developed by Kaufmann, Kraay and Matruzzi. The indicators cover quite comprehensively the definition of good governance by the OECD (2006), which this book follows, and, despite wide criticism, they constitute the most commonly utilised governance indicator for cross-country studies at this time (Arndt and Oman, 2006). As a robustness check, I use the Polity IV project's *polity2* measure. Unlike the WGI, *polity2* is rules-based and can hence compensate for the perceived weaknesses of outcome-based indicators such as the WGI. The policy index utilised by Burnside and Dollar (2000), which measures the quality of countries' economic policies, is not used in this study as it is arguably not as relevant for food security as it is for growth.

In the qualitative country-level analysis in Chapter 4, these data from international databases are supplemented with more country-specific, descriptive data from reports and analyses produced by governments, international organisations, or non-profit think-tanks, as well as with secondary data from research monographs and academic articles.

Data in four-country quantitative household study

Moving to the household-level analysis, the study in Chapter 5 works with data from household surveys collected by the Young Lives project. These data were selected due to their good information on both food security and development aid received by respondents, particularly when compared to other contenders including the World Bank's Living Standard Measurement Study (LSMS) surveys and national health surveys (NHSs). The Young Lives datasets contain information on Peruvian, Ethiopian, Indian and Vietnamese young children and their families from 2002, 2006 and 2010.[3]

The relevant food-security variables include children's nutritional indicators such as their weight-for-age, height-for-age and BMI-for-age scores. Furthermore, the surveys contain modules on household perception of food security, on which basis food-security indices can be estimated. As such, the data are able to capture household food insecurity in a more complex manner and more precisely than the data available on the country level. The surveys also contain modules on development assistance received by the households surveyed, which do not enquire precisely about the total amount of aid obtained but do enquire about the type of aid, its delivery mechanism and about the implementing institution.[4] The most problematic part are data on the quality of local governance, which is finally measured through the quality of local public institutions (the police, the professional judge, the water supply, the electricity supply, public phones, public internet and banks) as rated by several local community leaders. The measure is not ideal as the community leaders may be biased in their ratings of the different communities, but the fact that three different ones were consulted in each case should at least to some extent reduce this bias.

Food security, aid and governance data in field study

For the fourth study, I collected data personally in a cluster of villages near Gorakhpur, Uttar Pradesh in India between 2012 and 2014, from households participating in or living nearby a multi-component development project operated by the Indian arm of the international NGO Grameen Development Services (GDS). The first field study took place in December 2012– March 2013, when, with the help of an Indian enumerator Vatsalya Sharma, we distributed question-naires to 146 participating and 23 non-participating households. We returned one year later (December 2013–March 2014) to conduct in-depth interviews with several households (ten from participating and five from non-participating in the project). The questionnaire and the starting interview questions are discussed in greater detail in Chapter 6.

However, as a brief introduction, the questionnaires measured household food security through an index adopted and adapted from the Young Lives survey. Aid in the survey was operationalised through questions about the type of external assistance received by each household and the quality of local governance through an average of perception ratings by three community leaders. The in-depth interviews enriched the quantitative data on food security, aid and governance with descriptive colour and explanatory power.

The data gathered in the field study have both advantages and disadvantages as compared to the sources used in the first three empirical parts. I designed the surveys and interview questions myself and therefore all the questions deemed truly necessary were in place. Moreover, conducting the in-depth interviews a whole year after the surveys provided enough time to analyse the results from the surveys and include questions about apparently important relationships or discrepancies into the open-ended questions in the interviews.

The downsides of the data arose primarily due to financial and time constraints. First, we failed to distribute the surveys to as many households as we initially desired. Furthermore, we could not socially afford to interview people without any financial compensation for longer than 30–40 minutes. Finally, for cultural reasons, we found it difficult to talk to females within the households as the male heads of households usually assumed the role of the appropriate spokespeople for their families. Despite these shortcomings, the data gathered offer a valuable resource for my study and compensate for some of the drawbacks of the data sources used in the previous levels of analysis.

Research methods utilised

With a view to the different types and sources of data utilised in each level of my study, the thesis uses an eclectic mixture of empirical research methods of analy-sis, briefly introduced in this section. The methods are discussed in more detail in the following empirical chapters.

Quantitative cross-country study

In this level of study, I work with quantitative data accessible freely from international databases, for all low- and middle-income countries (World Bank definition) available for the years 1990–2010. The data are both cross-sectional and longitudinal – that is, they constitute a 'panel'. The most common approach to examining data collected for many countries over several years in social science is through fixed-effects ordinary least squares (OLS) panel regressions, which allow researchers to control for unobservable characteristics at both the country and at the time level. Nevertheless, the data in question suffer from both autocorrelation and endogeneity (both issues discussed more in the next chapter), and hence statistical methods such as two-stage least squares (2SLS) and generalised method of moments (GMM) equations are used as the primary tools, with the fixed-effects OLS employed only in the context of sensitivity analyses.

Four-country case study

In the second study, my analysis remains at the country level but focuses on four specific countries – Peru, Ethiopia, India and Vietnam. As stated already, the same international databases as in the previous study are used here as the sources of basic data on the countries' food security, development aid and governance. The numerical data, however, are supplemented by qualitative information obtained from policy and research reports and from secondary literature. The main approach employed to analyse these data is analytical narrative, which combines the rigours of rational-choice theory with the richness of detail of traditional historical narratives (Rodrik, 2003). Within this framework, the data collected are analysed using the methods of process tracing, pattern matching and explanation building, with a particular focus on brandishing the relationships examined in the previous chapter with more understanding of process and detail. The study further serves to set the stage for the household-level data analysis in the following chapter.

Quantitative household-level study in four countries

The data used in this section were collected on the level of individuals and households. Even though in their current form the data are both cross-sectional and longitudinal (available for three different time periods), the data on development assistance received were collected in all countries except for Ethiopia only once, in 2010. In Ethiopia the collection was carried out twice, in 2006 and 2010. In none of the four countries, however, did the surveys examine the households prior to receiving any external development assistance. This is partially because it was not the surveys' main objective to investigate the impact of the development projects implemented in the areas under study, but, regardless, it would have been impossible to do so given that most of the areas have been sites of development projects for many decades.

With this reality in mind, the best approach to analysing the effect of the various development projects on recipients' food security is via a method called propensity score matching (PSM), which allows for statistically rigorous impact evaluation even in the absence of pre-treatment data. This quasi-experimental method is based on the construction of a suitable control group to the treated one on the basis of observable relevant indicators. The output indicators of the 'constructed' control group are then subtracted from the indicators of the treated group (those households that received aid) to determine the significance and size of the treatment's impact. In the case of Ethiopia, where the available data are longitudinal, a panel-level version of PSM is used, unlike in the other three countries with a simpler version of PSM.

Household-level study in northern India with own data

The data collected for this study are both quantitative and qualitative, gathered through surveys as well as longer semi-structured interviews. The methods selected to analyse the data are thus also double-pronged, both quantitative and qualitative.

PSM is used, first, to analyse the survey data and establish the size and significance of the impact of the different development interventions received by the households under study. Second, I use the information collected in the long interviews to enlighten the processes that took place to bring about the discovered effects as well as to enrich the quantitative results with greater depth and detail.

Conclusion

This short chapter broadly introduced the methodological contours of this book, including its ontological and epistemological stance, its data sources and its methods of analysis. Each of the four empirical chapters that follow explains the specific methods utilised in more detail.

Notes

1 For which sufficient data are available.
2 'Stunted' means too short for age, 'underweight' means too light for age.
3 Results on the fourth data collection round were published by Young Lives in 2016.
4 Unfortunately, these detailed data are not available for all four countries in the same manner. In the case of Ethiopia, they were collected twice, in 2006 and in 2010. In India and Vietnam, they were collected once, in 2010, and in Peru not at all. Therefore, the data on development assistance in Peru is the most limited in scope.

References

Arndt, C., and Oman, C. (2006). *Uses and Abuses of Governance Indicators*. Paris: Development Centre, OECD.
Burnside, C., and Dollar, D. (2000). 'Aid, policies, and growth', *American Economic Review,* 90(4), pp. 847–68.

Creswell, J. (2011). 'Controversies in mixed methods research', *Sage Handbook of Qualitative Research*, 4, pp. 269–84.

FAO (2011). *Outcome of Roundtable to Review Methods Used to Estimate the Number of Hungry*. Available at: http://www.fao.org/docrep/meeting/023/mc204E.pdf

Greene, J. (2008). 'Is mixed methods social inquiry a distinctive methodology?', *Journal of Mixed Methods Research*, 2(1), pp. 7–22.

Halperin, S., and Heath, O. (2012). *Political Research: Methods and Practical Skills*. Oxford: Oxford University Press.

Hudson, D. (2015). *Global Finance and Development*. London: Routledge.

Jick, T. D. (1979). 'Mixing qualitative and quantitative methods: triangulation in action', *Administrative Science Quarterly*, 24(4), pp. 602–11.

Johnson, R., Onwuegbuzie, A., and Turner, L. (2007). 'Toward a definition of mixed methods research', *Journal of Mixed Methods Research*, 1(2), pp. 112–33.

Klein, K., and Kozlowski, S. (2000). 'From micro to meso: critical steps in conceptualizing and conducting multilevel research', *Organizational Research Methods*, 3(3), pp. 211–36.

OECD (2006). *DAC Guidelines and Reference Series Applying Strategic Environmental Assessment: Good Practice Guidance for Development Co-operation*. Paris: OECD.

Petrikova, I. (2016). 'Promoting "good behaviour" through aid: do "new" donors differ from the "old" ones?', *Journal of International Relations and Development*, 19(1), pp. 153–92.

Rodrik, D. (ed.) (2003). *In Search of Prosperity: Analytic Narratives on Economic Growth*. Princeton, NJ: Princeton University Press.

Yin, R. (2006). 'Mixed methods research: are the methods genuinely integrated or merely parallel?', *Research in the Schools*, 13(1), pp. 41–7.

3   Cross-country view

Introduction

This chapter marks the beginning of the empirical examination whether there is any relationship between development aid and food security, whether this relationship is positively conditioned on the quality of governance and whether it differs with the type of aid provided. This study explores these questions using cross-country data and quantitative research methods. The main aim of this chapter is to identify global trends and causal links in the relationships between aid, governance and food security.[1]

In order to re-establish the context of the research and its expected results, the following section offers a brief recap of the hypotheses formulated earlier in the text. This overview is followed by a detailed discussion of data sources, their summary statistics and the empirical approach chosen to analyse the data. The presentation of results focuses first on the general relationship between aid and food security, followed by a series of sensitivity tests to assess the robustness of the initial findings. Then it proceeds to debate the results obtained vis-à-vis the impact of different aid modalities on food security. The discussion and conclusion highlight the chapter's main findings, point out its main weaknesses and consider how the subsequent levels of analysis can improve upon them.

Founding expectations

In light of the existing research discussed in Chapter 1, I formulated a set of hypotheses to test in my empirical examinations. Most importantly, this study expects to find that aid in general has a small but significant positive impact on countries' food security and that this impact is conditioned on the quality of governance (H1). Looking at the heterogeneous impact of aid on food security, it is anticipated that multilateral aid is more beneficial for food security than bilateral aid (out of which DAC aid is expected to be more beneficial than non-DAC aid) (H2.1), that financial aid is more beneficial than food aid (H5) and that aid volatility harms food security (H6). Furthermore, short-term aid and agricultural aid are expected to bolster food security to a greater extent than other types of aid (H7 and H8). Regarding the different impact of loans versus grants and of budget support versus programme/project aid on food security, given that both loans and budget support require significant cooperation of the recipient governments, one can plausibly expect that, especially in these aid mechanisms, the quality of recipients' institutions plays a significant conditioning role (H3.1 and H4).

Data and methodology

Food (in)security

Due to the complexity of the food security concept, no perfect global measure exists. Available approximations, described in Chapter 2, include the FAO's undernourishment prevalence ratio (the percentage of population lacking sufficient calories) and depth-of-hunger measure (indicates how much food-deprived people fall short of minimum food needs in terms of dietary energy, expressed in kilocalories) and the WHO's measures of the percentage of under-five children that are underweight (too light for their age) and those that are stunted (too short for their age).[2] As Svedberg (2000) posited, none of these variables fully captures the complexity of food security, but using them together bolsters the results' overall validity – that is, if similar results are found on all of them, they are more likely to represent a real trend with regard to global food insecurity than if the different results contradict each other.[3]

However, one should simultaneously keep in mind that although the measures are mutually highly correlated, they capture slightly different aspects of populations' food security. The prevalence of undernourishment and the depth of hunger speak about whole populations while the WHO's variables only about children younger than five years. On the one hand, parents generally do their utmost to feed their children adequately even if they lack the resources to do so for themselves (Dinour et al., 2007), but, on the other hand, children are more susceptible to nutritional deficiencies than adults. Consequently, the rates of underweight and stunted children generally differ from countries' overall undernourishment rates, but the discrepancy might occur in either direction. On a different note, the depth of hunger and the percentage of underweight children are indicators of more immediate food insecurity than the percentage of stunted children. A sudden or severe food shortage is likely to push some people into deep hunger, leading to high caloric intensity of food deprivation and low-weighing children; however, milder but more chronic food insecurity tends to be reflected by children's shorter statures.

Development aid

Data on aid flows are available from the QWIDS and CRS databases of the OECD. Data regarding aid flows in general and the divisions into bilateral and multilateral aid[4] and into grants and loans are available since 1990 in constant 2010 USD disbursements. Unfortunately, disbursement data divided according to the sectors where the aid was spent are available only after 2002 and known for their unreliability (Petrikova and Chadha, 2011). Therefore, in these instances data on committed aid, available from 1995 onwards, are utilised.

When examining the impact of aid in general on food security, this chapter follows the majority of researchers and uses a measure of aid disbursed per recipient's GDP (natural logarithm, lagged by one time period). However, since the categorisation of aid is available only for gross aid flows, instead of using only net aid receipts as most researchers do, data on gross aid receipts are used and controlled for repayments (following Clemens *et al.*, 2004). Moreover, as a robustness check, one analysis uses also data on net aid per capita.

In examining the impact of multilateral versus bilateral aid and grants versus concessional loans, the general aid flow data is substituted with the two different measures per GDP. The same is done with respect to the divisions into DAC and non-DAC aid; financial and food aid; long-term, short-term and humanitarian aid; and agricultural, economic, social and other aid. When dividing aid into long-term, short-term and humanitarian categories, this chapter follows Clemens *et al.* (ibid.) – defining short-term aid as budget support and programme/project aid for real-sector investment, transportation, communications, energy, banking, agriculture and industry; long-term aid as technical cooperation, research and development, investment in education, health, population control and water sanitation; and humanitarian assistance as any emergency aid.[5] Aid is categorised into financial versus food aid and into agricultural, economic, social and other aid according to the delineated groupings within the CRS database.

However, in exploring the impact of general budget support on recipients as opposed to the effect of programme and project aid and of aid channelled via public–private partnerships versus via other modes, ratios of aid provided as budget support and through PPPs are included, together with a measure of general aid per GDP. This is because often the amounts of aid provided as budget support or through PPPs are very small relative to the rest of aid and if included in dollar terms their impact would be hard to detect. Similarly, when considering the effect of aid volatility on food security, the study utilises a general aid flow per GDP along with a coefficient of variation measure, calculated for each recipient as the ratio of the mean of aid received from 1990–2010 to its standard deviation. A higher coefficient of variation corresponds to a greater degree of aid volatility.

Governance

Two measures of governance are utilised. For theoretical reasons, as the main indicator the study uses the WGIs, an outcome measure based on an aggregate expert evaluation of institutional quality (Kaufmann and Kraay, 2008). The WGIs rate six different dimensions of governance – voice and accountability, political stability and absence of violence, government effectiveness, regulatory quality, rule of law and control of corruption – on a scale from –2.5 (worst) to 2.5 (best). Even though criticised by many, to date the indicators have remained the most widely used measure of cross-country governance (Arndt and Oman, 2006). However, as a robustness check, the study examines the impact of aid also when conditioned on *polity2*. Polity IV's *polity2* score is a rules-based indicator, which measures countries' 'authoritarianism' on a scale from −10 to 10. The main downside of *polity2* is that it only evaluates the nature of countries' regimes; the main downside of the WGI is its availability only after 1995.

Other factors

As discussed in Chapter 1, my main control variables on the country level are GDP per capita (logarithm), debt repayments, cereal yield, a dummy variable for least developed countries (LDCs), total population (logarithm), urban population (share), a domestic food-production index, a local food-price index and a global food-price index, a dummy variable for conflict, a trade-openness measure and a measure of social and economic rights. All the control variables, just like the measures of aid and governance, are used in regressions lagged by one time period. The conflict data come from the Uppsala Conflict Data Programme and the rights data from the Cingranelli and Richards' dataset; data on the rest of the variables were obtained from the World Bank's World Development Indicators (WDI) and the FAO.[6]

Final dataset

The final dataset is an unbalanced panel, comprising data in three-year averages from 1990–2010 for 81 low- and middle-income countries.[7] The year 2010 is the last year for which data were available at the time of conducting the analysis; 1990 was chosen as the lower cut-off point due to the unavailability of data on most independent variables prior to that date. The data were averaged over three-year periods to take into account the potentially cumulative effects of aid.

Summary statistics

Table 3.1 displays summary statistics of all the variables employed for the second time wave (1993–5)[8] and the last time wave (2008–10). As expected, the level of the four dependent variables – prevalence of undernourishment, depth of hunger and percentage of underweight and stunted children under five – declined between 1993–5 and 2008–10. However, the improvement in overall undernourishment rates has been more remarkable than in children's nutritional status. This finding is disappointing to some extent, as undernourishment in the first years of life carries more significant negative long-term consequences for human development than undernourishment later in life.

Regarding the main independent and conditioning variables, Table 3.1 shows that, on average, the countries examined received in 2008–10 less aid in per GDP terms but more aid in per capita terms than in 1993–5. Looking at the temporal evolution of the different aid types, the trend among donors has clearly been

Table 3.1 Summary statistics of all the variables utilised

	1993–5					2008–10				
	Obs	Mean	St Dev	Min	Max	Obs	Mean	St Dev	Min	Max
Food security										
Undernourishment (%)	67	21.18	16.30	0.00	64.00	66	14.51	12.95	0.00	65.00
Depth of Hunger (kCal)	67	237.2	61.3	120.0	380.0	66	213.0	52.4	120.0	350.0
Underweight (%)	40	20.80	14.72	0.70	56.70	28	18.63	11.78	2.20	41.30
Stunted (%)	40	33.62	14.49	3.70	66.50	28	27.78	12.57	7.10	43.20
Development aid										
ODA pg	67	0.10	0.12	0.00	0.53	66	0.07	0.09	0.00	0.35
ODA pc	67	38.03	53.56	1.65	253.07	66	43.94	43.27	1.13	229.66
Multilateral aid (share)	67	0.35	0.20	0.00	1.00	66	0.37	0.21	0.00	0.98
Concessional loans (share)	67	0.35	0.29	0.00	0.95	66	0.18	0.21	0.00	0.78
Budget support (share)	67	0.08	0.15	0.00	0.88	66	0.06	0.11	0.00	0.52
Aid through PPPs (share x 100)						48	0.08	0.39	0.00	2.68
Food aid (share)	67	0.04	0.11	0.00	0.84	66	0.02	0.05	0.00	0.37
Short–term aid (share)	67	0.45	0.27	0.00	1.00	66	0.34	0.23	0.00	0.99
Long–term aid (share)	67	0.44	0.25	0.00	1.00	66	0.57	0.22	0.01	0.98
Agricultural aid (share)	67	0.07	0.09	0.00	0.64	66	0.06	0.12	0.00	0.85
Social aid (share)	67	0.32	0.24	0.00	1.00	66	0.46	0.20	0.01	0.96
Economic aid (share)	67	0.21	0.23	0.00	0.99	66	0.16	0.18	0.00	0.75
Governance										
WGI	67	-0.46	0.52	-1.66	1.01	66	-0.50	0.55	-1.46	1.20
Polity2	67	1.06	6.22	-9.00	10.00	66	2.71	5.98	-9.00	10.00
Control variables										
GDP pc (PPP, 2010 USD)	67	3457	2998	358	11560	66	4720	3665	599	12752
Remittances pg	67	0.03	0.04	0.00	0.20	66	0.07	0.09	0.00	0.45
Population (in millions)	67	64.70	197.0	0.44	1220.0	66	65.90	199.0	0.84	1320.0

(*continued*)

Table 3.1 Summary statistics of all the variables utilised (continued)

	1993–5					2008–10				
	Obs	Mean	St Dev	Min	Max	Obs	Mean	St Dev	Min	Max
Urban population (%)	67	45.71	20.56	10.09	91.15	66	49.83	20.71	15.33	94.00
Food Production Index	67	91.17	11.24	49.00	122.00	66	119.40	20.55	66.00	172.00
Emergency food aid pc	67	3.69	9.42	0.00	82.51	66	3.70	7.47	0.00	41.49
Trade openness	67	63.30	31.10	14.93	165.61	66	79.56	35.39	25.21	199.45
Social and economic rights	67	7.28	3.51	0.00	13.00	66	8.40	3.09	3.00	14.00
Conflict	67	0.27	0.45	0.00	1.00	66	0.16	0.37	0.00	1.00
Local food prices	67	1971	1054	236	7049	66	2571	1645	470	10026
Global food prices	67	124.13				66	154.06			
Repayment (in millions USD)	67	1130	3420	0	27000	66	2610	7020	0	40000
LDC	67	0.34	0.47	0.00	1.00	66	0.30	0.50	0.00	1.00
Cereal yield	67	1955	1090	274	6499	66	2319	1419	88	7793

Source: Author's own calculations

away from providing aid in loans, as budget support and as food aid. Donors have also begun to disburse more aid to social infrastructure and to long-term sectors at the expense of aid to agriculture, to economic infrastructure and to short-term sectors. Interestingly, the two governance measures display a varying time trend. Whereas the WGI scores on average slightly worsened between the two waves of data examined, the *polity2* scores improved.

Turning attention briefly to the summary statistics of the control variables utilised, most measures increased on average between the first and the last time period under study – including GDP per capita, remittances per GDP, the food-production index, trade openness, local and global food prices, repayments, cereal yield, population and urban population share. It is encouraging to see that fewer countries were involved in an active conflict in 2008–10 than in 1993–5, as well as that the mean score on social and economic rights improved in that time frame.

Empirical methods

As mentioned in Chapter 2, data on aid and food security suffer from both auto-correlation and endogeneity. The Arellano-Bond (1991) test showed that food security data are correlated to the first order – that is, that the food-security levels in one time period are correlated with the levels in the previous time period. Regarding endogeneity, aid can hardly be expected to be completely exogenous to food security as countries with higher insecurity levels are more likely to receive larger amounts of aid.

The common method of resolving these problems in the cross-country aid litera-ture is to either use 2SLS regressions or dynamic panel regressions (e.g. Clemens *et al.*, 2004; Michaelowa and Weber, 2006; Dreher *et al.*, 2008). My primary analysis, which examines the impact of aid in general on food security, uses both approaches. First, to account for the data's endogenous nature, the data are analysed with a 2SLS regression with fixed effects, using the following model:

$$f_{it} = \beta_0 + \beta_1 A'_{it} + \beta_2 G_{it} + \beta_3 \left(A'_{it} * G_{it} \right) + \beta_4 X_{it} + \gamma_t + \varepsilon^f_{it} \tag{1}$$

$$A'_{it} = \delta_0 + \delta_1 IV_{it} + \delta_2 X_{it} + \gamma_t + \varepsilon^a_{it} \tag{2}$$

where β_0 and δ_0 are constants, f_{it} is the level of food insecurity observed for country i in year t, A_{it} are aid receipts per GDP, G_{it} is the quality of governance, $A_{it}*G_{it}$ is the aid–governance interaction term (which represents the impact of aid on food insecu-rity that is conditional on governance), IV_{it} are variables that affect aid but are exog-enous to undernourishment, X_{it} are other exogenous variables that affect food security and the allocation of aid, γ_t are unobserved time effects and ε^f_{it} and ε^a_{it} are error terms. Time dummies are included to capture worldwide business cycles.

As aid instruments I considered using Hansen and Tarp's (2001), which include several variables interacted with policy. However, since policy, even in its lagged term, is most likely endogenous to food security, I turned to Rajan and Subramanian's (2008) model instead. In it, they utilised the reality that aid is extended for many non-economic reasons and as instruments used variables capturing strategic and colonial ties between donors and aid recipients. Inspired by their choice of instruments, I have elected to use the following: three dummy variables denoting if the recipient country were ever a British colony, a French colony, or another European colony; countries' political and civil rights' scores; and the number of deaths in a major disaster. The rationale behind the selection is that donors are influenced in their aid-disbursement decisions by old colonial ties, political and civil rights records and natural disasters. Overall, the variables account for more than 20 per cent of the donors' allocation decision and are reasonably exogenous to the dependent variable.

Another concern is that the instruments could be correlated with governance, thereby violating the exclusion restriction underlying the instrumentation. However, the fact that the correlation coefficient between the instruments and the WGI is low (<0.2) and not statistically significant in my sample should allay this worry. The general insignificance of the Sargan tests of over-identifying restrictions and the Durbin–Wu–Hausman tests comparing the IV and OLS estimates further strengthen the instruments' validity.[9]

The second method utilised, which should account for both endogeneity and serial correlation, is the system generalised method of moments (GMM) estimator developed by Blundell and Bond (1998) and implemented into Stata by Roodman (2009) as the xtabond2 command.[10] The relevant equation in this case is the following:

$$ f_{it} = f_{it-1} + \beta_0 + \beta_1 A_{it} + \beta_2 G_{it} + \beta_3 \left(A_{it} * G_{it} \right) + \beta_2 X_{it} + \gamma_t + \varepsilon_{it} $$

where f_{it} is the level of food insecurity observed for country i in year t, f_{it-1} is the level of food insecurity observed in the previous time period ($t-1$), A_{it} are aid receipts per GDP, G_{it} is the quality of governance, $A_{it}*G_{it}$ is the aid–governance interaction term (which represents the impact of aid on food insecurity that is conditional on governance), X_{it} are control variables, γ_t is the unobserved time effect and ε_{it} is the error term.

The model corrects for the first-order autocorrelation of the dependent variable and treats aid as endogenous, instrumenting for it with its own lag. The Arellano-Bond test of second-order autocorrelation and the Hansen test of the exogeneity of instruments confirm the model's validity.

When scrutinising the impact of general aid flows on food security, this study reports results from both the 2SLS and GMM regressions. However, since it would be difficult to find relevant instruments for the different types of aid investigated and since the GMM model is arguably the most accurate one of the three, the study proceeds using only the GMM (xtabond2) estimator with robust standard errors.[11]

Results with aid in general

Table 3.2 displays results on the impact of total aid flows on food security, obtained using 2SLS and GMM regressions with three-year averaged data.

Table 3.2 The effect of aid on food security and the conditioning effect of governance (FE, 2SLS and GMM models)

Food insecurity	2SLS with 3‑y periods				GMM with 3‑y periods			
	Undernourished	Hunger	Underweight	Stunted	Undernourished	Hunger	Underweight	Stunted
ODA per GDP	**-2.20**	**-5.53**	-0.68	**-3.80**	-1.21	**-3.94**	**-0.31**	-0.36
	4.58	**5.89**	0.85	**4.92**	1.92	**2.10**	**1.88**	1.17
Governance	-0.14	-0.76	**-0.46**	-0.56	-0.44	**-0.85**	-0.19	-0.05
	0.95	1.11	**2.46**	**1.90**	1.96	**2.31**	1.19	0.90
ODA × governance	**-0.01**	**-0.06**	-0.03	-0.02	-0.04	**-0.08**	-0.02	**-0.04**
	2.75	**2.95**	0.43	**1.74**	**2.24**	**2.46**	0.58	**1.94**
GDP(PPP) pc	**-7.96**	**-24.42**	**-4.45**	**-5.98**	**-7.50**	**-26.04**	**-3.94**	**-7.55**
	2.88	**2.21**	**1.87**	**2.88**	**2.27**	**2.37**	**2.33**	**3.89**
Population	**-7.54**	**-36.93**	**-5.70**	-4.51	**-1.58**	**-1.55**	0.36	**-1.44**
	2.87	**3.35**	**1.97**	1.24	**2.13**	**1.91**	0.45	**1.86**
Urban population (share)	**-0.14**	0.48	-0.15	-0.07	**-0.02**	-0.03	-0.01	-0.02
	1.73	1.25	**1.82**	0.50	**1.86**	1.21	0.75	**1.71**
Food production index	**-0.07**	**-0.81**	**-0.05**	**-0.05**	**-0.03**	**-0.11**	**-0.01**	0.00
	3.69	**1.71**	**2.88**	**1.95**	**2.37**	**2.10**	**1.69**	0.33
Trade openness	0.00	0.06	-0.03	-0.02	0.00	-0.03	0.00	**-0.02**
	0.01	1.16	**1.79**	1.08	0.21	**1.77**	0.32	**1.81**
Social and economic rights	0.02	0.02	-0.03	0.06	-0.13	**-0.26**	-0.04	-0.07
	0.36	0.02	0.52	0.83	1.29	**1.84**	0.78	0.23
Conflict	**1.65**	3.10	0.64	1.14	**3.29**	**10.03**	**1.62**	**1.28**
	1.97	0.86	0.99	1.19	**1.97**	**2.99**	**1.85**	**1.78**
Local food prices (xth)	**0.00**	**0.00**	0.00	0.00	-0.28	**-0.64**	-0.20	-0.08
	3.05	**2.78**	0.37	0.55	0.63	**2.46**	0.50	0.35
World food price index	0.02	**0.07**	**0.02**	0.01	0.01	**0.07**	0.01	0.00
	1.58	**2.06**	**2.69**	1.07	1.12	**1.82**	1.17	0.93
N	340		240		358		212	
N of groups	81		67		82		62	
R2 within	38%	29%	46%	35%				
R2 (first stage regression)	24%	22%	24%	22%				
DWH test (Prob>z)/AR2 test (Prob>z)	0.74	0.36	0.06	0.16	0.132	0.687	0.249	0.47
Sargan test (Prob>χ2)/AR2 test (Prob>z)	0.81	0.37	0.32	0.44	0.103	0.242	0.28	0.838
Hansen test (Prob>χ2)					0.774	0.927	0.804	0.816

Notes: Regressions were run with robust standard errors and time dummies. The first number next to each variable is the coefficient; the number below is the corresponding t‑statistic. Bold font represents significance at least at the 10% level. Regressions were also controlled for the following undisplayed control variables: conflict, LDC status, cereal yield and repayments

The effect of aid on food security and the conditioning role of governance

Aid is consistently supportive of food security in both sets of regressions employed. When using the 2SLS estimator, the aid term is significant in half the regressions; with the GMM estimator it is significant in three-quarters of cases. The lower significance of the 2SLS results can likely be attributed to the relative weakness of the instruments employed. The size of the impact varies quite widely based on the model but overall, it seems that a ten-time increase of aid per GDP (= one logarithm) leads to a reduction in countries' undernourishment rates by 1 to 2 percentage points and in the proportion of underweight children by 0.2 to 0.6 percentage points. Depth of hunger is in this manner reduced by somewhere between 2 and 5 points while child underweight and stunting by between 0.3 and 3 percentage points. Despite the variation in the size of the coefficients, taken together the findings lend solid support to the hypothesis that aid has a significantly positive impact on food security.

Similar to aid, the governance variable is negative and often significant. This suggests that, as expected, countries with better governance suffer from lower levels of food insecurity. However, the size of the effect is relatively small. With a one-unit increase in the WGI score, undernourishment prevalence falls on average by 0.4 to 1.6 percentage points and the rates of underweight and stunted children by 0.4 to 1.4 percentage points. Hence, even if a country improved from the worst-rated governance possible to the best-rated one (5-point change), its undernourishment levels would not decrease on average by more than 2 to 8 percentage points.

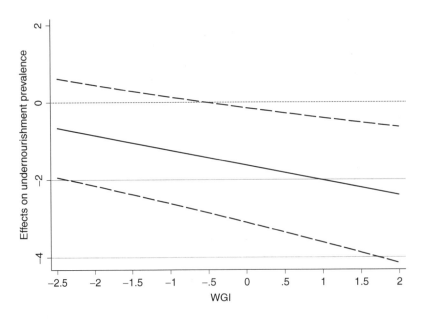

Figure 3.1 Marginal effect of aid on undernourishment (90% c.i.).

Source: Author's own graphic, reproduced from Petrikova (2015)

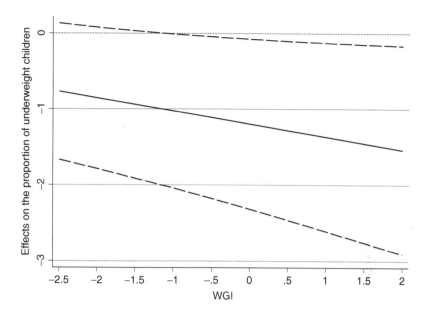

Figure 3.2 Marginal effect of aid on stunting (90% c.i.).

Source: Author's own graphic, reproduced from Petrikova (2015)

Looking at the aid–governance term, it is also negative and mostly significant. This outcome indicates that aid influences food security more positively in countries with better governance and supports the hypothesis that aid effectiveness is conditioned on the quality of recipients' governance. Graphs in Figures 3.1 and 3.2 show the interactive relationship graphically, for undernourishment prevalence and for the proportion of under-five children that are stunted.

The marginal effects, obtained with the GMM regressions, indicate that, as WGI scores increase, the positive effect of aid on recipients' food security increases in strength and significance as well. In fact, in countries with WGI scores lower than −1, aid appears to have no statistically measurable impact on food security, whereas in countries towards the high end of the WGI spectrum, a one-decade increase in aid per GDP leads to the reduction of stunting by more than 1 percentage point and of undernourishment by more than 2 percentage points.

In order to explore the aid–governance–food security interactive relationship deeper and find out which aspects of governance condition the positive effects of aid the most, Table 3.3 reports results from disaggregation of the WGI into its six components – voice and accountability, political stability and the absence of violence, government effectiveness, regulatory quality, the rule of law and control of corruption.[12]

The regressions in Table 3.3, which looked at the undernourishment and stunting measures of food insecurity, suggest that political stability, regulatory quality and control of corruption are the most important governance aspects in this regard, with voice and accountability, government effectiveness and the rule of

Table 3.3 Disaggregating the governance term

Food insecurity	Undernourished		Stunted	
ODA per GDP	−1.19	−0.93	−0.39	−0.290
	2.17	**1.98**	**2.41**	**1.93**
Voice and accountability	0.10	−0.53	1.36	1.12
	0.43	0.34	1.57	1.35
Political stability	−2.23	−3.12	−2.44	−2.61
	1.66	**1.75**	**1.91**	**1.99**
Government effectiveness	−0.08	−0.48	0.85	0.97
	0.25	0.20	0.80	0.98
Regulatory quality	−2.06	−3.61	−0.82	−1.26
	1.78	**2.27**	1.06	**2.32**
Rule of law	0.13	0.30	0.24	1.06
	0.47	0.15	0.25	1.27
Control of corruption	−2.17	−3.53	−1.70	−1.83
	1.36	**1.68**	**1.99**	**2.50**
Voice and accountability × gov		−0.04		0.16
		0.43		0.69
Political stability × gov		−0.17		−0.53
		1.78		**2.05**
Government effectiveness × gov		−0.03		0.11
		0.23		0.73
Regulatory quality × gov		−0.20		−0.78
		2.27		**2.43**
Rule of law × gov		0.01		0.15
		0.05		0.52
Control of corruption × gov		−0.22		−1.07
		1.72		**2.42**
N of observations	358		212	
N of groups	82		62	
AR2 test (Prob>z)	0.335	0.265	0.253	0.414
Hansen test (Prob>χ2)	0.982	0.631	0.948	0.997

Notes: Regressions were run using the GMM estimator, with robust standard errors, time dummies and the same control variables as regressions in Table 3.2. The first number next to each variable is the coefficient; the number below is the corresponding t–statistic. Bold font represents significance at least at the 10% level

law playing seemingly no significant role in ensuring aid's positive effect on food security. If the coefficients from the interactions between the different governance aspects and aid were to be taken at their face value, then it would appear that the control of corruption has the largest conditioning impact, followed by regulatory quality and political stability. Nevertheless, as touched on further in the Discussion section, the different components of the WGI have been accused of being overly mutually correlated, and hence drawing conclusions on their basis could be problematic (e.g. Langbein and Knack, 2010).

The effect of control variables

Briefly looking at the effect of control variables on food security, the most consistently significant are GDP per capita, population, urban population share and food production, all boosting food security. I expected this result regarding GDP per capita, food production and urban population share, but was somewhat surprised by such a strong and positive association between food security and population, as existing literature – except for my own previous study (Petrikova, 2013) – does not hint at its existence. In further research, it would be interesting to investigate why countries with larger populations, *ceteris paribus*, are better at keeping their inhabitants well-nourished than countries with smaller populations. Other variables with a positive but less significant impact on food security are trade openness, local food prices, cereal yield and social and economic rights. Global food prices, repayments, being in a conflict and being an LDC all have a negative effect on food security, but only in the case of global food prices is the effect steadily significant.

Most of the relationships discovered between control variables and food security were predicted by theory; one exception is the different direction of the food security–food prices association based on whether the prices are local or global. According to my findings, higher global food prices reduce food security while higher local food prices bolster it. The underlying explanation could be that in developing countries, often the most food insecure people are small farmers, who benefit from a rise in prices for which they can sell their produce. However, they are simultaneously harmed by the increase in global food prices as they tend not to be fully self-sufficient in their production and buy some imported food from stores. The inverse relationship also suggests the discrepancy between global and local food prices and implies the difficulty with which global prices translate into local ones (Benson *et al.*, 2008).

Sensitivity analysis

Results from the sensitivity tests are all presented in Table 3.4.[13] The first sensitivity test substituted WGI with *polity2*. The results show that the substitution does not majorly alter the general conclusions reached above. Aid still seems to strengthen the recipients' food security and the impact is stronger in countries with more democratic institutions, suggesting that authoritarian regimes use aid less effectively in bolstering food security than democratic regimes.

The second sensitivity test involves an addition of remittances per GDP into the equations. I chose not to use this variable as a constant control due to a large number of missing data points, which significantly restricted my sample. Nevertheless, the sensitivity test displayed in the upper-right corner of Table 3.4 demonstrates that the positive effect of aid on food security is not erased by the inclusion of remittances. It further shows that remittances strengthen food security but only when measured through the prevalence of undernourishment and child stunting, the more long-term measures. The impact of the flows on depth of hunger and underweight children is not statistically significant.

The third sensitivity check pertains to the fact that throughout the analyses data on gross aid rather than on the more commonly employed net aid are utilised. The study does so because data on aid categorisation were available only for gross aid and as an attempt at remedy controlled for repayments. Nevertheless, Table 3.4 examines the impact of aid on food security using data on net aid per capita. The

Table 3.4 Sensitivity analysis: substituting WGI with *polity2*, ODA per GDP with net ODA per capita and including remittances and aid squared

	with polity2				with remittances			
	Undernourished	Hunger	Underweight	Stunted	Undernourished	Hunger	Underweight	Stunted
ODA per GDP	**-1.07** / 2.17	**-2.00** / 5.14	**-1.85** / 2.46	**-0.39** / 2.13	**0.78** / 2.96	**-0.55** / 2.73	**-0.64** / 2.89	-0.22 / 1.73
Governance	0.14 / 1.46	**0.59** / 2.70	-0.18 / 1.28	0.08 / 0.98	-0.08 / 0.95	-0.06 / 1.42	**-0.99** / 2.18	0.02 / 1.39
ODA × governance	**-0.07** / 2.97	-0.04 / 1.67			-0.05 / 2.85		-0.05 / 2.85	-0.04 / 1.75
Remittances per GDP					**-0.12** / 2.17	-0.06 / 1.42	0.04 / 1.07	0.01 / 0.74
N of observations	406	406	253	253	234	234	135	135
N of groups	76	76	56	56	68	68	45	45
AR2 test (Prob>z)	0.136	0.111	0.14	0.117	0.135	0.113	0.119	0.113
Hansen test (Prob>χ²)	0.948	0.859	0.872	0.888	0.945	0.971	0.982	0.971

	with net ODA per capita				with ODA per GDP squared			
	Undernourished	Hunger	Underweight	Stunted	Undernourished	Hunger	Underweight	Stunted
ODA per GDP	**-0.78** / 2.33	**-1.59** / 3.09	**-3.55** / 4.95	-0.66 / 0.99	**-5.92** / 2.24	**-9.76** / 2.75	**-12.51** / 3.29	**-5.75** / 2.08
Net ODA per capita	**-0.36** / 1.68	-0.54 / 1.83	**-1.51** / 2.75	-0.03 / 1.18				
ODA per GDP squared					**2.52** / 2.70	**3.75** / 2.14	**4.49** / 2.39	**2.44** / 3.56
Governance	0.55 / 0.99				-0.35 / 1.81	-0.60 / 0.91	-2.42 / 1.74	-0.85 / 1.85
ODA × governance					**-0.35** / 3.29		-0.10 / 1.92	
Net ODA × governance	-0.33 / 1.87	**-0.54** / 2.01	**-0.77** / 2.12	-0.08 / 1.81				
N of observations	358	358	212	212	358	358	212	212
N of groups	82	82	62	62	82	82	62	62
AR2 test (Prob>z)	0.116	0.137	0.162	0.156	0.111	0.118	0.196	0.187
Hansen test (Prob>χ²)	0.954	0.893	0.904	0.946	0.796	0.956	0.863	0.918

Notes: Regressions were run with robust standard errors, time dummies and the same control variables as regressions in Table 3.2. The first number next to each variable is the coefficient; the number below is the corresponding t–statistic. Bold font represents significance at least at the 10% level

results show that the difference is not overwhelming. The coefficients do vary but the broad inference remains the same: aid reinforces food security and its effect on food security seems to be conditioned on governance.

The final robustness check introduced an aid-squared variable into the regressions, to examine whether aid in its positive impact on food security has diminishing returns as it does in its effect on growth (e.g. Rajan and Subramanian, 2008). The aid-squared coefficients are, indeed, significant and positive, corroborating the claim of diminishing returns. However, the core results do not change dramatically: ODA per GDP is still negative and significant, as is the interaction between aid and governance.

Overall, the sensitivity tests have strengthened the robustness of the finding that aid has on average a positive impact on recipients' food security, which is conditioned on the quality of their institutions and policies. Second, the tests have proven that the results attained via the GMM regressions with gross aid per GDP and WGI as governance do not significantly differ from results obtained using different estimators or different specifications of aid and governance. Consequently, they provide support to the decision to proceed with the remaining empirical investigations using only one model.

The impact of distinct types of aid on food security

Consequently, the impact of the different types of aid on food security is analysed using only GMM regressions with three-year averaged data. This part of the investigation does not use 2SLS regressions because finding relevant instruments for the different aid modalities would be very difficult.

Aid divided by the type of donor

Table 3.5 presents the results of regressions, first, with aid divided into bilateral and multilateral and, second, with bilateral aid divided into DAC and non-DAC. On its own, multilateral aid is uniformly negative (that is, reduces food insecurity) and significant, more consistently so than bilateral aid. However, the interaction of governance with bilateral aid is negative and significant more frequently than the interaction with multilateral aid. One can thus deduce that while multilateral aid confers a more consistently positive effect on food security than bilateral aid, the quality of governance matters more in ensuring the positive impact of bilateral aid. The most likely reasons are that bilateral donors distribute aid for more political reasons than multilateral donors whereas multilateral donors practice greater supervision of their aid implementation, and therefore a higher quality of institutions and policies is required to guarantee a positive effect of bilateral aid.

Turning to the division of bilateral aid into aid provided by DAC and non-DAC donors (while still controlling for multilateral aid), the lower part of Table 3.5 demonstrates that both types of aid influence food security positively, but only DAC aid is consistently significant in this effect. The finding on DAC aid is not surprising as bilateral aid – predominantly constituted by DAC donors – had a generally positive effect. Non-DAC donors were theoretically expected to be less

Table 3.5 The impact of *who* gives aid on recipients' food security

Panel A — Bilateral and multilateral aid

	Undernourished	Undernourished	Hunger	Hunger	Underweight	Underweight	Stunted	Stunted
Bilateral aid	**−0.37**	**−0.86**	**−0.82**	**−3.32**	**−0.31**	0.21	0.13	0.77
	1.88	**2.58**	**2.57**	**3.35**	**1.96**	0.58	**1.65**	1.23
Multilateral aid	**−0.60**	**−0.68**	**−2.22**	**−2.93**	**−2.11**	**−2.56**	**−0.21**	**−1.66**
	2.17	**2.19**	**4.52**	**4.67**	**3.41**	**3.49**	**1.81**	**2.05**
Governance	**−0.41**	**−6.11**	**−0.66**	**−1.67**	0.16	−0.02	−0.01	−0.04
	1.88	**3.52**	**2.22**	**3.65**	1.45	0.24	0.36	0.29
Bilateral aid × governance		**−0.36**		**−0.68**		−0.02		**−0.24**
		2.58		**2.17**		1.37		**2.05**
Multilateral aid × governance		0.05		**−0.86**		−0.11		−0.02
		1.48		**4.28**		1.56		0.43
N of observations	356	356	356	356	356	356	240	240
AR2 test (Prob>z)	0.177	0.082	0.161	0.164	0.135	0.160	0.402	0.558
Hansen test (Prob>χ2)	0.950	0.911	0.200	0.844	0.942	0.936	0.973	0.961

Panel B — DAC and non-DAC aid

	Undernourished	Undernourished	Hunger	Hunger	Underweight	Underweight	Stunted	Stunted
DAC aid	**−0.09**	**−0.11**	**−0.44**	**−0.43**	**−0.10**	**−0.07**	0.00	−0.04
	1.83	**2.31**	**1.96**	**1.97**	**1.71**	**2.29**	0.91	0.84
Non−DAC aid	**−0.08**	**−0.09**	−0.19	**−0.27**	0.02	0.02	0.02	0.04
	1.96	**1.97**	1.64	**1.79**	0.98	0.91	1.14	1.40
Governance	**−0.04**	**−0.72**	**−0.14**	**−0.97**	−0.03	−0.18	**−0.05**	**−0.21**
	2.22	**1.85**	**2.46**	**1.97**	0.54	1.53	**2.39**	**1.66**
DAC aid × governance		**−0.34**		**−0.42**		−0.21		**−0.25**
		1.87		**1.95**		1.53		**2.08**
Non−DAC aid × governance		**−0.81**		**−0.84**		**−0.67**		**−0.69**
		2.08		**4.12**		**2.58**		**2.63**
N of observations	356	356	356	356	356	356	240	240
AR2 test (Prob>z)	0.566	0.293	0.843	0.352	0.619	0.428	0.684	0.371
Hansen test (Prob>χ2)	0.933	0.875	0.959	0.902	0.963	0.895	0.912	0.878

Notes: Regressions were run with robust standard errors, time dummies and the same control variables as regressions in Table 3.2. The first number next to each variable is the coefficient; the number below is the corresponding t–statistic. Bold font represents significance at least at the 10% level

responsive to recipients' needs in their aid giving than DAC donors and thus, by extension, their aid expected to also have a less positive impact on recipients' food security. While the lower significance of the non-DAC aid term may be a validation of this hypothesis, it could also be due to the current paucity of data on non-DAC donors. Non-DAC aid is also conditioned more consistently on governance than DAC aid. This result is, again, not too surprising given that, in general, aid provided by non-DAC donors faces fewer conditions on how and to whom it can be disbursed and hence is likely to be used more effectively by countries with a better quality of institutions in place.

Aid divided by how it is disbursed

Table 3.6 displays the results of regressions examining how the way in which aid is disbursed affects its impact on food security. The upper left part of the table looks at aid disbursed in grants versus in concessional loans. Aid in grants is negative and significant in all regressions while aid in loans is negative and significant in fewer than half the regressions. Conversely, the loans–governance interaction term is significant more frequently than the grants–governance term. These results suggest that grants have a more consistently positive effect on food security than concessional loans, at least in the relatively short run (three to six years) examined. Furthermore, confirming one of my original hypotheses, the quality of governance plays a larger role in ensuring the positive effect of loans than grants.

The upper right part of Table 3.6 presents results vis-à-vis the different impact of financial versus food aid. Financial aid seems to have a considerably more positive effect on food security than food aid, with negative coefficients and significant t-statistics in all eight regressions as compared to food aid's significance in two out of eight. The aid–governance interaction terms are not particularly informative in this case, significant for financial aid in two out of four regressions and for food aid in three. One can hence conclude that while better governance most likely improves the impact on food security of both financial and food aid, only financial aid strengthens recipients' overall food security, at least in the short run.[14]

The lower left part of Table 3.6 focuses on the impact of aid delivered as budget support and through public–private partnerships. The ratios of aid disbursed as budget support and through PPPs are predominantly positive but insignificant. Nevertheless, the interaction variable of the budget-support ratio and governance is negative and significant in most regressions where it is included. The results thus imply that while food security is not widely affected by whether aid is implemented through programmes/projects, as budget support or through collaborations with private enterprise, in countries with better institutions budget support has the ability to bolster food security more than in countries with worse institutions. There is also some indication that aid channelled through PPPs may actually be harmful to recipients' food security but more research is needed to verify this claim.

Finally, the lower right part of Table 3.6 explores the effect of aid volatility on food security and its interaction with the quality of governance. The results show that aid volatility, not unexpectedly, has a negative impact on food security, as its coefficients are negative and significant in most regressions. The findings on the

Table 3.6 The impact of *how* aid is provided on recipients' food security

Note on reading the table: for each variable the first number is the coefficient and the number directly below it is the corresponding t-statistic (shown in parentheses). Bold t-statistics denote significance at least at the 10% level.

Panel 1 (aid form: grants/financial aid vs. loans/food aid)

Variable	Undernourished	Hunger	Underweight	Stunted	Undernourished	Hunger	Underweight	Stunted
Grants/financial aid	−3.32 (**3.29**); −2.64 (**2.38**)	−5.99 (**2.34**); −9.98 (**2.41**)	−0.31 (**2.08**); −0.15 (**1.95**)	−0.26 (**2.12**); −0.85 (**3.09**)	−0.71 (**1.91**); −0.42 (1.73)	−1.71 (**2.21**); −1.42 (**2.48**)	−0.25 (**2.41**); −0.73 (**3.27**)	−1.10 (**3.28**); −0.59 (**2.54**)
Loans/food aid	0.12 (0.35); 0.68 (1.32)	1.25 (0.95); 3.32 (**1.66**)	−0.17 (**1.68**); −0.04 (0.98)	−0.36 (**1.96**); −0.38 (**2.46**)	0.06 (1.25); −0.09 (1.53)	−0.63 (**2.31**); −0.08 (0.33)	−0.15 (**1.72**); 0.05 (0.59)	−0.14 (1.41); −0.02 (0.22)
Governance	−0.39 (**3.81**); −4.79 (**1.67**)	−0.94 (**1.69**); −0.88 (**1.78**)	0.31 (**1.72**); −0.51	0.84; −0.08 (**1.82**)	−0.54 (0.94); 0.94	−0.84 (**2.31**); −1.00 (**2.29**)	−2.73 (**3.09**); −0.10 (1.18)	−0.07 (1.06); 0.21
Grants × gov / financial aid × gov	0.40 (1.07); −0.33 (**1.71**)	0.01 (0.23); 0.40	0.16 (0.90); 0.01	−0.01 (0.16); 0.07 (1.11)	−0.08 (**1.72**); 0.01 (**1.79**)	—	−0.09 (**1.79**)	−0.10 (1.44)
Loans × gov / food aid × gov	0.08 (1.07); −1.45 (**1.68**)	−0.04 (**2.10**)	−0.02 (**1.72**)	0.01 (0.58)	−0.08 (**1.96**)	−0.14 (**2.88**)	0.01 (0.58)	−0.07 (**1.98**)
N	362	362	230	230	271	271	188	188
AR2 test (Prob>z)	0.059; 0.165	0.172; 0.190	0.156; 0.984		0.107; 0.096	0.152; 0.126	0.090; 0.137	0.825; 0.598
Hansen t. (Prob>χ2)	0.262; 0.919	0.899; 0.951	0.935; 0.985		0.341; 0.508	0.954; 0.819	0.948; 0.935	0.968; 0.994

Panel 2 (aid form: ODA per GDP, GBS share, PPP share/volatility)

Variable	Undernourished	Hunger	Underweight	Stunted	Undernourished	Hunger	Underweight	Stunted
ODA per GDP	−0.72 (**1.80**); −0.69 (**1.72**)	−3.57 (**2.18**); −3.80 (**2.26**)	−0.20 (**1.75**); −0.08 (1.09)	−0.21 (**1.79**); −0.09 (1.14)	−1.16 (**1.98**); −1.13 (**1.95**)	−4.15 (**2.75**); −4.73 (**3.29**)	−0.37 (**1.76**); −0.28 (**1.70**)	−0.04 (0.27); −0.02 (0.14)
GBS share	5.29 (1.48); 8.87 (**1.82**)	25.33 (**2.65**); 48.63 (**2.65**)	5.83 (1.59); 5.73 (1.53)	−1.73 (0.93); 7.34 (1.41)				
PPP share/volatility	2.68 (0.96); 2.07 (**1.82**)	7.54 (1.48); 9.39 (**2.58**)	3.13 (**1.70**); 0.26 (0.96)	5.41 (**2.59**); 3.69 (**1.99**)	1.07 (**1.71**); 3.85 (0.95)	3.69 (**1.99**); 10.54 (**3.29**)	15.22 (**4.15**); 5.41	10.54 (**3.29**); 15.22 (**4.15**)
Governance	−0.20; −0.40 (0.58)	0.11 (0.12); 0.58	−0.16 (0.71); 0.09 (0.00)	−0.03 (0.67); −0.02	−0.41 (0.48); −0.11 (0.40)	−0.75 (**1.78**); −1.67 (**2.75**)	−0.06 (1.01); −0.10 (0.35)	0.94; −0.11 (**2.03**)
GBS × gov	−14.40 (**3.29**); 1.95 (1.11)			−0.22 (**1.67**); 0.90				
PPP × gov/volatility × gov	−1.76 (**1.78**); 3.45 (1.54)		−1.13 (0.56); 2.47 (**2.47**)	0.84	1.11 (**3.09**)		0.75 (**2.81**); −0.16 (**2.54**)	−2.55 (**3.85**)
N	340	340	230	230	336	336	230	230
AR2 test (Prob>z)	0.101; 0.216	0.145; 0.158	0.150; 0.908	0.148; 0.908	0.161; 0.142	0.133; 0.079	0.132; 0.839	0.156; 0.908
Hansen t. (Prob>χ2)	0.319; 0.306	0.190; 0.959	0.957; 0.986	0.960; 0.986	0.181; 0.814	0.889; 0.889	0.928; 0.963	0.941; 0.951

Notes: Regressions were run with robust standard errors, time dummies and the same control variables as regressions in Table 3.2. The first number next to each variable is the coefficient; the number below is the corresponding t-statistic. Bold font represents significance at least at the 10% level interaction term between volatility and governance are more confusing. In all four regressions they are significant – however, in two they are positive while in two they are negative. This outcome most likely indicates that the influence of governance on the aid volatility–food security relationship is not singular but could go in both directions. Countries with better governance could be in a better position to deal with aid volatility but they may simultaneously be countries that are more deeply involved in development partnerships with their donors and thus aid volatility could have a more detrimental effect on their economies.

Aid divided by where it flows

Table 3.7 looks at the heterogeneous effects of aid on food security when classified by the sector to which it is provided. The upper part of the table presents regressions that compare the impact of aid divided into long-term, short-term and humanitarian. Unexpectedly, long-term aid is uniformly significant and negative, while emergency aid only sometimes and short-term aid not at all. The aid–governance interaction term is similarly significant for both long-term and short-term aid. These results suggest that long-term aid strengthens food security generally whereas short-term aid only in countries with better governance, at least in the three-to-six-year window after the aid's disbursement. Clemens *et al.* (2004), who used this aid typology, found only short-term aid to have a discernibly positive effect on growth in this time horizon. Thus, the impact of aid on food security differs from that on growth in this regard, suggesting that the positive effect of short-term aid on growth fails to reach the most vulnerable, food-insecure sections of society in the time frame examined.

However, the positive impact of humanitarian aid should be felt immediately, especially with regard to certain types of food insecurity. Indeed, emergency aid seems to reduce the depth of hunger and the percentage of underweight children, the two most immediate measures of food insecurity in my study. The fact that it does not strengthen the other two dependent variables – the prevalence of undernourishment and stunting – indicates that, unsurprisingly, humanitarian aid cannot serve as an effective long-term tool for combating food insecurity.

The lower part of Table 3.7 compares the effects of agricultural, social, economic and other aid. Social aid is most consistently significant while agricultural aid, despite expectations, is not significant at all. The first finding, that social aid bolsters food security, is interesting yet not completely unforeseen. This category includes aid intended to improve health services, encourage population control and improve water and sanitation and, as such, was anticipated to strengthen food security at least to some extent. The more surprising finding is with regard to agricultural aid, which I expected to have the most positive effect on food security of the four types of aid but apparently has none. This lack of significance does not imply that agricultural aid cannot play a meaningful role in strengthening food security, given that the contrary has often been proven on the micro level (e.g. IYCN, 2011). Instead, the more likely explanation is that not *all* aid to agriculture strengthens food security, a suspicion reinforced by the fact that

Table 3.7 The impact of *where* aid is provided on recipients' food security

	Undernourished		Hunger		Underweight		Stunted	
Long–term aid	**−3.39**	**−2.61**	**−0.35**	**−1.23**	**−3.48**	**−1.38**	**−0.39**	**−1.05**
	2.81	**2.24**	**2.18**	**3.28**	**3.15**	**1.74**	**1.92**	**2.27**
Short–term aid	0.10	0.96	−0.12	−0.17	0.08	−0.38	−0.15	0.13
	1.36	1.42	1.28	1.49	0.89	0.85	1.18	0.84
Humanitarian aid	0.09	−0.32	0.05	−0.19	0.09	**−1.17**	0.10	−0.13
	1.55	1.38	0.95	1.74	1.19	**2.24**	1.12	1.58
Governance	−0.40	**−0.70**	**−0.14**	**−0.11**	**−2.93**	**−1.35**	**−0.53**	**−1.06**
	0.70	**1.68**	**1.77**	**1.91**	**3.31**	**3.32**	**2.33**	**1.82**
Long–term aid × gov		**−0.12**		**−0.52**		0.00		**−0.07**
		2.30		**2.97**		0.08		**2.11**
Short–term aid × gov		**−0.12**		**−0.68**		−0.01		**−0.07**
		2.29		**3.29**		0.42		**2.06**
Humanitarian aid × gov		−0.09		**−0.14**		0.02		−0.01
		1.71		**2.09**		1.13		0.57
N	325	325	228	228	325	325	228	228
AR2 test (Prob>z)	0.172	0.151	0.169	0.830	0.167	0.177	0.158	0.808
Hansen test (Prob>χ2)	0.979	0.808	0.976	0.970	0.987	0.656	0.940	0.961

	Undernourished		Hunger		Underweight		Stunted	
Agricultural aid	0.09	0.09	0.38	0.04	0.07	−0.16	0.34	0.29
	1.48	1.21	0.99	0.40	0.76	1.27	1.63	1.52
Social aid	**−1.77**	0.07	**−1.98**	**−1.80**	0.06	0.06	**−0.36**	**−0.27**
	2.88	0.74	**2.97**	**2.65**	0.90	0.56	**1.85**	**1.69**
Economic aid	**−1.67**	**−1.17**	**−3.98**	**−3.35**	−0.31	−0.82	**−0.97**	**−0.88**
	2.35	**2.11**	**3.09**	**2.65**	0.59	1.27	**2.51**	**2.16**
Other aid	0.06	−0.07	0.40	**−1.09**	**−0.30**	−0.01	−0.11	−0.51
	0.15	0.74	0.90	**1.70**	**2.70**	0.06	0.77	1.61
Governance	**−0.43**	**−1.96**	**−0.93**	**−7.46**	**−0.08**	−0.28	−0.04	−0.73
	1.97	**2.48**	**2.39**	**2.08**	**2.17**	0.41	1.15	0.91
Agricultural aid × gov		−0.04		**−0.35**		**−0.06**		0.03
		1.70		**3.29**		**2.18**		0.54
Social aid x gov		0.02		−0.04		0.01		−0.10
		1.14		0.61		1.07		1.06
Economic aid × gov		0.01		**−0.63**		**−0.16**		**−0.05**
		0.14		**2.81**		**2.29**		**3.32**
Other aid × gov		**−0.19**		**−0.51**		0.08		−0.06
		2.88		**2.54**		1.37		0.87
N	325	325	325	325	228	228	228	228
AR2 test (Prob>z)	0.080	0.232	0.190	0.163	0.134	0.167	0.959	0.977
Hansen test (Prob>χ2)	0.830	0.844	0.883	0.902	0.976	0.988	0.979	0.982

Notes: Regressions were run with robust standard errors, time dummies and the same control variables as regressions in Table 3.2. The first number next to each variable is the coefficient; the number below is the corresponding t–statistic. Bold font represents significance at least at the 10% level

agricultural aid is also the type of aid whose influence is most significantly conditioned on governance.

On a different note, the results presented offer an insight also into the different measurements of food security utilised. Throughout the different regressions, depth of hunger appeared bolstered by aid most significantly, followed by the prevalence of undernourishment, the rate of underweight children, and the rate of stunted children. Moreover, depth of hunger and the underweight variable seemed more frequently significant in relationship with food and other types of emergency aid. The greater overall significance of the FAO variables – depth of hunger and undernourishment – can probably be attributed to the fact that their observations are more numerous than of the other two variables, and hence regressions that work with them are more powerful. Undernourishment and stunting exhibited lower significance with humanitarian aid most likely because they measure more chronic food insecurity, unlike the other two, more short-term, indicators.

Does aid foster food security cross-nationally?

Most data available for quantitative cross-country studies are believed to be imperfect. This may not apply to data on aid but is almost certainly true regarding data on food security and governance, two main concepts examined here. This study has done its best to overcome this problem, however, by providing a number of robustness checks on the results obtained. Consequently, the findings paint a picture that perhaps does not reflect but surely at least closely resembles the reality.

The most salient finding that emerged in this chapter is that development aid has a significant positive impact on recipient countries' food security, whether embodied by their prevalence of undernourishment, their depth of hunger or their rate of underweight and stunted children. The attained coefficients are quite fragile to changing specifications and sample sizes in their magnitude but not in their direction or significance. The conclusion that development aid strengthens food security is further supported by the fact that there is a slight downward bias in the results as aid and food insecurity have a naturally positive association – given that more assistance goes to countries with higher food insecurity rates (e.g. Brückner, 2013).

Less hearteningly, the size of the positive effect of aid on food security is small. Raising the amount of aid per GDP by one logarithm – so, for example from 1 USD per GDP to 10 USD per GDP – would, according to my results, translate into less than 1 percentage-point reduction in the proportion of stunted and underweight children and less than 2 percentage-point reduction in countries' overall prevalence of undernourishment. For comparison, the effect of aid is approximately seven times smaller than the impact of GDP per capita on the prevalence of undernourishment and on depth of hunger and ten times smaller than the impact of GDP per capita on children's stunting and low weight. Additionally, it is unfortunate that the positive influence of aid is less notable on children's nutritional status than on adults' since nutritional deficiencies in early childhood are considerably more detrimental to human development than later on in life. However, particularly in countries with low levels of per capita incomes and large populations, even this small impact of aid can theoretically translate into improved food security for millions of people.

The second most salient result in this chapter is that the effect of aid on food security is strengthened by better governance – that is, in countries with better-rated institutions, aid bolsters food security more than in countries with worse-rated institutions. Looking at the impact's magnitude, visualised marginal effects of aid showed that while in countries with WGI scores lower than −1 aid had no positive effect on food security, in countries with WGI scores above 2 aid contributed to the reduction in child stunting by more than 1 percentage point and in undernourishment prevalence by more than 2 percentage points. The magnitude of the coefficients with *polity2* was similar.

The positive conditioning effect of governance is also stronger in countries that receive higher volumes of aid per GDP. This is not altogether surprising, as countries that receive more aid relative to the size of their economies understandably need increasingly better institutions to be able to use all that aid productively. Unfortunately, highly aid-dependent countries have generally worse quality of governance. My data clearly show this: countries in the lowest quarter of the aid per GDP distribution have an average WGI score of −.84 while countries in the highest quarter of this distribution have an average WGI score of −.1. Both these findings – that aid has a greater positive effect on food security in the presence of better governance and that governance matters more in countries that receive relatively more aid – strongly underscore the need for donors to take individual country situation into consideration when making decisions about aid disbursements.

Turning to the specific type of governance that matters the most in the aid–food security relationship, when the WGIs were disaggregated into their separate components – voice and accountability, political stability, government effectiveness, regulatory quality, rule of law and control of corruption – control of corruption was found to have the largest positive conditioning effect, followed by regulatory quality and political stability. The effect of the other three aspects did not appear to be statistically important. This discovery, as interesting as it appears, should, however, be explored further in the following qualitative case-study chapter. The different WGI indicators have been accused by researchers (e.g. Bjørnskov, 2006; Langbein and Knack, 2010) of being highly collinear and consequently not genuinely measuring different aspects of countries' governance. Kaufmann and Kraay (2008) countered this criticism but conceded that the aggregate WGI scores had a higher external validity than their separate components.

Jointly, the findings discussed provide solid support to the first research hypothesis (H1), which theorised that aid had a significant positive effect on food security, conditioned on the quality of governance. Results on the heterogeneous impact of different aid modalities on food security are not equally robust but some interesting discoveries have emerged. Both multilateral aid and bilateral aid bolster food security – albeit multilateral aid, as was expected, seems to do so more consistently. When bilateral aid is separated into DAC and non-DAC aid, DAC aid appears to affect food security more positively while the effect of non-DAC aid is influenced more by the quality of governance. Moreover, bilateral aid overall is more positively influenced by the quality of governance than multilateral aid. Together, these findings not only support my second hypothesis (H2.1) but also make sense in light of existing literature, which argues that bilateral aid tends to be more political and less development-oriented than multilateral aid and that this is even more true of aid provided by the 'new', non-DAC donors.

Looking at the different mechanisms of aid delivery, grants seem a more beneficial tool for strengthening food security than concessional loans and financial aid better than food aid. Budget support and aid channelled through PPPs do not seem to have a very different impact on food security from other aid and aid volatility predictably dampens aid's positive effect on food security. Taking the intervening role of governance into account, both concessional loans and budget support are more conditioned on governance than their counterpart instruments, suggesting that only countries with reasonably good institutions should be receiving these aid modalities. The scandal over the misuse of US budget support provided to Afghanistan, used in large part for 'kickbacks and bribes', nicely, if only anecdotally, illustrates this point (Brinkley, 2013). It is also not surprising to see financial aid to be more supportive of food security than food aid, as the study uses three-year averaged data on aid lagged by one time period and consequently does not capture the short-term fluctuations in food security that might be more positively affected by food aid. All of the conclusions in this section have aligned with my initially formulated research hypotheses (H3.1, H4, H5, H6, and H7).

However, that is not the case when it comes to examining the heterogeneous relationship between food security and aid divided according to the sector where it flows. Looking to Clemens *et al.* (2004), who found short-term aid to be more supportive of economic growth than long-term aid in the time frame examined (five years in their case), I expected to find the same with respect to the impact of aid on food security. Nevertheless, I discovered just the opposite – long-term aid to be most consistently positive and significant, followed by humanitarian and, finally, by short-term aid. The underlying reasons for this divergent finding could be many but the most likely one is that short-term types of aid that encourage growth, such as aid to industry, finance, tourism, or even agriculture, on the one hand, are not directly beneficial to the most vulnerable strata of the society, who are most likely to be food insecure. On the other hand, long-term aid includes a lot of initiatives in the social sector (health, education, water and sanitation), which may strengthen recipients' food security quickly and directly without ever translating into higher rates of economic growth.

Results vis-à-vis the last aid classification, into agricultural, social, economic and other aid, strongly support these conjectures. Formulated as the ninth hypothesis (H9) was my expectation to discover agricultural aid to have a more positive effect on food security than aid provided to any other sector, primarily because agricultural aid is generally aimed at helping countries boost their agricultural production, which should, in theory, promptly reinforce their food security. Nevertheless, not only did the regressions reveal social aid to have a more significant positive effect on food security than agricultural aid, also they did not find a significant relationship between agricultural aid and food security at all. Since most sectors that fall under social aid are also classified as long-term aid, the results are congruent with those discussed in the previous paragraph and to some extent illuminate the previous finding. Aid to health, education, water and sanitation probably has a fast-acting positive impact on countries' food security levels. However, the impact of agricultural aid on food security might be more ambiguous, as is supported by the finding that agricultural aid is, in its effect on food security, highly conditioned on the quality of governance. However, it is difficult to find out anything more specific about the underlying causes using cross-country quantitative data analysis alone.

Conclusion

This last point illustrates well the main weakness of this chapter's empirical approach. While using quantitative methods to test the originally formulated hypotheses on cross-country data is perfectly valid, the data and methods are unable to yield nuanced explanations about process and development. Cross-sectional time-series regressions demonstrate merely the average effects of development and governance on countries' food security, without displaying any country specificities or accounting for outliers. Relying on such results alone in policy decisions could lead to serious mistakes (e.g. Agénor *et al.*, 2008).

This realisation leads me naturally to the chapter's conclusion. This empirical study has presented an analytical overview of the relationships between development aid in its various modalities and countries' food security. On the one hand, the findings discovered have provided support to most of the hypotheses formulated in Chapter 1, strengthening both the credibility and validity of the theoretical underpinnings of my research. On the other hand, they illustrated that the relationship between aid and food security, with the intervening role of governance, is often non-linear, and that in order to better understand its complexities it should be studied further using other data sources and empirical methods. The next chapter does just that, by examining the impact of aid on food security through a four-country case study, using primarily qualitative analytical methods.

Notes

1 Some results presented in this chapter were published previously in the *International Journal of Development Issues* (Petrikova, 2015).
2 Children are considered to be too light or too short for their age if they fall below 1.96 standard deviations from the mean in the respective categories.
3 All the dependent variables used here measure food *in*security, not food security, and hence finding negative signs on independent variables means that those actually strengthen food security.
4 The division includes also private aid, but the OECD database contains virtually no data in this category.
5 I use the terms 'humanitarian aid' and 'emergency aid' interchangeably.
6 Initially, a measure of political and civil rights and a dummy variable for disaster were also included; however, as both appeared consistently insignificant, they were excluded from the final analysis.

7 The countries examined are the following: Albania, Algeria, Antigua and Barbuda, Armenia, Azerbaijan, Bangladesh, Belarus, Belize, Bolivia, Bosnia and Herzegovina, Brazil, Burkina Faso, Burundi, Cambodia, Cameroon, Cape Verde, Chile, China, Colombia, Congo, Costa Rica, Côte d'Ivoire, Dominican Republic, Ecuador, Egypt, El Salvador, Eritrea, Ethiopia, Fiji, Gambia, Georgia, Ghana, Guinea, Honduras, India, Indonesia, Iran, Jamaica, Jordan, Kazakhstan, Kenya, Kyrgyzstan, Laos, Lebanon, Madagascar, Malawi, Malaysia, Mali, Mauritius, Mexico, Mongolia, Morocco, Mozambique, Namibia, Nepal, Nicaragua, Niger, Nigeria, Pakistan, Panama, Paraguay, Peru, Philippines, Moldova, Rwanda, Saint Lucia, South Africa, Sri Lanka, Sudan, Suriname, Tajikistan, Thailand, Togo, Trinidad and Tobago, Tunisia, Turkey, Turkmenistan, Ukraine, Uruguay, Venezuela, Yemen.
8 Summary statistics of the second-wave, not first-wave, data are listed because comparatively more data were missing from the first wave.
9 In 2SLS regressions where the interaction term with WGI is used, I instrument for it by its multiplication with all the instrumental variables.
10 The xtabond2 command includes Windmeijer's (2005) finite sample correction.
11 All the regressions were run with robust standard errors to control for potential heteroskedasticity.
12 For more information, see http://info.worldbank.org/governance/wgi/index.aspx#home
13 All sensitivity tests except for the first one were estimated with GMM regressions and three-year averaged data.
14 That is not to say that food aid does not have an important role to play in famines and other emergency situations.

References

Agénor, P., Bayraktar, N., and El Aynaoui, K. (2008). 'Roads out of poverty? Assessing the links between aid, public investment, growth, and poverty reduction', *Journal of Development Economics*, 86(2), pp. 277–95.

Arndt, C., and Oman, C. (2006). *Uses and Abuses of Governance Indicators*. Paris: OECD.

Arellano, M., and Bond, S. (1991). 'Some tests of specification for panel data: Monte Carlo evidence and an application to employment equations', *Review of Economic Studies*, 58(2), pp. 277–97.

Benson, T., Mugarura, S., and Wanda, K. (2008). 'Impacts in Uganda of rising global food prices: the role of diversified staples and limited price transmission', *Agricultural Economics*, 39(1), pp. 513–24.

Bjørnskov, C. (2006). 'The multiple facets of social capital', *European Journal of Political Economy*, 22(1), pp. 22–40.

Blundell, R., and Bond, S. (1998). 'Initial conditions and moment restrictions in dynamic panel data models', *Journal of Econometrics*, 87(1), pp. 115–43.

Brinkley, J. (2013). 'Money pit: the monstrous failure of US aid to Afghanistan', *World Affairs*, 6(1).

Brückner, M. (2013). 'On the simultaneity problem in the aid and growth debate', *Journal of Applied Econometrics*, 28(1), pp. 126–50.

Clemens, M., Radelet, S., and Bhavnani, R. (2004). 'Counting chickens when they hatch: the short-term effect of aid on growth', *Center for Global Development Working Paper*, 44. New York: Center for Global Development.

Dinour, L., Bergen, D., and Yeh, M. (2007). 'The food insecurity–obesity paradox: a review of the literature and the role food stamps may play', *Journal of the American Dietetic Association*, 107(11), pp. 1952–61.

Dreher, A., Nunnenkamp, P., and Thiele, R. (2008). 'Does aid for education educate children? Evidence from panel data', *World Bank Economic Review*, 22(2), pp. 291–314.

Hansen, H., and Tarp, F. (2001). 'Aid and growth regressions', *Journal of Development Economics*, 64(2), pp. 545–70.

IYCN (2011). *Nutrition and Food Security Impacts of Agriculture Projects*. Washington, DC: Infant and Young Child Nutrition Project.

Kaufmann, D., and Kraay, A. (2008). 'Governance indicators: where are we, where should we be going?', *World Bank Research Observer*, 23(1), pp. 1–30.

Langbein, L., and Knack, S. (2010). 'The worldwide governance indicators: six, one, or none?', *Journal of Development Studies*, 46(2), pp. 350–70.

Michaelowa, K., and Weber, A. (2006). 'Aid effectiveness in the education sector: a dynamic panel analysis', *Frontiers of Economics and Globalization*, 1, pp. 357–85.

Petrikova, I. (2013). 'Bolstering food security through agricultural policies: cross-country evidence', *International Journal of Development Issues*, 12(2), pp. 92–109.

Petrikova, I. (2015). 'Aid for food security: does it work?', *International Journal of Development Issues*, 14(1), pp. 41–59.

Petrikova, I., and Chadha, D. (2011). '"More power to the Commission?" Comparison of the European Commission's and EU Member States' adherence to recommended practices in aid provision'. Paper presented at EADI/DSA Conference in York. Available at: http://eadi.org/gc2011/petrikova-245.pdf

Rajan, R., and Subramanian, A. (2008). 'Aid and growth: what does the cross-country evidence really show?', *Review of Economics and Statistics*, 90(4), pp. 643–65.

Roodman, D. (2009). 'How to do xtabond2: an introduction to difference and system GMM in Stata', *Stata Journal*, 9(1), pp. 86–136.

Svedberg, P. (2000). *Poverty and Undernutrition: Theory, Measurement, and Policy*. Oxford: Oxford University Press.

Windmeijer, F. (2005). 'A finite sample correction for the variance of linear efficient two-step GMM estimators', *Journal of Econometrics*, 126(1), pp. 25–51.

4 Peru, India, Ethiopia and Vietnam

Introduction

Having examined the links between aid, governance and food security quantitatively, using a large cross-country dataset, this chapter delves into the relationships deeper, through a case study of four developing countries. The selection of cases was driven primarily by the availability of appropriate household data on development aid and food security as one of the main goals of the qualitative country analysis is to provide background information to the subsequent household-level research. The most appropriate countries from this perspective have been Peru, Ethiopia, India and Vietnam, where the Young Lives initiative gathered a series of suitable survey data between 2002 and 2010.

The graph in Figure 4.1, which plots the relationship between aid received by countries and their corresponding level of food insecurity (approximated by undernourishment prevalence) between 1990 and 2010, demonstrates, however, that the choice of country case studies from this perspective could have been worse. Vietnam, India, and Peru lie close to the fitted line, representing thus 'typical' cases to different degrees. Vietnam is the most average case, falling directly on the line, with India exhibiting slightly higher than average and Peru slightly lower than average prevalence of undernourishment for the amount of aid received. Ethiopia is an outlier, with undernourishment prevalence significantly higher than the average expected given the amount of aid per capita received. The addition of an outlier in an opposite manner to Ethiopia – a country with significantly lower levels of undernourishment than the amount of aid received would suggest – would have strengthened the study's validity; unfortunately, no such country with a suitable household dataset was identified.

The four countries under study reflect a wide range of contexts faced by developing countries globally, enabling the case study to explore the aid–food security links in diverse conditions. Geographically, the countries represent Latin America, sub-Saharan Africa, South Asia and East Asia – four of the six main global developing regions.[1] Each of the countries has different cultural and religious traditions. Politically, Peru, Ethiopia and India are nominal democracies, of varying degrees of liberalism, and Vietnam is one of only four remaining 'communist' countries in the world. In the past two decades, all four experienced significant rates of economic growth but not in all of them has it been consistent

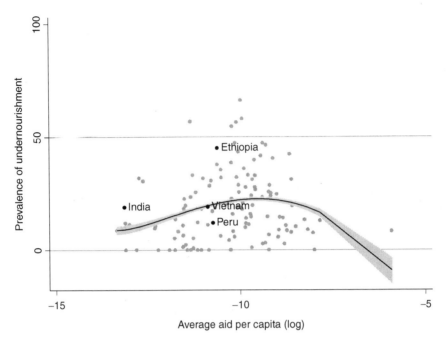

Figure 4.1 The relationship between aid and food security (1990–2010).

Source: Author's own graphic

and translated into steady poverty reduction. Moreover, despite the growth, in all four countries social and economic inequality not only persists but has intensified. Another commonality is that each country has recently struggled with at least some of the issues currently widespread in developing countries, such as high debt burden, post-conflict reconstruction, minority rights, rural–urban divide and adverse environmental conditions (WDI, 2014; Young Lives, 2014).

However, each of the countries faces realities that make it a unique case study of the effects of aid on food security. Peru is a resource-rich country that has always received a big part of its aid in support or tied to the mining sector (Brown, 2014). Ethiopia was one of the world's largest recipients of food aid between 1990 and 2010 (FAO, 2014). India is home to the largest number of malnourished children in the world despite recent high levels of economic growth (WHO, 2014). Finally, Vietnam is one of the world's greatest recent successes in poverty reduction, not least in response to a successful agricultural 'Green Revolution' (Hazell, 2009). As such, each country case study contributes a distinct perspective with regard to the aid–food security relationship – Peru on the influence of mining companies on the provision of foreign aid, Ethiopia on food aid, India on unrelenting food insecurity despite economic growth and Vietnam on the agricultural sector and its connections with development aid.

Structurally, this chapter proceeds in the following manner. The next section introduces the methodological approach utilised, including the choice of data and methods of analysis. Then the chapter describes each country's food-security situation, experience with development assistance, performance in governance and some of the key control variables that emerged in the previous chapter, including economic and trade performance, agricultural production, population and its growth, conflicts, and environmental factors. Finally, it analyses the information collected and summarised with the aim to illuminate the process through which aid in its different types may have influenced food security and interacted with the quality of governance. At the same time, the descriptive parts of the chapter constitute a background to the household-level analysis in Chapter 5.

Chapter methodology

Analytical approach

This chapter uses analytical country narrative, which combines the rigours of rational choice theory with the richness of detail of traditional historical narratives. The method takes as its foundation the basic aid–food security statistical model utilised in Chapter 3 and enhances its complexity, using specific country experiences as a backdrop. The country narratives hence constitute a complementary tool to the cross-country empirics, on one hand attempting to verify the findings from the statistical models, but, more importantly, on the other hand deepening our understanding of the relationships between the key variables examined (Rodrik, 2003).

The basic statistical model tested in Chapter 3 was the following:

$$f_{it} = \beta_0 + \beta_1 A_{it} + \beta_2 G_{it} + \beta_3 \left(A_{it} * G_{it} \right) + \beta_2 X_{it} + \gamma_t + \varepsilon_{it}$$

where f_{it} is the level of food insecurity observed for country i in year t, A_{it} are its aid receipts per GDP, G_{it} is the quality of governance, $A_{it}*G_{it}$ is the aid–governance interaction term (which represents the impact of aid on food insecurity that is conditional on governance), X_{it} are control variables (which can be generally divided into economic, trade and social factors, agricultural factors, population factors and environmental factors), γ_t is the unobserved time effect and ε_{it} is the error term.

For the purposes of the statistical analysis, the equation strived for parsimony and assumed the effect of aid on food security to be mostly direct, conditioned only on the quality of governance. Nevertheless, the discussion of the four different aspects of food security and its influents in Chapter 1 indicated that the relationship between aid and food security is in reality much more complex than the equation suggests. Aside from the direct effect that aid confers on food security, it can also affect food security indirectly, via various factors that were mostly used as control variables in the regressions. Figure 4.2 models this more complex version of the aid–food security relationship graphically.

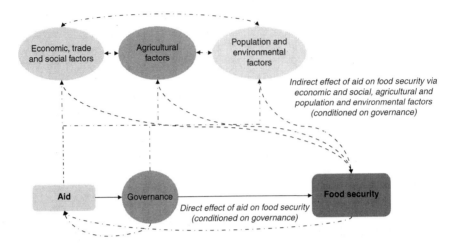

Figure 4.2 The direct and indirect effects of aid on food security.

Source: Author's own graphic

Translating the figure into words, aid can influence countries' food security directly as well as indirectly via other factors and in both cases the effect is likely conditioned on the quality of the countries' governance. Directly, aid can improve food availability, people's access to food and even food utilisation through activities/mechanisms such as budget support, food distribution, direct cash transfers, provision of nutritionally fortified foods and water-sanitising tablets and building of toilets, just to name a few. Indirectly, aid can influence countries' economic, social and trade factors, agricultural factors and population and environmental factors, which can, in turn, affect food security. For example, aid can help raise growth or ameliorate social inequality, raise agricultural yields or contribute to undermining local food production and destroying local environ-ment, curb or encourage population growth – all results that can impact food security. How strong these effects on food security are is undoubtedly also a function of how representative, responsive and responsible institutions and poli-cies are in any given country.

Data sources and analysis

Data sources for this study range from primary data to secondary documents. The primary data used, on food security, aid, governance and all the control variables, come from the same sources as the data used in the quantitative cross-country study – from the FAO, the WHO, the OECD's QWIDS and CRS databases, the Polity IV project, the WDI, the Uppsala University conflict database and the EMDAT disaster database. These data, which in themselves provide no more information than raw numbers, are then supplemented with information obtained from the

WFP's and IFPRI's food security portals, the FAO's and IFAD's analysis papers and briefs, the World Bank's and other donor agencies' country reports, own country aid analyses and from research articles and books. Most of the data examined come from the period between 1990 and 2010,[2] as this is the time frame considered in the previous study.

Within the framework of analytical country narrative, the data collected are analysed using the specific empirical methods of process tracing, pattern matching and explanation building, with a focus on examining the relationships that were found to hold true in the previous chapter. Hence, first the chapter inspects whether aid may have had a positive influence on food security in the four countries, whether the relationship has been influenced by the countries' quality of governance, and if so, through what mechanisms the positive influence has played out.

Second, the chapter considers the heterogeneity of aid's impact on food security. Looking at *who* provides aid, it inspects whether there seems to be any difference between the aid disbursed by bilateral and multilateral donors. Regarding *how* aid is provided, it examines if loans have a less positive effect on food security than grants and are more conditioned on governance, if budget support has a different influence as compared to programme and project aid, if aid channelled through public–private partnerships has a different effect from aid channelled through other sources, if food aid differs from non-food aid and if aid volatility has had a negative impact. Finally, the chapter reviews the sectors where aid in the four countries has been provided, in order to explore whether long-term or short-term aid may have influenced food security more positively, whether aid to social infrastructure or aid to agriculture has been more useful and whether governance has had a different conditioning impact in these relationships.

The state of food (in)security

Overview of food security in case-study countries

In all four countries under study food security improved between 1990 and 2010, albeit the rates of improvement differ. Graphs in Figures 4.3 and 4.4 show that the prevalence of undernourishment and depth of hunger decreased significantly, especially in Ethiopia. The prevalence of undernourishment – the proportion of people in a population believed to lack access to a sufficient amount of daily calories – declined there from more than 70 per cent in 1990 to less than 40 per cent in 2010. The reduction in Vietnam and Peru was also notable, from 47 per cent to 10 per cent in Vietnam and from 32 per cent to 14 per cent in Peru. The slowest rate of change occurred in India, where undernourishment decreased by mere 7 percentage points, from 25 per cent to 18 per cent.

Looking at the depth of hunger, Ethiopia again performed relatively the best, reducing the index of caloric inequality from more than 600 kilo calories (kCal) prior to 1995 to 335 kCal in 2010. The reductions in Vietnam and Peru were also

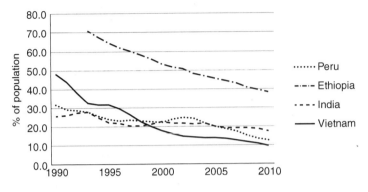

Figure 4.3 Prevalence of undernourishment.

Source: FAO

quite noteworthy, from 357 in Vietnam and 212 in Peru in 1990 to less than 90 in 2010 in both countries. India managed to reduce the calorie gap as well, but only by a small margin, from 167 kCal in 1990 to 124 in 2010. As a result, while in 1990 India was the most food-secure country of the four, by 2010 it was the second least food-secure one.

The evolution of the prevalence of low weight and stunting in children younger than five years tells a similar story (Figures 4.5 and 4.6). The reduction in the rate of underweight children in Ethiopia was proportionally the largest, from 42 per cent in 2000 to 29 per cent in 2010. Peru started with a low number already, 9 per cent, and managed to decrease it to 5 per cent by 2010. In Vietnam, the rate of underweight children declined from 37 per cent in 1990 to 20 per cent in 2010. However, even in 2010 the rate in India still hovered above 40 per cent.

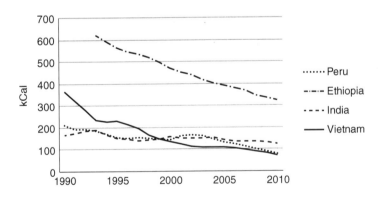

Figure 4.4 Depth of hunger.

Source: FAO

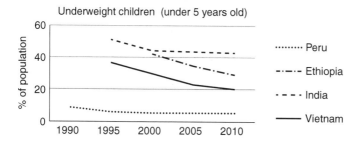

Figure 4.5 The prevalence of underweight children.

Source: WHO

Stunting experienced the largest drops in Vietnam, from more than 61 per cent to 30 per cent, and in Peru, from 37 per cent in 1990 to less than 20 per cent two decades later. The decrease in Ethiopia and India was less momentous, from more than 50 per cent in both countries to 44 per cent in Ethiopia and to 48 per cent in India. It is interesting to note here that the 2010 stunting rate in India was the highest in the world, at least from countries with records available (Drèze and Sen, 2013).

Food-security narratives: what lies beneath the numbers?

PERU

Currently categorised as an upper middle-income country, Peru is considered a small economic miracle. Between 2000 and 2010, its GDP per capita increased by more than 50 per cent (WDI, 2014). This high rate of growth was fuelled primarily by an increase in the exploitation of mining and extraction of other natural resources. Agriculture has conversely decreased in its relative importance to GDP and Peru now imports most of its staple agricultural commodities (IFPRI, 2014).

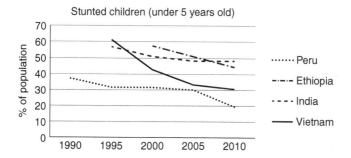

Figure 4.6 The prevalence of stunted children.

Source: WHO

Despite this economic success, however, poverty remains an indelible part of life for many Peruvians, particularly in the countryside. The national poverty rate lies around 30 per cent but in rural areas it exceeds 50 per cent, with 20 per cent living in extreme poverty (IFAD, 2011b). The rural–urban income divide fuelled a high rate of urbanisation, with three out of four inhabitants in 2010 living in cities (WDI, 2014).

As a result, food insecurity remains a concern primarily in the rural areas, even though some people inhabiting slums in Peruvian cities also go to bed hungry every night. The WFP estimates that among smallholder farmers 38 per cent lack access to minimum daily calorie intake and that 14 out of 25 Peruvian regions are extremely vulnerable to chronic child undernourishment (WFP, 2014). As the main causes underlying the issue, IFAD cites high rates of rural illiteracy, primarily among women; the lack of essential services such as education and electricity; insecure land, forest and water rights; inadequate agricultural research, training and financial services; and poor transportation infrastructure and marketing systems (IFAD, 2011b).

The most affected by food insecurity in Peru are minority groups. The history of inequality and discrimination in Peru dates back to the Inca Empire, which encouraged social stratification (Gispert, 1999). The situation worsened after the arrival of Spanish colonisers, who institutionalised discrimination against the natives and mestizos (De la Cadena, 1997). The arrival of African slaves and Asian indentured labourers added to the complexity of the Peruvian population composition and its discriminatory nature. However, the indigenous populations, primarily the Quechua and Aymara Indians residing in remote Andean regions, still remain the most marginalised and most food insecure social groups (IFAD, 2011b).

Ethiopia

Even though the economic growth in Ethiopia between 1995 and 2010 averaged over 5.5 per cent, Ethiopia remains one of the poorest countries in the world (WDI, 2014). The national poverty rate in 2010 was estimated to be 'only' 30 per cent, but since the national poverty line was set at a very low level, from an international point of view the rate likely lay upwards of 50 per cent (IFAD, 2012). Moreover, as the food-security overview suggested, despite major recent progress the state of food insecurity in Ethiopia remains still highly unsatisfactory, at a level deemed by IFPRI to be 'alarming' (IFPRI, 2014).

The relatively steady rate of economic growth in the country after 1995 was achieved primarily thanks to the liberalising institutional and policy reforms set in place by Ethiopia's ruling party, Ethiopian People's Revolutionary Democratic Front (EPRDF), after overthrowing a Marxist regime led by Haile Marian Mengistu. The effect of the reforms has been strengthened to some extent by the government's poverty-reducing efforts and increased investments in agriculture, education, health, water, transport and telecommunications, all fully or partially financed by foreign donors (IFAD, 2012). However, the more than 80 per cent of population that still live on and off small farms, accounting for 95 per cent of Ethiopia's agricultural production, are, despite the recent economic growth, still highly vulnerable to food insecurity and seasonally dependent on free food-aid shipments (IFPRI, 2014).

Only 25 per cent of Ethiopia's arable land was under cultivation in 2010, with subsistence rain-fed agriculture and low productivity the norm. Approximately half of the non-cultivated land is used by migrant tribes as pastures for their herds. Some see this situation as one of opportunity to boost production by introducing irrigation, high-yielding seeds, fertiliser, pesticides and increasing cultivated land area (IFAD, 2012). Others, however, warn against relying on large-scale agriculture to fuel further Ethiopian growth, since the non-cultivated land is environmentally fragile and susceptible to erosion (Devereux, 2000). Moreover, Ethiopia suffers from recurrent droughts and has a small number of natural water aquifers, which could further complicate attempts at agricultural intensification (ibid.).

Setting aside considerations about the correct way to proceed with agricultural policy in the future, however, Ethiopia currently produces a significantly lower amount of food per capita than it consumes and since it generally does not hold enough foreign currency to import the rest at market prices, it continuously relies on foreign food assistance. The availability of nationally produced food per capita has been declining ever since the 1960s, not due to a decline in overall production but due to a 3 per cent population growth, through which the country's population increased from 48 million in 1990 to more than 94 million in 2013 (WDI, 2014). During the Horn of Africa drought of 2011, 5 million Ethiopians relied on food assistance. Due to an ongoing drought brought about by the El Niño phenomenon and exacerbated by climate change, more than 10 million people are estimated to need food aid in 2016 (Meyer, 2016). However, even in 2012, which brought good rains and harvests, more than 3 million Ethiopians needed food assistance (IFPRI, 2014).

Ethiopian persisting food insecurity can be traced partially to the lack of food availability on the country level, and due to inadequate infrastructure and restrictions on transporting food from one district to another, also on the local level. Nevertheless, not always have bad drought and harvests translated into famines and not all famines were triggered by complete harvest failures, suggesting that insufficient food access is a major factor to blame (Webb and Von Braun, 1994). Finally, poor sanitation conditions and scarcity of health services add poor food utilisation as another major driving cause of Ethiopia's lacking food security (IFAD, 2012).

Vietnam

The statistical overview earlier in this chapter suggested that Vietnam is quite a success story when it comes to reducing food insecurity. The reduction can be at least partially attributed to a steady rate of economic growth ever since the Vietnamese communist government abandoned the ship of centrally planned economy and launched a set of liberal market reforms under the name of 'doi moi'.[3] Between 1990 and 2010, GDP growth in Vietnam averaged more than 7 per cent (WDI, 2014). National poverty rate decreased as a result, from 58 per cent in 1993 to less than 15 per cent in 2010 (ibid.). Nonetheless, food insecurity did not fully disappear; it continues to be a problem particularly for the rural poor, female-headed households, children and ethnic minorities (IFPRI, 2014).

Vietnamese economic growth has been largely fuelled by growth in agricultural productivity. Vietnamese economy remains closely tied to agricultural production, which in 2010 constituted 22 per cent of the country's GDP, 30 per cent of exports, and 52 per cent of employment (WDI, 2014). Initial agricultural growth was based on increasing the area of land under use, irrigation, labour and new technologies. A further increase in productivity was engendered through institutional restructuring, including agricultural price liberalisation and land titling. Consequently, Vietnam transformed from a net food-importer in the 1980s to one of the largest net rice exporters in the world by 2010 (IFAD, 2011c).

However, smallholder farmers in rural areas have not always benefited from the enhanced agricultural productivity on large industrialised farms. Lacking adequate access to basic financial services and infrastructure and faced with the effects of frequent natural disasters, many have remained vulnerable to seasonal variation in food availability and often find themselves in highly food-insecure situations (Imai *et al.*, 2011). Some researchers have also argued that the increase in Vietnamese food availability through higher levels of production failed to translate into an improved access or quality of food and in turn deepened the existing income inequalities (Trang, 2012). Nevertheless, the government has made a conscientious effort to combat poverty with the National Targeted Programme for Poverty Reduction (NTP-PR), a large-scale 'safety net' that provides poor people with various support ranging from land, agricultural extension, credit and vocational training to education and health (WB, 2010), and as a result the overall state of food security in the country continues to improve.

As in Peru, minorities in Vietnam are among those worst affected by poverty and food insecurity. Even though the 53 ethnic minorities represent only 13 per cent of Vietnam's total population, they make up 30 per cent of the poor (IFAD, 2011c). The national government has tried to encourage smallholding ethnic farmers to switch away from growing traditional rice varieties to higher-yielding hybrid rice. Nonetheless, the hybrid varieties are also less resilient, exposing farmers to greater seasonal vulnerability and subsequently making some more food insecure in bad-weather years (Bonnin and Turner, 2012).

India

Similar to the other three countries, India experienced a significant rate of economic growth between 1990 and 2010, averaging at more than 6 per cent. Its development indicators improved, with the national poverty rate declining from 37 per cent in 2005 to 30 per cent in 2010 (IFPRI, 2014). However, as the overview of food-insecurity data shows, despite the substantial economic growth, undernourishment among adults and even more among children has remained high.

The underlying reasons for India's sluggish improvement on the food-security front, dubbed the 'South Asian enigma', are not clear (Ramalingaswami *et al.*, 1997). National food availability is not an issue: for the past two decades, India has been a net exporter of major staples including rice, wheat and maize. It is also the world's largest producer of milk, pulses and spices (IFPRI, 2014). However, one third or more of the country's grains procured by the government for distribution through social support schemes does not reach consumers due to deficient storage, administrative delays and/or corruption. Moreover, small subsistence farmers, who constitute the majority of India's rural population, generally lack access to basic financial services and productive resources and thus often fall prey to food insecurity due to unfavourable weather conditions or seasonal fluctuations in local food availability (IFAD, 2011a). Social stratification and ethnic discrimination are other very serious issues in India, with scheduled castes (the 'untouchables') and indigenous tribes suffering from much higher rates of food insecurity than other groups.

Focusing purely on undernourishment trends among children, Pathak and Singh (2011) concluded that the improvement that did occur in India has been quite uneven throughout the different Indian regions, with southern states experiencing a much higher reduction than northern states. However, in those states where positive change occurred, it was predominantly in higher income brackets, thus simultaneously fuelling an increase in nourishment inequality across different economic and social strata. The fact that even high-income groups in northern Indian states experience high rates of child undernourishment indicates that at least some portion of Indian food security problems is caused by deficient food utilisation rather than by scarce food availability or inadequate food access. The problems with food utilisation can be traced to the poor quality of public health institutions along with deficient sanitation and hygiene infrastructure (IFAD, 2011a). In 2013, more than half of the Indian population still lacked access to toilets and almost a fifth to safe drinking water (Drèze and Sen, 2013).

How much and what kind of aid the countries receive

Aid in general

Ethiopia, India, Peru and Vietnam all have a long history of receiving development assistance and all of them could at some point in their history be described as 'aid darlings'. Nevertheless, as Table 4.1 shows, there are significant differences among the amounts of aid disbursed to the four countries between 1990 and 2010, whether aid is considered in its total amount, per capita or per GDP.

Looking at total aid disbursements, in 1990 India was a clear leader, receiving more than 3 billion USD annually, followed by Ethiopia with half that amount, Peru with one quarter and Vietnam with less than one tenth. Throughout the two decades under examination, this order changed significantly. By 2010, Ethiopia came first, having received more than 3.5 billion USD, followed by Vietnam with almost the same amount, India with 3 billion and Peru with 250 million. Between 1990 and 2010, the amount of annual aid to Ethiopia roughly doubled and to Vietnam increased by more than ten times. However, India received approximately the same amount as before and aid to Peru declined to one third of the 1990 amount.

Table 4.1 General trends in net aid provision between 1990 and 2010

ODA total (million 2011 USD)	1990	1995	2000	2005	2010
Ethiopia	1595.48	1332.27	1301.40	2314.75	3777.72
India	3260.99	2612.30	2259.46	1567.62	2976.35
Peru	713.68	482.11	605.70	553.04	257.14
Vietnam	276.13	1264.35	2241.06	2345.88	3613.42
ODA per GDP (*10)	1990	1995	2000	2005	2010
Ethiopia	2.32	1.85	1.44	1.88	1.88
India	0.09	0.06	0.04	0.02	0.02
Peru	0.16	0.08	0.09	0.07	0.02
Vietnam	0.16	0.48	0.61	0.44	0.49
ODA per capita	1990	1995	2000	2005	2010
Ethiopia	33.21	23.36	19.71	30.39	43.37
India	3.75	2.73	2.17	1.39	2.47
Peru	32.78	20.14	23.30	19.95	8.79
Vietnam	4.18	17.56	28.87	28.47	41.57

Sources: QWIDS, WDI

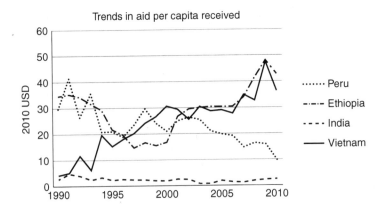

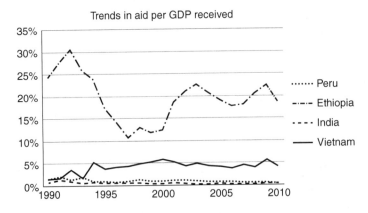

Figure 4.7 Trends in aid per capita and per GDP receipts between 1990 and 2010.

Sources: QWIDS, WDI

The aid figures expressed as a percentage of the countries' GDP and population are perhaps more informative, however, since the four countries' GDP and population levels are very different. In per-GDP terms, Ethiopia in 2010 received the highest amount of aid, with Vietnam second and Peru and India sharing the last place. Given the high rate of economic growth between 1990 and 2010 in all four countries, the per-GDP amount of aid disbursed in the two decades declined in all the countries except for Vietnam, where apparently the growth of aid disbursements was three times faster than the rate of the country's economic growth.

In terms of per-capita aid, Ethiopia started with Peru in 1990 as the largest receiver and finished as the largest receiver in 2010 with Vietnam as a very close second. India was receiving around 3.7 USD per person in 1990, the lowest amount of the four countries, and finished with 2.5 USD per person in 2010, still last. The largest reduction throughout the decades occurred in Peru, from 33 to 9 USD per person and the largest increase in Vietnam, from 4 to 42 USD.

Aid heterogeneity

Figure 4.8 demonstrates *who* provided aid to the four countries under study between 1990 and 2010. Looking at the division of aid into multilateral and bilateral, while India was initially the largest recipient of multilateral aid proportionally, in 2010 it was Ethiopia followed closely by Vietnam. Peru always received majority of its aid from bilateral donors, even though, as Figure 4.8 suggests, this trend might be changing. The figure also looks at the division of bilateral aid into aid provided by DAC and non-DAC donors and indicates that only Ethiopia receives a sizeable portion of its aid from non-DAC countries. The graph likely underestimates the reality, given that many non-DAC donors, particularly China, do not share data on their aid giving with the OECD. Available information on China's development activity suggests, however, that out of the four case-study countries China is notably active only in Ethiopia.

Figure 4.9 shows *how* aid to Peru, Ethiopia, India and Vietnam had been provided. Considering the division of aid into concessional loans and grants, the pattern of their provision appears rather erratic. For example, while India received often about half of its aid in loans, in the 2004–6 years it received virtually none. The proportion of concessional loans to Ethiopia was low and to Peru almost non-existent. Given Ethiopia's persistent reliance on emergency assistance, providing mostly grant aid makes sense. However, the low amount of loan aid to Peru is surprising since it is now classified as an upper middle-income country and hence more likely able to shoulder the burden of loan repayments. Economic growth in Vietnam *has*, however, been accompanied by an increasing loan portion of aid, which by 2010 constituted more than 70 per cent of all its aid.

General budget support, an aid instrument through which donors provide funds to governments in recipient countries to use according to their best judgement, became particularly popular in the aid community after 2000 (Lawson *et al.*, 2005) and the graph depicting the budget-support portion of aid mirrors this rise in popularity. In Vietnam, budget support in 2000 constituted 10 per cent of all aid receipts;

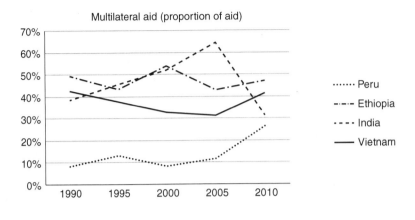

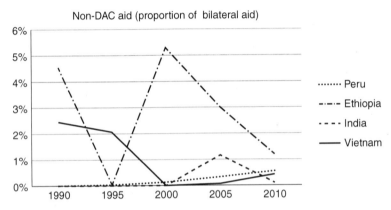

Figure 4.8 Trends in *who* provides aid.

Source: QWIDS

India and Ethiopia collected around 7 per cent of their aid as budget support in 2005. However, as with many development 'panaceas', the budget-support hype died down as donors realised the instrument's drawbacks, particularly its high susceptibility to 'bad' governance, and in 2010 from the four countries only Ethiopia received any money as general budget support.[4]

Even though public–private partnerships (PPPs) in development aid gained popularity in the 1990s, Figure 4.9 demonstrates that by 2010 it had not become a commonly used mode of delivery in the four countries analysed. In 2010, only 2 per cent of aid to Peru was channelled through PPPs; in Ethiopia, India and Vietnam the proportion was lower than 0.5 per cent.

Looking at the division of aid into food and financial and at aid volatility, no clear trends or unforeseen findings emerged. Not surprisingly, Ethiopia received a significantly higher portion of its aid in food donations than the other countries,

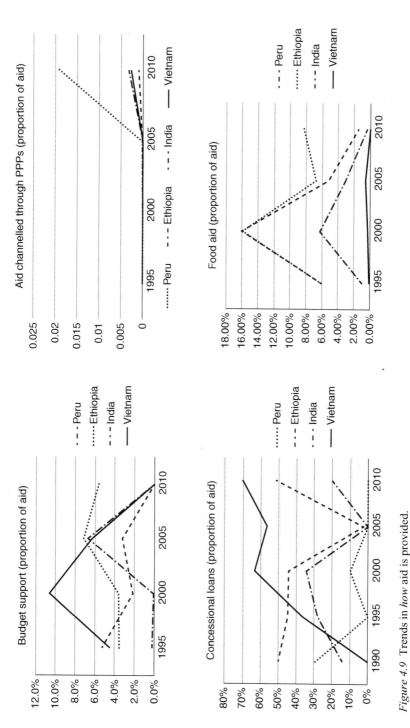

Figure 4.9 Trends in *how* aid is provided.

Sources: QWIDS, CRS

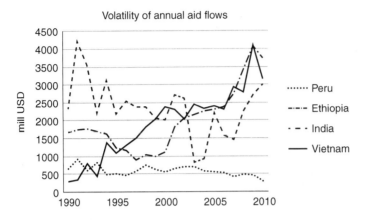

Figure 4.9 Continued.

Sources: QWIDS, CRS

by a factor of four. Aid volatility was high in all four countries but, as calculated coefficients of variation indicate, it was highest in Vietnam and lowest in India.

Finally, Figures 4.10 and 4.11 display trends vis-à-vis *where* aid goes. One of the most salient observations is that the amount of aid disbursed to social infrastructure has been on the rise in all four countries. Aid to agriculture constitutes a small portion of total aid in all four countries, but everywhere except for in India it has also recently increased. Long-term aid has exhibited an upward trend as well, partially driven by the rise in aid to social infrastructure, which is all classified as long-term. Humanitarian assistance has steadily intensified in Ethiopia and experienced a bump in Vietnam after 2005, in response to several severe floods and typhoons between 2006 and 2009.

Aid narratives: what lies beneath the numbers?

Peru

Peru has an extensive history of receiving Western development aid, primarily from the United States (US). Prior to 1990, during the government of Alan García, Peru experienced a dramatic economic meltdown with very high inflation rates, decline in GDP, increase in external debt and a violent civil war between the government forces and the rebel movement Shining Path. Furthermore, since García was not a favourite of the US, aid to the country reached a historic low (Muller, 1985). With the 1990 election of Alberto Fujimori, who promised a return to neo-liberal economic policies and serious government restructuring, aid flows rose above 700 million USD annually and remained at levels above 500 million USD until 2005 (Hudson, 1992; Table 4.1). As the Peruvian economy grew and poverty rates declined in 2000s, however, many donors began to close

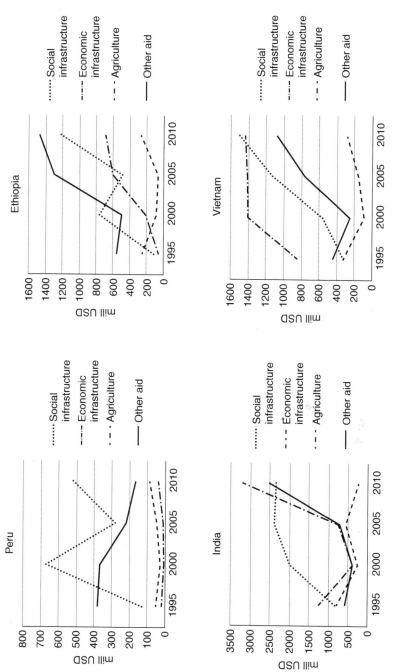

Figure 4.10 Trends in *where* aid is provided (1): Sector distribution.

Source: CRS

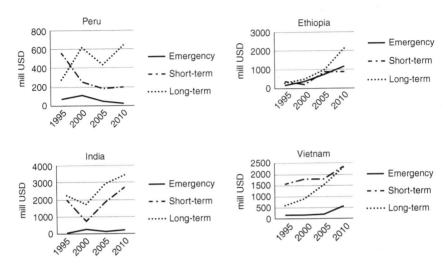

Figure 4.11 Trends in *where* aid is provided (2): Division into 'short-term', 'long-term' and emergency.

Source: CRS

their aid programmes in the country and hence the annual aid flows in 2010 constituted less than half of those in 1990 (Table 4.1).

It is hard to evaluate the nature of the partnership between the Peruvian government and donors as little scholarship exists on the topic. Given that aid represents currently only 0.2 per cent of the country's GDP, it seems unlikely that donors can majorly influence public policies. However, throughout the two decades under study (1990–2010), Peru received the majority of its aid from bilateral donors in project grants, which is the type of aid most often used to attain political goals. Two pieces of recent news indirectly confirm the conjecture that donors continue to exercise power over Peru in some ways. First, since Peru recently surpassed Colombia as the largest global grower of coca, the US pledged up to 100 million USD annually to help the country with anti-drug efforts, primarily with destruction of the crops and offering the growers alternative development routes (*Fox News Latino*, 2013). Second, Canada announced a large aid package to the Peruvian mining sector in 2013, seen by most as really intended to help private Canadian mining companies expand their operations in Peru (*Associated Press*, 2013). In both cases, development aid appears to have been used by donors to encourage the Peruvian government to formulate its policies in line with the donors' own goals and strategies.

Ethiopia

The history of aid flows to Ethiopia is full of dramatic changes. In the 1950s and 1960s, Ethiopia, the only country in sub-Saharan Africa never to have been truly colonised, received only small amounts of aid as it lacked ex-colonial ties that would encourage a particular donor to engage with it extensively (Furtado and Smith, 2007). This situation deteriorated further after 1974, when the Derg rebel movement led by Mengistu overthrew the royal Selassie family and established a Marxist regime. Despite several famines that plagued Ethiopia between 1975 and 1990, aid to the country, due to Cold War considerations, was very scarce.[5] In 1991, after the EPRDF brought down the Derg regime and officially disavowed socialism, the amount of aid dramatically increased and continued to rise throughout the next two decades with two dips, one following Ethiopia's war with Eritrea in 1998 and the other following the 2005 explosion of post-election violence. Regardless of the slight reductions, in 2010 Ethiopia was the recipient of the highest amount of total development aid in the world with the exception of Iraq and Afghanistan (Feyissa, 2011; Furtado and Smith, 2007; Hayman, 2011).

Unlike in Peru or in India, aid in Ethiopia constitutes a very significant portion of the government's expenditures. Throughout the 2000s, annual aid flows accounted for more than 30 per cent of the government's budget (Feyissa, 2011). As Table 4.1 shows, aid also constitutes almost 19 per cent of the country's annual GDP.

Nevertheless, despite the high relative importance of aid to Ethiopia's economy, the Ethiopian government can hold its own in its negotiations with donors (Feyissa, 2011). Although the EPRDF is no longer officially Marxist, it still believes in the supreme role of the state in the development process. Twenty-six of Ethiopia's bilateral and multilateral donors, organised in the Development Assistance Group (DAG), tried pushing the government on issues such as privatising telecommunications and fertiliser distribution and centralising local government expenditure reporting. The government refused to agree to these conditions yet the total aid flows only increased (Furtado and Smith, 2007; Geberegziabher, 2006).

The underlying reasons are multiple. First, Ethiopia has been praised for a long time for its lack of corruption and relative government efficiency and the donor community is reluctant to sully this reputation by overt criticism, which would reflect badly on its own judgement. Second, Ethiopia's humanitarian and development needs are truly pressing and therefore decreasing the amount of aid provided could be regarded as immoral. More importantly, after 9/11 Ethiopia became a strategic Western ally in the War on Terror and reducing the amount of aid it receives could compromise this partnership. Finally, Ethiopia also receives a large amount of Chinese aid – although unclear how much exactly since China does not reveal such information – and by reducing the amount of aid disbursed, Western governments would risk losing even the little control that they have over the country to the Chinese (Feyissa, 2011; Hackenesch, 2013).

This increasing strategic importance of Ethiopia to its donors can be also observed in the reality that, despite the country's worsening governance ratings and increase in violence, Ethiopia has continued to receive various forms of budget-support assistance (Geberegziabher, 2006) – an aid instrument preferred by the government to project and programme aid due to its greater fungibility. In the same line, the government has started to prefer bilateral aid over multilateral aid, which tends to be more burdened with conditionality (Feyissa, 2011).

Vis-à-vis the specific activities financed by donors in the country, food shipments constitute a very significant portion of the portfolio. In fact, in the past ten
years Ethiopia has been one of the largest recipients of food aid in the world
(FAO, 2014). With a view to Ethiopia's often acutely dismal food-security situation, food aid to the country undeniably saved millions of lives in the short run.
However, some research has suggested that its longer-term impact on food security might not be equally positive, as food aid in places reduced local food prices
and hence discouraged local food production (Gelan, 2007; Tadesse and Shively,
2009). Moreover, the food aid to Ethiopia has been described as deficient in
targeting, often failing to reach the poorest and slow to respond to food insecurity
in new localities (e.g. Clay *et al.*, 1999).

In an attempt to make aid effects more sustainable, a large portion of foreign
funds to Ethiopia after 2005 has been spent on supporting large public poverty-
reduction programmes: the Public Sector Capacity Building (PSCAP), the
Productive Safety Net Programme (PSNP) and the Promotion of Basic Services
(PBS). The objective of the PSCAP is to improve the scale, efficiency and
responsiveness of public service delivery and to strengthen good governance and
public-sector accountability (WB, 2013). The PNSP provides food or cash to
food-insecure households in exchange for work at public projects or directly to
people unable to work. Finally, the PBS helps regional and district governments in
financing services such as education, health, water, agricultural extension and
construction of roads (Feyissa, 2011). PPSs in agriculture have also been promoted
as useful aid tools in strengthening food security (Spielman *et al.*, 2010).

India

Western donors have provided aid to India ever since its independence in 1947.
However, while initially aid flows were significant enough to finance a large
portion of India's public investment and imports, as the Indian economy grew,
the size of aid flows became relatively much smaller (Lipton and Toye, 1991). In
1990, aid constituted 1 per cent of Indian GDP and by 2010 it decreased to only
0.2 per cent (QWIDS, 2014).

The small relative importance of aid is undoubtedly one of the fundamental
factors that have allowed the Indian government to be a strong aid-negotiating
partner. All aid provided to India, even if earmarked for various states, has to go
through the national government. There the money is pooled and then disbursed
to the different states according to a national plan, at a stable proportion of 70 per
cent concessional loans and 30 per cent grants (Colclough and De, 2010; Lipton
and Toye, 1991). The Indian government is generally clear about its policy objectives and not open to accepting aid conditions (Colclough and De, 2010).
Unsurprisingly then, studies have found aid in India to be fully fungible – that is,
to merely substitute for spending that the government would have undertaken
regardless (Jha and Swaroop, 1998; Swaroop *et al.*, 2000).

Another sign of India becoming ever more assertive in its relationship with
donors has been the gradual decline of the amount of multilateral aid that India
receives, which – even if less political – tends to be burdened with a greater

amount of conditionality (Figure 4.8). However, in 2003 the Indian government led by the nationalist Bharatiya Janata party terminated aid agreements with all but six of its largest bilateral donors, citing excessively high transaction costs attached to aid received from the smaller donors. This ban was withdrawn the following year, when the Congress Party came to power, but only three smaller donors subsequently renewed their aid agreements (Colclough and De, 2010).

Nevertheless, the small relative importance of aid to the Indian economy means neither that aid has never had any positive impact on India's poor nor that donors have no more influence over the funds that they provide to India. Initially, through the 1960s and 1970s, foreign aid in India was used to fund primarily large infra-structural projects and foreign exchange reserves and as such did not directly trans-late into poverty reduction (Lipton and Toye, 1991). Later, aid focused on support to agriculture, particularly on encouraging the cultivation of 'Green Revolution' crops, might have had some positive impacts on ameliorating poverty. Unfortunately, due to the lack of access to credit necessary to purchase essential inputs, the poorest farmers in India were largely left out of the 'Green Revolution' (e.g. Frankel, 2015).

Recent aid flows, however, have concentrated on providing support to social infrastructure sectors such as education, health and sanitation, which have the high-est poverty-reducing potential. Amis (2001) examined the impact of slum-upgrading projects on slum inhabitants in several Andhra and Madhya Pradesh cities and concluded that they significantly raised recipients' quality of life. The same can be concluded about projects aiming at increasing primary school enrolment rates, described by Colclough and De (2010). Moreover, while the enrolment efforts were largely coordinated by the government of India, foreign donors designed several innovative pilot projects – for example, small school desks for small chil-dren, radio utilisation for teaching – which, due to their positive impact, were eventually adopted and scaled up by the government. In this manner, the donors retained their ability to shape concrete Indian policies despite their decreasing clout in negotiations with the government.

Vietnam

The causes underlying the changing aid flows to Vietnam are multiple, both economic and political. In 1990, the Cold War was only drawing to a close and Vietnam was still under the influence of the Soviet Union. At that time, the US was not disbursing any except for humanitarian aid to the country. Other donors were also committing only small aid amounts, citing worries about human rights abuse (Hay, 1978). However, as the government at the beginning of the 1990s committed itself to a full market liberalisation *à la* China, Western donors started disbursing increasingly larger sums of money. Vietnam thus became a true 'donor darling', with aid programmes in 2003 administered by 25 official bilateral donors, 19 multilateral donors and about 350 international NGOs (Acharya *et al.*, 2006). Together, these donors accounted for more than 8,000 development projects or approximately one project per every 9,000 inhabitants (ibid., p. 4).

This situation is naturally not completely beneficial to the country as donor proliferation and lack of coordination take a toll on the recipients.

Countries dealing with too many donors at one time often focus too much on accommodating the myriad of different donor requirements and too little on identifying own development goals in line with true population needs (Morss, 1984). Donor proliferation also weakens countries' administrative capacity by drawing human capital away from public to the non-profit (donor) sector (Knack and Rahman, 2004). The list of related afflictions extends to high transaction costs, duplication or even cross-purposes of project efforts, and a lack of project scale.

Another characteristic of the aid to Vietnam is its generally unequivocal support for 'Green Revolution' agricultural methods focused on raising industrial agricultural productivity and increasing outputs, without due consideration for smallholding farmers and ethnic minorities (Bonnin and Turner, 2012). By supporting the government's major push for all farmers to grow hybrid rice at the expense of traditional rice varieties and other crops, the donors likely helped the country reduce overall food insecurity but might have simultaneously contributed to small farmers' increased vulnerability to crop failures due to drought or floods.

Governance

The previous chapter discovered that the positive effect of aid on food security is conditioned on the quality of recipients' governance. The two indicators used in the quantitative cross-country study – WGIs and the *polity2* measure – are first examined here for the four case-study countries. This overview is supplemented with some descriptive narrative.

As a reminder, the WGI is an index of six indicators – voice and accountability, political stability and absence of violence, government effectiveness, regulatory quality, rule of law and control of corruption. The score varies from –2.5 to 2.5, with higher numbers denoting a better quality of governance.

Figure 4.12 shows that, from the four countries under study, Ethiopia always scored by far the worst on the WGI. In contrast, India used to be the best performer but was superseded by Peru after 2005. Vietnam's performance has generally been quite dismal and deteriorated further after 2005, which is a little puzzling in view of Vietnam's rapid and conversely India's sluggish improvement on the food-security front. However, disaggregation of the WGI index in the quantitative study suggested that it is particularly the political stability, regulatory quality and control of corruption components that reinforce the positive effect of aid on food security. Figure 4.13 displays the evolution of these three components only and the picture changes a little. While Ethiopia's average score remains the worst, Vietnam swaps places with India and moves behind Peru as the second best performer. India's relatively worse score in these three components is driven primarily by its low mark in political stability and a declining mark in control of corruption.

The *polity2* rates countries on the basis of their observed democracy/authoritarianism. The score varies from –10 to 10, with higher numbers denoting a higher quality of democracy. As Figure 4.14 shows, the score is less temporally transient than the WGI, remaining flat for some countries for long periods of time. In 2010, Peru and India scored the highest number – 9, with Ethiopia at 1 and Vietnam at –7. Since Vietnam has been officially ruled by one-party communist

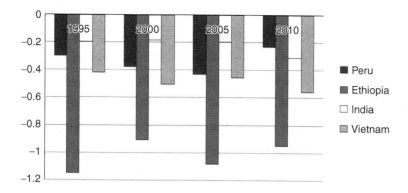

Figure 4.12 Trend in WGI scores between 1995 and 2010.

Source: WGI

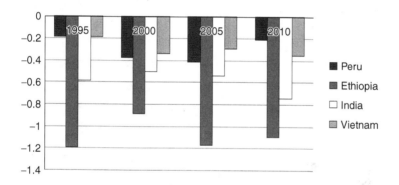

Figure 4.13 Trend in political stability, regulatory quality and control of corruption.

Source: WGI

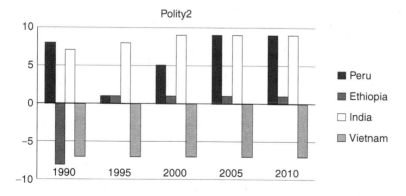

Figure 4.14 Polity2 scores between 1990 and 2010.

Source: Polity IV project

government ever since its reunification in the 1970s, it is easy to understand why its score has been consistently so low. Ethiopia's score improved dramatically after 1991, when its communist dictatorship was overthrown by the EPRDF. India, as a multi-party democracy, scores consistently high while Peru's score improved dramatically after the reintroduction of more democratic government in 2000.

With a view to the WGI and *polity2*, Ethiopia and Vietnam seem quite stable at their low quality of governance, India appears to have somewhat deteriorated and Peru improved. The main areas of India's governance to have experienced a turn for the worse are political stability and rule of law, as evidenced, for example, by an increasing number of government–Maoist clashes and the rise in sectarian violence (Bahree, 2010; Swamy, 2016).

Has aid influenced food security indirectly?

In addition to affecting food security directly, development aid may influence social factors that can, in turn, influence food security. The possible factors, discussed here, are divided into economic and trade factors, agricultural factors, population factors and conflict/disaster/environmental factors – the same divisions as those utilised in Chapter 1.

Economic and trade factors

Literature reviewed in the previous chapters suggests that aid may positively impact countries' economic growth and GDP per capita. Aid can also influence trade flows but the direction of the relationship is more ambiguous (Lloyd *et al.*, 2000). The quantitative cross-country study indicated that GDP per capita and GDP growth have a positive impact on countries' food security quite consistently and that trade has a positive impact sometimes. The effect of aid on food security via economic factors is hence likely to range from none to positive.

Table 4.2 shows that all four countries under study experienced a steady rate of growth after 1995. Consequently, their GDP per capita doubled or even tripled in the 1990–2010 period. All four countries also became much more open to trade although from the trade-openness indicator (exports + imports/GDP) it is not clear whether this opening has been more due to an increase in exports or in imports. Nevertheless, Peru, India and Ethiopia, with trade openness still under 50 per cent, remain significantly less engaged with the world economy than Vietnam, with its trade openness of more than 160 per cent.

Has aid played a role in these developments and did they translate into improved food security? To respond to the latter part of the question first, the country narratives on food security suggest that, indeed, higher rates of growth and trade openness might have strengthened food security in all four countries to at least some degree. Whether economic growth and trade openness were bolstered by development aid receipts is harder to answer, however. With a view to the relative size of foreign aid to the four countries' economies and the accounts above, this case can be argued persuasively only for Ethiopia, where aid

Table 4.2 Overview of economic and trade control variables

	GDP growth	GDPpc, PPP	Trade (%GDP)	GDP growth	GDPpc, PPP	Trade (%GDP)
	Peru			Ethiopia		
1990	2.17	4465.18	27.14	−7.14	491.97	13.24
1995	7.98	5198.44	30.08	7.25	495.91	24.06
2000	1.36	5465.93	33.37	6.51	527.65	35.83
2005	6.51	6375.71	43.97	12.08	619.75	49.18
2010	5.50	8461.04	48.71	8.68	881.71	44.92
	India			Vietnam		
1990	1.06	1205.58	16.69	5.96	941.32	66.95
1995	7.26	1418.45	21.25	9.24	1232.40	81.63
2000	5.79	1747.31	25.56	6.15	1599.64	108.94
2005	8.80	2238.22	41.15	8.15	2163.66	144.56
2010	8.45	3086.39	49.31	6.02	2870.15	163.47

Source: WDI

has constituted on average more than 20 per cent of GDP in the past two decades and has also been quantitatively found to increase growth under positive policy conditions (Girma, 2015). This is an interesting finding, given that the level of undernourishment in Ethiopia is significantly above the fitted line of the average aid–food insecurity relationship. The links between aid and growth in Vietnam, India and Peru may also be positive, but the information surveyed here is not sufficient to enable such conclusion in any of the three cases.

Agricultural factors

Let us now shift focus to agricultural variables – food production, cereal yield, the amount of GDP composed by agricultural production and the proportional employment in agriculture. Chapter 1 found the first two variables – domestic food production and cereal yield – to strengthen countries' food security. The other two variables might not have a direct effect on food security but they are discussed here in order to paint a more complete picture of the countries' agricultural situation. Regarding the effect of aid on these four variables, aid might contribute positively to raising countries' cereal yield, through supporting agricultural research. Its effect on food production can vary from negative to positive, however – as, for instance, food aid might lower domestic production, on the one hand, while support for agricultural extension might, on the other hand, boost it.

Table 4.3 displays the performance of Peru, Ethiopia, India and Vietnam in the four agricultural indicators. Food production rose from 1990–2010 in all four countries. However, population numbers also increased in that time frame and hence per capita food production has likely stayed roughly the same or even declined – particularly in Ethiopia, with its extremely high population growth. Cereal yield per hectare increased as well, but remained at very different levels for the four countries. At less than 1,700 kilograms per hectare, it was by far the

Table 4.3 Overview of agricultural control variables

	Food production	Cereal yield (kg per ha)	Agriculture (%GDP)	Employed in agriculture (%)	Food production	Cereal yield (kg per ha)	Agriculture (%GDP)	Employed in agriculture (%)
	Peru				*Ethiopia*			
1990	49.61	2603	8.54			1238	54.34	
1995	63.05	2639	8.78		57.27	1034	57.48	89.30
2000	85.43	3084	8.50	6.80	69.88	1116	48.69	
2005	99.84	3558	7.21	10.80	102.25	1361	45.59	79.30
2010	129.63	3898	6.77	6.50	124.42	1682	45.62	
	India				*Vietnam*			
1990	70.29	1891	29.02		49.21	3073	38.74	
1995	81.20	2112	26.26	60.50	61.26	3570	27.18	70.00
2000	91.67	2294	23.02	59.90	76.88	4112	22.73	65.30
2005	100.02	2412	18.81	55.80	100.42	4726	19.30	54.80
2010	123.39	2676	17.98	51.10	119.25	5177	18.89	48.40

Source: WDI

lowest in Ethiopia, followed by India, Peru and, finally, by Vietnam, with more than 5,000 kilograms per hectare. The relative productivity increase between 1990 and 2010 was also the lowest in Ethiopia and in India.

In Ethiopia, agriculture is clearly the most important productive sector, accounting for almost half the annual GDP and more than 80 per cent of employment. In India, the importance of agriculture to GDP declined by almost half between 2000 and 2010, but more than half the population is still employed agriculturally. Vietnam has very similar numbers to India, with agriculture actually contributing more to the Vietnamese GDP – the major difference is the much higher productivity of Vietnam's industrialised agricultural sector (Bonnin and Turner, 2012). Finally, in Peru agriculture seems economically quite negligible, contributing only 7 per cent to annual GDP and employing fewer than 7 per cent of the population.

The food-security and aid narratives suggested that aid had a particularly significant impact on agriculture in Vietnam, in India and in Ethiopia. In both Vietnam and India, donors for several decades[6] supported the countries' efforts at modernising their agriculture through 'Green Revolutions', which helped them increase agricultural yields and food production in general. However, while in Vietnam the Green Revolution arguably translated into improved local food security, in India the link is less clear as the poorest farmers have been left out of most improvements and food insecurity, particularly at the child level, improved only marginally throughout the two decades under study (Drèze and Sen, 2013; Frankel, 2015; Tran and Kajisa, 2006). Ethiopia has also received significant amounts of agricultural development aid, but its cereal yields and agricultural productivity are yet to experience a significant improvement and the aid has been accused of lending support to human rights' abuse, by enabling the government to enforce resettlements of certain social groups (Smith, 2014). At the same time, the country has been, for many years, a consistent recipient of food aid, which is suspected to have depressed the levels of domestic food production (Gelan, 2007). Consequently, aid appears to have plausibly bolstered food security via the agricultural route only in Vietnam.

Population and environmental factors

Looking at population variables, in Chapter 1 I found that countries with larger populations were generally better at ensuring food security, although the impact was not very significant. Increasing population density as a result of population growth is, however, associated with lower food security, particularly in poor countries (Ezra, 1997). Both the percentage of people annually affected by natural disasters and air pollution, the two environmental variables considered here, are likely to impact food security negatively, even though my quantitative cross-country study failed to find a significant relationship between disaster occurrence and countries' food security.

While aid may have an impact on these four variables, it is not easily evident. It seems improbable that aid could significantly affect population levels in the short run, although aid initiatives in education and reproductive health might contribute to reducing population growth in the long run. Vis-à-vis environmental factors, aid is naturally unable to directly influence the occurrence of natural disasters, but it can counteract their negative impact on food security via the provision of humanitarian assistance. Aid might also influence countries' level of environmental degradation. This influence can be either positive or negative – a lot of aid has recently been earmarked in support of projects aimed at improving environmental conditions, but, at the same time, projects focused on agricultural mechanisation or large infrastructure projects can have major harmful effects on the environment.

Table 4.4 shows that between 1990 and 2010 the number of inhabitants in Ethiopia, India, Peru and Vietnam increased, but to varying degrees. In 1990, Ethiopia had a population of 48 million; by 2010 the number increased to 87 million and by 2015 it was more than 97 million. This population jump occurred thanks to a high rate of population growth, which was higher than 2.5 per cent in 2010. India also experienced a large increase in population in the two decades under study, from less than 870 million in 1990 to more than 1.2 billion in 2010, but its recent population growth slowed down significantly, to 1.3 per cent in 2010. Peru and Vietnam started out the 1990s decade also with high rates of growth but slowed down to 1 per cent by 2010.

Regarding natural disasters, all four countries experienced one most of the 20 years examined. Ethiopia suffers a drought virtually every single year, only its intensity varies, while India annually goes through both droughts and floods, and usually also cyclones, landslides and earthquakes. Vietnamese coastal areas are annually affected by cyclones and floods, while Peru is particularly prone to earthquakes and landslides. The highest proportion of population annually affected is in India and in Ethiopia, followed by Peru and Vietnam.

In terms of conflicts, only Ethiopia was involved in a full-on international war in the time period examined. Between 1998 and 2000, Ethiopia fought a 'border' war against Eritrea; in addition, the Ethiopian military was involved in a conflict with

Table 4.4 Overview of population and environmental control variables

	Population (millions)	Population growth %	Disaster affected %	Air pollution (PM2.5 mg/m3)	Population (millions)	Population growth %	Disaster affected %	Air pollution (PM2.5 mg/m3)
	Peru				*Ethiopia*			
1990	21.8	2.01	↑	7.84	48.0	3.48	↑	15.99
1995	23.9	1.80		8.21	57.0	3.25		16.02
2000	26.0	1.51	1.95	8.92	66.0	2.87	3.26	16.08
2005	27.7	1.16		10.59	76.2	2.80		16.82
2010	29.3	1.13	↓	11.31	87.1	2.63	↓	17.04
	India				*Vietnam*			
1990	868.9	1.99	↑	30.25	66.0	1.84	↑	19.09
1995	955.8	1.83		31.78	72.0	1.64		20.20
2000	1042.3	1.67	4.36	33.66	77.6	1.37	1.60	21.27
2005	1127.1	1.48		38.71	82.4	1.16		23.20
2010	1205.6	1.29	↓	43.40	86.9	1.05	↓	25.14

Source: WDI

Somalia towards the end of the 2000s and the country experienced also domestic unrest from various terrorist groups. In that time, the Indian army had been deployed to fight Maoist and other insurgents throughout the country and cross-border skirmishes with Pakistan also occurred several times. The Peruvian army waged a protracted war against the Shining Path guerrillas, which was finally brought to a close in the middle of 1990s. Only in Vietnam the situation was quite peaceful.

Finally, vis-à-vis environmental degradation, all four countries have been faring quite poorly. Table 4.4 shows a steady deterioration in air quality, with India most and Peru least afflicted. Other environmental issues common to the countries have included deforestation and accompanying soil erosion and degradation, water pollution and depletion of ground water aquifers and a loss of biodiversity – all negative factors for future agricultural production.

Has development aid affected the four countries' food security through any of these mechanisms? The evidence fleshed out here does not suggest that it could have happened via the population variables, not because they had no impact on food security but because aid had at best a very marginal impact on the countries' population growth. Turning to the case of natural disasters and conflicts, humanitarian aid provided in their wake certainly helped to compensate for the damage to countries' food security but the measures have generally been short term, involving primarily deliveries of food aid, without a long-term positive effect on food security. However, the evidence available indicates that aid might, to a small degree, have indirectly influenced the four countries' food security negatively, via reinforcing environmental degradation through projects aimed at the mechanisation and intensification of agriculture. While raising cereal yields, these initiatives generally contributed to worsening soil conditions and increasing the rate of water-aquifer depletion, both factors with harmful effect on food security, particularly in the long run. However, it is unlikely that in any of the four countries this negative effect was significant enough to offset the positive impacts of aid.

Has aid strengthened food security in Peru, Ethiopia, India and Vietnam and, if so, *how*?

Taking into account the information presented above, this section considers the three central questions of the thesis in the context of the four country case studies: 1) Has aid influenced food security in Peru, Ethiopia, India and Vietnam positively? 2) Has its impact been affected by governance? And 3) Have different types of aid had different impact? This chapter cannot provide a definitive answer to most of these questions due to insufficient evidence. What it can do, however, is to supply the relationships examined with a depth of detail and understanding of the processes at play that the previous chapter was unable to. In addition, it paints a descriptive background against which results from the household-level analysis in the following chapter can be explained and understood more complexly.

Aid in general

The strongest conclusion of the previous chapter was that development aid has a positive impact on food security and that this positive effect is strengthened by the quality of the recipients' governance. The case studies do not disprove that the relationship might be positive in some countries but neither do they confirm it very strongly. As the passages above have suggested, aid likely strengthened food security directly in Ethiopia and indirectly in Vietnam. It is harder to say whether any such a relationship holds for India and Peru, but equally there is no strong evidence suggesting that the aid disbursed had no positive effect on food security.

Between 1990 and 2010, Ethiopia received annually a significant portion, frequently more than 50 per cent, of its budget in aid (Oakland Institute, 2013). Aid has financed most of the food-aid shipments from abroad on which millions of Ethiopians have relied for their year-to-year survival, as well as large parts of public safety-net and transfer programmes. Aid has also been empirically shown to raise Ethiopian growth under positive policy conditions and higher growth has translated into improved food-security outcomes (Girma, 2015). Thus, it is quite indisputable that aid has had a positive impact on the country's food security, at least in the short term and particularly on the reduction of acute undernourishment. However, a few important caveats need to be highlighted here.

First, the Ethiopian government has been reluctant to accept donors' suggestions on certain policies – for example, on reducing the firm territorial division of the country, which does not allow for large amounts of food to be transported from one section of the country to another, even in famine situations (Feyissa, 2011; Webb and Von Braun, 1994). Moreover, according to the Human Rights Watch, the Ethiopian government has commonly used aid as a tool for the repression of political dissent, refusing to provide food aid to activists and opponents and using donor money for indoctrination in schools (HRW, 2010). Donors have also indirectly provided financial support to Ethiopia's 'villagisation' scheme, under which farming and nomadic populations have been resettled to different regions within Ethiopia under the guise of improving agricultural productivity (HRW, 2012). Hence, it is almost certain that if the Ethiopian government were more democratic and its institutions more responsive to people's needs and less corrupt, the impact of aid on food security would have been stronger.

Box 4.1 Aid, governance and food security in Ethiopia

In 2011, a major drought in the Horn of Africa resulted in a poor harvest and major loss of livestock (Reta, 2015). However, thanks to the reaction of the international aid community, more than 13 million people in Ethiopia, Somalia, Kenya and Djibouti received food aid that year, thus keeping the death toll down to 'tens of thousands' (Tisdall, 2012). In contrast, a similar drought in 1984 without an appropriate international response resulted in the deaths of more than 400,000 people in Ethiopia alone (*BBC*, 2000).

However, despite good rains and harvests in the following two years, even in 2014 almost 3 million Ethiopians had to rely on food aid to ensure survival (*Ayyaantuu*, 2014). According to most researchers, Ethiopia has become chronically dependent on food aid (Gelan, 2007; Tadesse and Shively, 2009), as evidenced by the fact that between 1990 and 2010 it received on average 1 million tonnes of food-aid cereals annually.

Agriculture-development programmes, aimed at tackling this dependency and largely funded through external aid, have translated into some improvements as of late. The 3 million people dependent on food aid in 2014 actually constituted an improvement as compared to the average 5 million from previous years (Reta, 2015). Ethiopia's agricultural production in 2014 also increased 1.52 per cent compared to the year before.

Nevertheless, much of the increase in production has come from large commercial farms set up on lands 'grabbed' from small farmers by the Ethiopian government and leased to foreign countries including India and Saudi Arabia (IRIN, 2011). Many former land occupants, such as the Kwegu tribe in the Lower Omo valley, have been forcefully moved to less fertile lands, with no means of securing food other than through reliance on external assistance (HRW, 2012; Survival International, 2015). More grassroots-friendly, democratic policies by the EPRDF government would, without a doubt, ensure a more positive effect of Ethiopia's aid on its food security.

Second, one third of all aid provided to Ethiopia is generally made up of food, which – as many researchers have pointed out – may have discouraged the country from adopting a more sustainable and long-term-oriented vision of national food security. Claims about Ethiopians becoming 'addicted' to food aid have been largely refuted by researchers on the individual level, on the basis that food-aid delivery in Ethiopia was too unreliable and poorly timed for farmers to grow dependent on it and complacent in response (Little, 2008; Siyoum *et al.*, 2012).

However, from a macro perspective researchers agree that the constant food-aid flows likely led to a depression in the levels of local agricultural production, hence indirectly harming the country's long-term food security. Having recognised this, foreign development agencies, in cooperation with the Ethiopian government, have tried to tackle it through the provision of greater support to the agricultural sector. However, an indirect negative impact of aid could have also been produced by these foreign-funded agricultural mechanisation efforts, which might have contributed to worsening soil conditions and, eventually, collapsed yields in certain areas. Even when summed up, these negative indirect effects of aid on food security in Ethiopia are probably smaller in size than the aid's positive direct effects, but perhaps only when viewed through a short-term lens.

In the same 1990–2010 time frame, aid to Vietnam increased from a relatively negligible amount to almost as much annually as provided to Ethiopia, despite Vietnam's significantly higher GDP per capita. By 2010, Vietnam managed to significantly reduce the country's poverty and food-insecurity rates. One of the main underlying reasons has been a dramatic increase in agricultural productivity thanks to industrialisation and adoption of high-yielding 'Green Revolution' crop varieties. Since foreign donors have invested quite heavily in Vietnamese agriculture (e.g. OECD, 2012), it seems plausible that aid had at least some positive impact on food security in Vietnam, via the agricultural factors.

Box 4.2 Aid, governance and food security in Vietnam

Vietnam is a global success story in poverty reduction in the past few decades. The poverty rate declined from more than 60 per cent in 1990 to 15 per cent in 2010, with similar reductions in adult and child undernourishment rates (WDI, 2014; WHO, 2014). This success owes its due largely to the country's rapid agricultural growth in the past 20 years, propelled, among other factors, by technology of the 'Green Revolution'. The Western donor countries, who supported the 'Green Revolution' financially, take at least partial credit for the country's successful transformation (OECD, 2012). However, researchers agree that it would not have been possible without beneficial supportive policies.

Devienne's (2006) analysis of agricultural transformation in the Red River Delta aptly illustrates this reality. The delta underwent a successful agricultural transformation in the 1990s and 2000s, helping Vietnam become the second largest rice exporter in the world. Part of this success was due to the high-yielding, fast-growing rice varieties provided with the help of donors such as the FAO (FAO, 2011c). Nevertheless, the achievement would not have been possible without further supporting factors, such as the government's land collectivisation in the 1980s, which allowed for the development of hydraulic irrigation systems, the subsequent land redistribution by the government in the 1990s, and the government's continued support for domestic agricultural research (Devienne, 2006; Tran and Kajisa, 2006).

Vietnam's institutions and policies played an important role in this impact, however. The quality of governance in Vietnam is generally rated low due to a very authoritarian nature of the regime (ruled by the Communist Party); nevertheless, Vietnam's level of corruption in project implementation, unlike its level of corruption in general, is not reputed to be very high. Moreover, the country is politically stable and non-violent as compared to Ethiopia or India, which, according to the quantitative study, is one of the major elements of governance that reinforces aid's positive effect on food security. Last, looking specifically at policies important in ensuring the positive effect of the 'Green Revolution' process on food security, the Vietnamese government has redistributed farming land and continuously encouraged domestic agricultural research (Devienne, 2006). It does appear consequently likely that aid has had at least some positive impact on food security in Vietnam and that the country's performance in certain forms of governance further strengthened this effect. Similar to Ethiopia and India, aid to agricultural intensification in Vietnam appears to also have had a roundabout negative effect on local food security through environmental degradation, but not sizeable enough – at least thus far – to counteract the positive influence.

The stories of India and Peru are quite different as aid to both countries declined throughout the two decades and became increasingly irrelevant economically due to the rapidly increasing size of the two economies. Aid to India moved from supporting large infrastructure projects in the 1960s and 1970s through support for 'Green-Revolution' agriculture in the 1980s and early 1990s to more support for social infrastructure, generally considered to be a sector with the most poverty-reducing potential. Analyses of early Indian aid and its effects were quite positive (Lipton and Toye, 1991) and hence it is likely that the later aid to India has had some positive impacts on poverty reduction and food security as well. However, unlike in Vietnam, where aid appears to have bolstered food security via the agricultural route, 'Green Revolution' in India did not have the same kind of positive effects on food security, most probably due to a lack of accompanying poverty-friendly policies and initiatives (Frankel, 2015). Unlike in Vietnam, where the introduction of higher-yielding cereal varieties was complemented by state support for irrigation and fertiliser, land redistribution and domestic agricultural research, land in India remained concentrated in the hands of traditional landowners, with the smallest farmers either unable to afford the cost of fertiliser needed to grow the new crop varieties or becoming excessively indebted in the process (Vasavi, 2012). Hence, aid in support of the 'Green Revolution' cannot be considered an unequivocally positive factor for India's food security.

Moreover, by now the proportion of aid to the Indian economy and population as a whole has become very small and the food security situation in India has improved only little in the last two decades, despite high rates of economic growth and relatively constant inflow of aid. Thus, it is difficult to draw any nation-wide conclusions about the effect of aid on Indian food security. However, in view of the lack of well-functioning redistributive public policies and the amount of corruption plaguing India's large public safety net programmes that have received also significant foreign funding (Shankar and Gaiha, 2013), it is easier to

Box 4.3 Aid, governance and food security in India

Between 1990 and 2010, PPP per capita increased in India from less than 2,000 USD to more than 4,500 USD (WDI). This increase, however, translated into little improvement in food security among Indian children, whose rates of stunting still hovered close to 50 per cent in 2010 (WHO). Researchers explained this reality, showing that social disparities in Indian child undernourishment widened or stayed the same between 1992 and 2005 and that there was very little, if any, association between average per capita growth and improvement in child undernutrition in developing countries (Subramanyam *et al.*, 2010; Vollmer *et al.*, 2014). Social welfare initiatives were recommended as necessary to ensure that growth led to stronger food security, with a particular emphasis on sanitation interventions in India (Subramanian *et al.*, 2014).

One of India's main problems in sanitation has been open defecation, practised by more than half the Indian population (Drèze and Sen, 2013). The resultant high levels of areal pollutants lead to frequent bouts of diarrhoea among children and over time reduce their ability to uptake nutrients from food (Keusch *et al.*, 2013). Nevertheless, a randomised-control trial conducted by the London School of Tropical Medicine and the Xavier Institute of Management recently suggested that toilet construction is not a panacea to India's food security problem either (Clasen *et al.*, 2014).

In cooperation with the Indian government, EU-funded NGOs Water Aid, United Artists Association and SHARE constructed toilets in 50 randomly chosen villages in Odisha, with 50 non-intervention villages acting as controls. During the 30-month intervention period, the proportion of households with toilet access increased from 9 to 63 per cent in treatment households as opposed to the 8- to 12-per cent increase in control households. However, the rate of diarrhoea among children under five years remained the same in both groups. The underlying explanation for the non-effect of toilets lie in people's reluctance to use the toilets (RICE, 2014), which could be remedied through more active support for their use by the local government (Reilly and Louis, 2014). In this way, this case illustrates how the quality of local governance plays a role in ensuring the success of aid interventions.

convincingly maintain that aid would have had a more positive impact on the country's food security in the presence of better governance.

In the past, Peru was a large recipient of foreign aid, primarily from the US and the World Bank. However, by 2010, the amount of aid received by Peru declined to one third of previous levels. The underlying reasons have included the rapid economic growth of the country, rising GDP per capita and decreasing poverty and food-insecurity levels (*El País*, 2012). Aid might have initially – in the 1950s through 1970s – contributed to higher economic growth in the country, but the

---

Box 4.4 Aid, governance and food security in Peru

In 2013, under the leadership of the conservative Prime Minister Stephen Harper, Canada doubled its aid commitments to Peru, becoming hence its third largest donor after the US and Spain (QWIDS, 2014). Many researchers and development practitioners in Canada questioned this move, wondering why at a time when other DAC donors were reducing their aid programmes in Peru due to the country's rapid economic growth, Canada was significantly increasing its commitments, while simultaneously slashing its aid commitments to other developing countries (Oved, 2014). The explanation for the increase in Canadian aid to Peru was its intent to reduce the amount of civil strife against Canadian mining companies in the country and thereby facilitate their further growth (Arnold, 2012). The Peruvian government under the leadership of Ollanta Humala was willing to 'play along', as mining constitutes the country's main growth engine (Oved, 2014).

In Quiruvilca, Barrick Gold, a Toronto-based company, started mining gold in 2004. At first sight, it may appear that the operation brought about economic development, since with the help of the companies' taxes, the local government built new electric lines, roads, schools and a hospital (ibid.). However, the mine did not fuel the promised growth of new jobs and caused environmental damage, primarily to water sources. Consequently, local farmers began to protest, culminating in a 2012 National March for Water (Arnold, 2012). In order to appease the locals, Barrick Gold launched a development project in cooperation with Canadian World Vision, aimed at reducing local poverty and social exclusion (Barrick beyond Borders, 2012). The project spurred some growth of micro-enterprises in the region; nevertheless, many people who were initially displaced to make space for the mine and promised jobs in return have remained jobless, food insecure and bitter about foreign intervention (Alonso, 2014; Oved, 2014).

---

exploration of new mining sites and exports of metals constituted a more robust driver in the recent decades. The same can be said with regard to poverty and food-insecurity reduction – while aid projects have likely had a positive impact in some places, the effect of nation-wide safety nets and transfer programmes such as Juntos, community kitchens and Vaso de Leche have been more significant. Hence, similar to the Indian case, it is difficult to draw any conclusions about the nation-wide effect of aid on food security based on the information presented in this chapter.

Heterogeneity of aid impact

Who gives aid?

Results in Chapter 1 suggested that while both multilateral and bilateral aid strengthen food security, the effect of bilateral aid is more conditioned on governance, particularly so in the case of non-DAC donors. This conclusion fits well with existing research as bilateral aid has long been known for its political nature and less conditionality, and hence countries with better institutions and policies are able to utilise bilateral aid more productively than countries with worse institutions and policies.

Out of the four countries studied, Ethiopia and India have historically received the largest proportion of multilateral aid, although by 2010 the amount had declined. According to analyses of the countries' relationships with donors, India and Ethiopia have become relatively keen on receiving more bilateral aid as it comes with fewer policy conditions and recommendations that neither government is happy to accept. In both countries, however, corruption in project implementation is rampant and pro-poor government policies often ineffective.

The only one of the four countries that receives a large portion of its aid from non-DAC donors is Ethiopia. The large amount of aid provided to Ethiopia by China has helped the government negotiate with more leverage with the DAC donors and thus evade more conditionality in aid implementation. Given the above-cited possibility of greater aid effectiveness in the case of stronger aid conditions, Chinese aid might have thus even weakened the overall positive effect of aid on food security in Ethiopia.

How is aid given?

The main findings regarding the way in which aid is provided from Chapter 1 were that grants have a more positive effect than loans but that loans are more conditioned on governance, that budget support is more conditioned on governance than programme/project aid, that food aid is often less useful for food security than non-food aid and that aid volatility dampens the positive effect of aid on food security. The four countries are not discussed with regard to every category but only focus on the main conclusions.

Looking at grants and concessional loans, Vietnam, followed by India, received the largest proportion of its aid as loans between 1990 and 2010. Neither of the countries had very high governance scores, but while it is possible that aid in Vietnam and in India would have had a more positive impact had it been provided as grants, there is no concrete evidence supporting this claim. Ethiopia obtained little of its aid in loans, which – if the result from Chapter 1 applies there – might have had a positive impact on the country's food security, given its poor quality of governance.

However, Ethiopia has been the largest recipient of budget support from the four countries, even after it became clear following the 2005 election that the EPRDF wanted to maintain an absolute control over power in the country. Coupled with the strong will that the government exhibits in its negotiations with donors and high levels of corruption, budget support is probably not the best aid instrument to be used in Ethiopia. In contrast, Peru, India and Vietnam all have better governance records than Ethiopia and yet in 2010 they received none of their aid disbursements as general budget support. This is most surprising in the case of Peru, which has the best governance and economic indicators of the four countries.

Concerning the classification of aid as food or financial, between 1990 and 2010 food aid constituted a significant portion of aid only in Ethiopia. As mentioned earlier, in many cases, particularly in famine situations, shipments of foreign food played an undeniably positive role in rescuing people from the brink of starvation or preserving their asset base. Nevertheless, Ethiopia has, throughout the past decades, come to consistently rely on foreign food aid, to the extent that local production suffered in consequence. Redirecting some of the food aid into aid aimed at increasing local production through raising agricultural productivity, as the PSNP has attempted, should constitute a better long-term food-security strategy, at least in theory. However, for the implementation to truly work in practice, the government needs to ensure that even the marginalised, most food-insecure groups are included – which might be hard to achieve in a country with such low governance scores as Ethiopia.

Finally, aid volatility seems to be a large problem, particularly in Vietnam, where it is connected also to the issues of donor proliferation and lack of donor coordination. It is quite possible that the volatility has diminished the positive effects of aid on food security as it is hard to plan public policies several years ahead when the source of foreign support varies greatly from one year to the next. Nevertheless, as Vietnam becomes increasingly less dependent on aid for its development, aid volatility should also wane in importance.

Where does aid go?

The main findings in Chapter 1 vis-à-vis this question were 1) that aid to social and economic infrastructure has the most outright positive impact on food security whereas aid to agriculture is most conditioned on governance and 2) that primarily long-term aid bolsters food security.

Regarding the division of aid according to the sector where it is disbursed, in all four countries between 1990 and 2010 the amount of aid provided to social and economic infrastructure increased. Anecdotal and case-study evidence from Ethiopia, Vietnam and India suggests that particularly aid to social infrastructure (health, sanitation) has had a positive effect, at least in places, on poverty and food-insecurity reduction.

Agricultural aid was found by the quantitative study to have a positive impact on food security only in the presence of good governance. This study helped to explain, at least to some extent, this finding. In India, the 'Green Revolution' firmly supported by foreign donors contributed to raising cereal yields, but the achievement did not translate into evidently stronger food security on the national level, due to the absence of accompanying pro-poor policies and land redistribution (e.g. Gupta, 1990; Frankel, 2015). At the same time, this study connected agricultural aid more strongly with bolstering food security, particularly through the case of Vietnam where increased yields, achieved with the help of aid, in the presence of supportive policies (land redistribution, fertiliser subsidies, agricultural research) did help bring about stronger food security.

Looking at the distribution of aid between long-term, short-term and emergency, the proportion of long-term aid increased in all four countries. This is an encouraging finding for food security, given that the quantitative study identified it as the type of aid more beneficial than either short-term or emergency aid in the relatively short term – and likely still more so in the longer term, as the name suggests. However, as the failure of the toilet project in India, discussed in Box 4.3, demonstrated, in ensuring the success of long-term aid initiatives (as in of all others, if not more so) the quality of recipients' governance is of crucial importance.

Conclusion

This chapter allowed me to assess the plausibility of the findings from the quantitative cross-country study on four case-study countries, to enrich the relationships examined with description and to delve deeper into the various aid–food security links. None of the findings here have outright contradicted the findings from the previous chapter and several have become strengthened in the process. The findings from this part of the study constitute a good starting point and background for the analysis of household data from the same four countries in the next chapter, which starts examining the aid–food security link on the micro level.

Notes

1 Not included are North Africa/the Middle East and Eastern Europe/Central Asia
2 Most tables and figures in this chapter present five data points for each country, for years 1990, 1995, 2000 2005 and 2010. However, each data point is an average of three annual observations; e.g. data point for 2010 is an average for 2009, 2010 and 2011.
3 'Doi moi' can loosely be translated as 'creating a socialist-oriented market economy'.
4 In 2015, DFID made the decision to stop providing general budget support to aid recipients altogether (DFID, 2015).
5 There was some Soviet aid, but it was insufficient to fully combat the effects of the famines (Patman, 1993).
6 Although primarily prior to 1990.

References

Acharya, A., De Lima, A., and Moore, M. (2006). 'Proliferation and fragmentation: transactions costs and the value of aid', *Journal of Development Studies*, 42(1), pp. 1–21.
Alonso, G. (2014). 'Barrick Gold and CSR: dynamics of Canadian extractive capitalism in Peru'. Master's thesis, St Mary's University, Halifax, Canada. Available at: library2. smu.ca/bitstream/handle/01/25853/alonso_georgina_masters_2014.pdf
Amis, P. (2001). 'Rethinking UK aid in urban India: reflections on an impact assessment study of slum improvement projects', *Environment and Urbanization*, 13(1), pp. 101–13.
Arnold, R. (2012). 'Peruvians oppose CIDA's joint CSR initiative with Barrick Gold and World Vision', *Mining Watch*, 9 March. Available at: www.miningwatch.ca/article/ peruvians-oppose-cida-s-joint-csr-initiative-barrick-gold-and-world-vision
Associated Press (2013). 'Canada's government announces new aid package for Peru closely linked to mining industries', 22 May. Available at: http://www.foxnews.com/ world/2013/05/22/canada-government-announces-new-aid-package-for-peru-closely-linked-to-mining.html

Ayyantuu (2014). 'Food crisis in Ethiopia: 2.7 million need food aid', 12 February. Available at: https://kafaforfreedom.wordpress.com/2014/02/12/food-crisis-in-ethiopia-2-7-million-need-food-aid/

Barrick beyond Borders (2012). 'Barrick and CIDA co-funding new World Vision project in Peru', 15 January. Available at: barrickbeyondborders.com/people/2012/01/barrick-and-cida-co-funding-new-world-vision-project-in-peru/#.VSTgiPmUfYg

Bahree, M. (2010). 'India's dirty war', *Forbes*, 23 April. Available at: http://www.forbes.com/forbes/2010/0510/global-2000-10-maoists-naxalites-tata-steel-india-dirty-war.html

BBC (2000). 'Flashback 1984: portrait of a famine', 6 April. Available at: http://news.bbc.co.uk/1/hi/world/africa/703958.stm

Bonnin, C., and Turner, S. (2012). 'At what price rice? Food security, livelihood vulnerability, and state interventions in upland northern Vietnam', *Geoforum*, 43(1), pp. 95–105.

Brown, S. (2014). 'Undermining foreign aid: the extractive sector and the re-commercialization of Canadian development assistance', *Rethinking Canadian Aid*, 277.

Clasen, T., Boisson, S., Routray, P., Torondel, B., Bell, M., Cumming, O., Ensink, J., Freeman, M., Jenkins, M., Odagiri, M., Ray, S., Sinha, A., Suar, M., and Schmidt, W. (2014). 'Effectiveness of a rural sanitation programme on diarrhoea, soil-transmitted helminth infection, and child malnutrition in Odisha, India: a cluster-randomised trial', *The Lancet Global Health*, 2(11), pp. 645–53.

Clay, D., Molla, D., and Habtewold, D. (1999). 'Food aid targeting in Ethiopia: a study of who needs it and who gets it', *Food Policy*, 24(4), pp. 391–409.

Colclough, C., and De, A. (2010). 'The impact of aid on education policy in India', *International Journal of Educational Development*, 30(5), pp. 497–507.

De la Cadena, M. (1997). 'La decencia y el respeto: Raza y etnicidad entre los intelectuales y las mestizas cuzqueñas', *Instituto de Estudios Peruanos Working Paper*, 86. Lima: Instituto de Estudios Peruanos.

Devereux, S. (2000). *Food Security in Ethiopia: A Discussion Paper for DFID*. Sussex: Institute for Development Studies.

Devienne, S. (2006). 'Red River Delta: fifty years of change', *Moussons. Recherche en Sciences Humaines sur l'Asie du Sud-Est*, 9–10, pp. 255–80.

DFID (2015). UK aid: tackling global challenges in the national interest. Available at: https://www.gov.uk/government/uploads/system/uploads/attachment_data/file/478834/ODA_strategy_final_web_0905.pdf

Drèze, J., and Sen, A. (2013). *An Uncertain Glory: India and Its Contradictions*. Princeton, NJ: Princeton University Press.

El País (2012). 'La ayuda debe ir a los más pobres, no a países con ingresos medios como Perú', 22 February. Available at: http://sociedad.elpais.com/sociedad/2012/02/22/actualidad/1329913536_647673.html

Ezra, M. (1997). *Demographic Responses to Ecological Degradation and Food Insecurity: Drought Prone Areas in Northern Ethiopia*. West Lafayette, IN: Purdue University Press.

FAO (2014). Available at: www.fao.org

Feyissa, D. (2011). 'Aid negotiation: the uneasy "partnership" between EPRDF and the donors', *Journal of Eastern African Studies*, 5(4), pp. 788–817.

Fox News Latino (2013). 'US ups anti-drug aid as Peru becomes world leader in coca production', 25 September. Available at: latino.foxnews.com/latino/news/2013/09/25/us-ups-anti-drug-aid-as-peru-becomes-world-leader-in-coca-production

Frankel, F. (2015). *India's Green Revolution: Economic Gains and Political Costs*. Princeton, NJ: Princeton University Press.

Furtado, X., and Smith, J. (2007). 'Ethiopia: aid, ownership and sovereignty', *Global Economic Governance Program Working Paper*, 8. Oxford: Global Economic Governance Programme.

Geberegziabher, S. (2006). 'Impact of conditionality on aid effectiveness in Ethiopia'. Doctoral dissertation, Ruhr University of Economics. Bochum: Ruhr University.

Gelan, A. (2007). 'Does food aid have disincentive effects on local production? A general equilibrium perspective on food aid in Ethiopia', *Food Policy*, 32(4), pp. 436–58.

Girma, H. (2015). 'The impact of foreign aid on economic growth: empirical evidence from Ethiopia (1974–2011) using ARDL approach', *Journal of Research in Economics and International Finance*, 4(1), pp. 1–12.

Gispert, C. (1999). *Enciclopedia Concisa del Perú*. Madrid: Océano Grupo Editorial.

Gupta, A. (1990). 'Sustainable development of Indian agriculture: Green Revolution revisited', *Indian Institute of Management Working Paper*, 896. Ahmedabad: IIM.

Hackenesch, C. (2013). 'Aid donor meets strategic partner? The European Union's and China's relations with Ethiopia', *Journal of Current Chinese Affairs*, 42(1), pp. 7–36.

Hay, A. (1978). 'Vietnam still looking for foreign aid', *Nature*, 275, pp. 6–7.

Hayman, R. (2011). 'Budget support and democracy: a twist in the conditionality tale', *Third World Quarterly*, 32(4), pp. 673–88.

Hazell, P. (2009). 'The Asian Green Revolution', *IFPRI Discussion Paper*, 00911. Washington, DC: IFPRI.

HRW (2010). *Development without Freedom: How Aid Underwrites Repression in Ethiopia*. Available at: https://www.hrw.org/sites/default/files/reports/ethiopia1010webwcover.pdf

HRW (2012). *'Waiting Here for Death': Displacement and 'Villagisation' in Ethiopia's Gambella Region*. Available at: https://www.hrw.org/report/2012/01/16/waiting-here-death/forced-displacement-and-villagization-ethiopias-gambella-region

Hudson, R. (1992). *Peru: A Country Study*. Washington, DC: GPO for the Library of Congress.

IFAD (2011a). *IFAD and India*. Available at: www.ifad.org/governance/replenishment/briefs/india.pdf

IFAD (2011b). *Peru: Country Results Brief*. Available at: www.ifad.org/governance/replenishment/briefs/peru.pdf

IFAD (2011c). *Vietnam: Country Results Brief*. Available at: www.ifad.org/governance/replenishment/briefs/vietnam.pdf

IFAD (2012). *Enabling Poor Rural People to Overcome Poverty in Ethiopia*. Available at: www.ifad.org/operations/projects/regions /Pf/factsheets/ethiopia.pdf

IFPRI (2014). *Food Security Portal*. Available at: www.foodsecurityportal.org

Imai, K. S., Gaiha, R., and Kang, W. (2011). 'Poverty, inequality and ethnic minorities in Vietnam', *International Review of Applied Economics*, 25(3), pp. 249–82.

IRIN (2015). 'Ethiopia: the great land-grab debate', 25 March. Available at: www.irinnews.org/report/92292/ethiopia-the-great-land-grab-debate

Jha, S., and Swaroop, V. (1998). *Fiscal Effects of Foreign Aid: A Case Study of India*. Washington, DC: The World Bank Group.

Keusch, G. T., Rosenberg, I. H., Denno, D. M., Duggan, C., Guerrant, R. L., Lavery, J. V., Tarr, P. I., Ward, H. D., Black, R. E., Nataro, J. P., Ryan, E. T., Bhutta, Z. A., Coovadia, H., Lima, A., Ramakrishna, B., Zaidi, A. K., Burgess, D. H., and Brewer, T. (2013). 'Implications of acquired environmental enteric dysfunction for growth and stunting in infants and children living in low-and middle-income countries', *Food and Nutrition Bulletin*, 34(3), pp. 357–65.

Knack, S., and Rahman, A. (2004). *Donor Fragmentation and Bureaucratic Quality in Aid Recipients*. Washington, D.C.: The World Bank Group.

Lawson, A., Booth, D., Msuya, M., Wangwe, S., and Williamson, T. (2005). *Does General Budget Support Work? Evidence from Tanzania*. London: Overseas Development Institute.

Lipton, M., and Toye, J. (1991). *Does Aid Work in India?: A Country Study of the Impact of Official Development Assistance*. London: Routledge.

Little, P. (2008). 'Food aid dependency in northeastern Ethiopia: myth or reality?' *World Development*, 36(5), pp. 860–74.

Lloyd, T., McGillivray, M., Morrissey, O., and Osei, R. (2000). 'Does aid create trade? An investigation for European donors and African recipients', *European Journal of Development Research*, 12(1), pp. 107–23.

Meyer, R. (2016). 'How to see a famine before it starts', *The Atlantic*, 3 February. Available at: http://www.theatlantic.com/technology/archive/2016/02/famine-fewsnet-forecasting/431478

Morss, E. (1984). 'Institutional destruction resulting from donor and project proliferation in sub-Saharan African countries', *World Development*, 12(4), pp. 465–70.

Muller, E. (1985). 'Dependent economic development, aid dependence on the United States, and democratic breakdown in the Third World', *International Studies Quarterly*, 29(4), pp. 445–69.

Oakland Institute (2013). *Development Aid to Ethiopia: Overlooking Violence, Marginalisation, and Political Repression*. Oakland, CA: Oakland Institute.

OECD (2012). *Managing Aid for Trade and Development Results: Vietnam Case Study*. Paris: OECD.

Oved, M. (2014). 'Fool's gold: the limits of tying aid to mining companies', *The Star*, 15 December. Available at: https://www.thestar.com/news/world/2014/12/15/fools_gold_the_limits_of_tying_aid_to_mining_companies.html

QWIDS (2014). Available at: stats.oecd.org/qwids

Pathak, P., and Singh, A. (2011). 'Trends in malnutrition among children in India: growing inequalities across different economic groups', *Social Science and Medicine*, 73(4), pp. 576–85.

Patman, R. (1993). 'Soviet-Ethiopian relations: the horn of dilemma', in M. Light (ed.), *Troubled Friendships: Moscow's Third World Ventures*. London: Royal Institute of International Affairs, pp. 110–39.

Ramalingaswami, V., Jonsson, U., and Rohde, J. (1997). 'Malnutrition: a South Asian Enigma', in *Malnutrition in South Asia: A Regional Profile*. Kathmandu: United Nations Children's Fund.

O'Reilly, K., and Louis, E. (2014). 'The toilet tripod: understanding successful sanitation in rural India', *Health and Place*, 29, pp. 43–51.

Reta, H. (2015). 'Ethiopia: curbing climate-related disasters', *All Africa*, 21 March. Available at: allafrica.com/stories/201503231588.html

RICE (2014). *Sanitation Quality, Use, Access, and Trends (SQUAT) Report*. Available at: squatreport.in

Rodrik, D. (ed.) (2003). *In Search of Prosperity: Analytic Narratives on Economic Growth*. Princeton, NJ: Princeton University Press.

Shankar, A., and Gaiha, R. (2013). *Battling Corruption: Has NREGA Reached India's Rural Poor?* New Delhi: Oxford University Press.

Siyoum, A., Hilhorst, D., and Van Uffelen, G. (2012). 'Food aid and dependency syndrome in Ethiopia: local perception', *Journal of Humanitarian Assistance*. Boston, MA: Tufts University.

Smith, D. (2014). 'Britain is supporting a dictatorship in Ethiopia', *Guardian*, 6 July. Available at: http://www.theguardian.com/world/2014/jul/06/britain-supporting-dictatorship-in-ethiopia

Spielman, D., Byerlee, D., Alemu, D., and Kelemework, D. (2010). 'Policies to promote cereal intensification in Ethiopia: the search for appropriate public and private roles', *Food Policy*, 35(3), pp. 185–94.

Subramanian, S., Huq, S., Yatsunenko, T., Haque, R., Mahfuz, M., Alam, M., Benezra, A., DeStefano, J., Meier, M., Muegge, B., Van Aredonk, L., Zhang, Q., Province, M., Petri Jr, W., Ahmed, T., and Gordon, J. (2014). 'Persistent gut microbiota immaturity in malnourished Bangladeshi children', *Nature*, 510(7505), pp. 417–21.

Subramanyam, M., Kawachi, I., Berkman, L., and Subramanian, S. (2010). 'Socioeconomic inequalities in childhood undernutrition in India: analysing trends between 1992 and 2005', *PLoS One*, 5(6), e11392.

Survival International (2015). 'Ethiopia: tribe starves as dam and land grabs dry up river', 10 March. Available at: www.survivalinternational.org/news/10691

Swamy, A. (2016). 'Modi fails to live up to high hopes', *East Asia Forum*, 11 January. Available at: www.eastasiaforum.org/2016/01/11/modi-fails-to-live-up-to-high-hopes

Swaroop, V., Jha, S., and Sunil Rajkumar, A. (2000). 'Fiscal effects of foreign aid in a federal system of governance: the case of India', *Journal of Public Economics*, 77(3), pp. 307–30.

Tadesse, G., and Shively, G. (2009). 'Food aid, food prices, and producer disincentives in Ethiopia', *American Journal of Agricultural Economics*, 91(4), pp. 942–55.

Tisdall, S. (2012). 'East Africa's drought: the avoidable disaster', *Guardian*, 18 January. Available at: www.theguardian.com/world/2012/jan/18/east-africa-drought-disaster-report

Tran, T., and Kajisa, K. (2006). 'The impact of green revolution on rice production in Vietnam', *Developing Economies*, 44(2), pp. 167–89.

Trang, T. (2012). 'Food security versus food sovereignty: choice of concept, policies, and classes in Vietnam's post-reform economy', *Philippine Journal of Third World Studies*, 26(1-2), pp. 68–88.

Vasavi, A. (2012). *Shadow Space: Suicides and the Predicament of Rural India*. New Delhi: Three Essays Collective.

Vollmer, S., Harttgen, K., Subramanyam, M., Finlay, J., Klasen, S., and Subramanian, S. V. (2014). 'Association between economic growth and early childhood undernutrition: evidence from 121 demographic and health surveys from 36 low-income and middle-income countries', *The Lancet Global Health*, 2(4), pp. 225–34.

WDI (2014). Available at: http://data.worldbank.org/data-catalog/world-development-indicators

Webb, P., and Von Braun, J. (1994). *Famine and Food Security in Ethiopia: Lessons for Africa*. Chichester: John Wiley and Sons.

WFP (2014). *Peru: Overview*. Available at: www.wfp.org/countries/peru/overview

WHO (2014). Available at: www.who.org

WB (2010). Partnership to support National Target Programs. Available at: go.worldbank.org/ZNBDMWACZ0

Young Lives (2014). Available at: www.younglives.org.uk

5 Aid, governance and food security from the recipients' perspective

Introduction

This chapter marks the beginning of the book's micro section, which examines the effects of aid in its different forms on food security using household-level data; it looks at households living in Peru, Ethiopia, India and Vietnam, the same countries as examined in Chapter 4. This study hence draws on some of the background information already discussed and provides a micro-level counterpart to the macro-level study in the previous chapter. If findings in this study align with those from the previous one, they will bolster the robustness of the conclusions. If they are at odds, they will indicate that the aid–food security relationships differ when observed on the household as opposed to the country level.

The chapter proceeds as follows. The next section offers a brief overview of the variables and hypotheses to be examined. After that, the chapter introduces the data used and their descriptive statistics and discusses the empirical models utilised to analyse them. The subsequent results section talks about the relationships discovered and finishes with a discussion and conclusions section.

Founding expectations

Main variables investigated

This part of the study considers the same basic questions as the previous ones – Does aid influence food security positively? Do good governance and the type of aid provided make a difference in the relationship? – but it focuses on the micro level and aid recipients' individual perspectives. The dependent variable is still food security but measured on the household and individual rather than on the country level. The specific outcome indicators, discussed in more detail in the data section, are thus related to individual nutritional status and perception of food security rather than to the national percentages of undernourished people.

Development aid remains the main independent variable but does not perfectly correspond to the measure utilised in the macro-level studies. First, as it is reported here by aid recipients rather than by donors, it cannot include those types of aid that do not affect recipients individually, such as budget support. Furthermore, since aid disbursed through development projects is often combined with domestic government support, it is likely that the amount reported as aid by households is inflated. This luckily does not constitute a major problem since this study's main objective is to discover whether and how precisely funds disbursed to poor families help them improve their food security, without too much regard for the precise origin of those funds. That is not to imply that it is irrelevant if certain projects were funded primarily through aid or through other resources – after all, the core topic of this book is the effect of *aid* on food security – but rather that the more political aspects of the question have already been examined on the country level, while the micro-level part of the book focuses more on the mechanisms through which funds strengthen food security and on families' experience with receiving them.

Finally, governance is still the main conditioning variable but here it is measured on the local level and hence constitutes a significantly different concept from the one used in the country-level studies. The quality of national policies and institutions influences how development aid affects food security on the household level as well, but in order to achieve a measurable level of variation in examining governance in household-level studies, one can only focus on the quality of local policies and institutions. These are likely affected by the quality of their national-level counterparts, yet cannot be equated with them.

Hypotheses

Bearing in mind the existing research discussed in Chapter 1 and the findings from the two preceding chapters, this study tests the following hypotheses. First, it examines whether aid has a positive impact on food security even when tested on the household level and whether the relationship is strengthened by the quality of local governance (H1). The study further explores whether aid implemented by NGOs is more effective at bolstering food security than other aid (H2.2), whether credit aid is less directly supportive of food security than non-credit aid, but simultaneously more conditioned on the quality of governance (H3.2), and whether non-food aid has a more pronounced impact than food aid (H5). With the help of the findings from the previous two studies in reformulating the last two original hypotheses, it also assesses whether long-term aid (H7a) and social-infrastructure aid (H8a) have more positive influence on food security than their counterpart types of aid at the household level as they appear to have at the country level.

Data, descriptive statistics and empirical methods

This section first introduces the data used to test the hypotheses specified above. Next, it presents descriptive statistics of all the key variables utilised and explains the empirical methods employed to analyse the data.

Data source

The data utilised come from the Young Lives project, an international longitudinal analysis of childhood poverty funded by the UK Department for International

Development (DfID) and the Netherlands' Ministry of Foreign Affairs. Information has been gathered on children and their families in four countries – India (Andhra Pradesh), Vietnam, Ethiopia and Peru – in three rounds. The first round took place in 2002, when a younger group of children examined was between six and 18 months old and an older one between seven and eight years old. The subsequent rounds of data collection took place in 2006 and in 2010.[1] This study uses only data on the younger cohort, approximately 2,000 children from each country. The main reason is that nutritional status variables are more precise in younger children (Moursi *et al.*, 2008) and, by 2010, the older cohort had reached mid-teenage years already. The survey respondents were the children's primary caretakers, predominantly their mothers, but in every round surveys were also carried out at the community level.

Detailed data on aid receipts, essential for this investigation, were collected in Ethiopia during the second and third rounds of data collection, in India and Vietnam only during the third round of data collection and in Peru not at all. As a result, while the analysis in Ethiopia can proceed using panel data, the analyses in India and Vietnam rely on cross-sectional data only and the analysis in Peru cannot answer any more refined questions beyond the general impact of project aid on recipients' food security. The first round of data was used to extract information about the children not available in the following rounds, such as their birth size and whether they were born prematurely. It was also used to obtain data about households' wealth, in order not to introduce bias into the subsequent analysis.

Descriptive statistics

Outcome variables

Table 5.1 presents descriptive statistics of the outcome variables. The primary outcome of interest, food security, is measured in two ways. First, children's nutritional status variables – the incidence of children that are underweight (too light for their age), stunted (too short for their age) and under-BMI (with a BMI too low for their age) – are utilised to capture outward manifestations of food insecurity (WHO, 2014). While all three indicators indicate nutritional deficiency, they are not identical. Rates of stunting are particularly relevant when looking at chronic undernourishment, underweight levels when examining the effects of sudden food crises, and under-BMI levels as children approach adulthood (ibid.). Since most parents go to great lengths to prevent their children from being affected by food insecurity, no incidence of underweight, stunted or under-BMI children does not necessarily equal food security, but only the absence of severe food insecurity.

The second type of outcome measurement used, a food-security index, is based on households' perceived food security. I constructed it from household responses to questions about the frequency of concern about not having enough to eat, inability to eat the foods desired, necessity to limit the variety of foods consumed, need to limit portion sizes or meal frequency, necessity to go to bed hungry and not eating 24 hours for lack of food. The responses varied from 'never' (0) to

Table 5.1 Descriptive statistics of outcome indicators

Outcome indicators	Peru				Ethiopia				India				Vietnam			
	Mean	StD	Min	Max	Mean	StD	Min	Max	Mean	StD	Min	Max	Mean	StD	Min	Max
Underweight children (prevalence)	0.06	0.23	0	1	0.32	0.47	0	1	0.44	0.50	0	1	0.24	0.43	0	1
Stunted children (prevalence)	0.21	0.40	0	1	0.20	0.40	0	1	0.28	0.45	0	1	0.19	0.40	0	1
Under-BMI children (prevalence)	0.01	0.09	0	1	0.20	0.40	0	1	0.27	0.44	0	1	0.11	0.32	0	1
Food-insecurity index (self-perception)	0.49	0.48	0	3	0.73	0.49	0	3	0.35	0.41	0	2.56	0.47	0.46	0	2.7
Consumption levels (monthly, USD)	70.0	50.5	0	626	16.9	12.4	2.2	129	21.8	11.6	4.8	86.6	36.0	28.4	0.0	339
N of observations	1946				1853				1927				1935			

Source: Author's own calculations

'almost always' (3). Because many responses were missing, an average of available responses was taken to construct the final index, on a 0 to 3 scale (3 = highest level of food insecurity). This index is, theoretically, more sensitive to capturing milder forms of food insecurity than nutritional indicators, but it is by nature less objective and more susceptible to cultural preconceptions regarding one's appropriate public image.[2] Furthermore, unlike the nutritional indicators, it captures household-level rather than individual-level food security.

Finally, because some projects may affect recipients' wellbeing without influencing their food security – whether because they already are food secure or because the benefits have not had time to translate into better food security – as a tertiary measure of outcome, and a form of robustness check, the study also looks at self-reported monthly household consumption levels.

The descriptive statistics of outcome indicators in Table 5.1 suggest that, when measured through children's nutritional status, food-insecurity situation is at its most dire in India, with 44 per cent of children underweight, 28 per cent stunted and 27 per cent under-BMI. Second in line is Ethiopia, with a third of the children underweight and one fifth stunted and under-BMI. The situation in Vietnam is better, with 24 per cent of children underweight, 19 per cent stunted and 11 per cent under-BMI. Finally, in Peru, the prevalence of stunting is relatively high at 21 per cent, but 'only' 6 per cent of the children examined are underweight and 1 per cent has too low BMIs.

These findings do not deviate too far from the picture of under-five child undernourishment painted by the WHO. As discussed in Chapter 4, the latest data from the source put child stunting in Ethiopia and India at 44 and 48 per cent (37 per cent in Andhra Pradesh) and in Vietnam and Peru at around 30 and 20 per cent, respectively (WHO, 2014). Hence, children in the Young Lives sample are less affected by stunting than children in their countries on average. The prevalence of underweight children was estimated by the WHO at 43 per cent in India (slightly below 40 per cent in Andhra Pradesh), 29 per cent in Ethiopia, 20 per cent in Vietnam and slightly over 5 per cent in Peru. These numbers are quite similar to the Young Lives statistics. The fact that the undernourishment rates in India are the highest from the four countries even though GDP per capita is the lowest in Ethiopia – reflected also by the lowest mean consumption level – confirms the existence of the 'South Asian enigma' even in Andhra Pradesh communities where the Young Lives data were collected.

Interestingly, however, the food-insecurity index tells a different story. The lowest number, suggestive of most food-secure households, can be found in India. Vietnam and Peru follow, with Ethiopia the most insecure from this viewpoint. India's number thus seems out of place, the lowest of all four countries when, on the basis of the other outcome variables, one would expect it to be the highest. Could this be because Indian parents expose their children to more food insecurity than parents in other countries? This seems improbable as a similar percentage of parents in India reported to allow their children to be affected by food insecurity as elsewhere. More likely explanations are that Indian parents have suffered from chronic food insecurity for so long that the situation does not seem out of the ordinary and that one needs to look beyond access to food to understand the causes of Indian child undernourishment. The data at hand somewhat corroborates both explanations. Whereas in Vietnam and Peru more than 60 per cent of respondents were worried about not having sufficient food to eat in the future, only 26 per cent of respondents were worried in India, despite lower average incomes per capita and consumption. Also, Indian households had the lowest proportional access to toilets within premises – 34 per cent, compared to Ethiopian 55 per cent, Vietnamese 61 per cent and Peruvian 91 per cent – pointing to deficient food utilisation as a possible contributor to high undernourishment among Indian children.

Project and governance variables

The first aim of this study is to find out whether the receipt of *any* type of external assistance has a positive impact on recipients' food security and whether this effect is conditioned on the quality of local governance. Measuring the receipt of external assistance in all four countries was relatively straightforward, as households were asked in the questionnaire conducted whether that was the case at the moment. Assessing the quality of local governance was trickier since no appropriate state- or regional-level data could be found. In the end, community-level data collected by the Young Lives, on the subjective quality of local government services including the police, the professional judge, the water supply, the electricity supply, public phones, public internet and banks, were used to construct an index. Unfortunately, while questions relevant to constructing the local-governance variable were meant to be asked in all four countries, this did not happen in Peru in the end.

The other task of this study is to examine how *who* gives aid, *how* it is given and *where* it flows influence aid's overall impact. In the first category – *who* gives aid – the division was made into governmental organisations (GOs) and NGOs.[3] Since it is impossible to know the original source of the money used to run the projects in question, the examination here relates to the influence of the organisation that implements the project rather than to the organisation that financed the project. The two categorisations made in the section on *how* aid is provided are into credit (CD) and non-credit aid (NCD) and into food (FA) and non-food aid (NFA). Finally, the divisions vis-à-vis *where* aid goes are, first, into humanitarian assistance (HA), short-term aid (ST) and long-term aid (LT) and, second, into agricultural aid (AGR), social infrastructure aid (SOC), economic infrastructure aid (EC) and other aid, which here constitutes direct transfers of both food and cash (DIR). Agricultural aid includes primarily agricultural extension and irrigation development projects, social aid health and education services and economic aid credit and business training. Following Clemens *et al.* (2004), who originally coined the first categorisation, HA includes primarily direct food and cash transfers, ST agricultural and business assistance and LT education-based activities.

From the descriptive statistics of the project and governance variables, displayed in Table 5.2, it is apparent that there is a large discrepancy between the percentage of people receiving external assistance in the four countries, ranging from only 22 per cent in Peru through 40 per cent in Vietnam to more than 70 per cent in

India and Ethiopia. The different levels of external assistance roughly mirror the GDP per capita and food-insecurity differences among the four countries. In all four countries, GOs (national and international) were responsible for the bulk of aid distributed, with 20 per cent of respondents receiving aid from them in Peru, 54 per cent in Ethiopia, 32 per cent in Vietnam and 73 per cent in India, whereas NGOs disbursed aid to only 5 per cent of respondents in Peru, 28 per cent in Ethiopia, 12 per cent in Vietnam and 3 per cent in India.

Looking at the distribution of the different types of aid, 16 per cent of households in Ethiopia and 35 per cent of households in India received microfinance loans, while 57 and 39 per cent received non-credit aid. Twenty per cent of the households surveyed in Ethiopia and in Vietnam were beneficiaries of food aid – surprisingly, this was true about only 3 per cent of the Indian population.

Divisions based on the specific sector where aid flows reveal that whereas long-term aid is the most popular in Ethiopia, short-term aid is in India and HA is in Vietnam. Thus, unsurprisingly, the highest percentage of direct-aid recipients is also in Vietnam. Agricultural and social infrastructural aid is most popular in Ethiopia while economic infrastructure aid is in India.[4]

The quality of governance, measured on a theoretical scale from 1 to 3, with 3 being the best, exhibits in reality only variation from 1.5 to 3 in Ethiopia and Vietnam and from 1.67 to 3 in India. India has the highest average score in this category, 2.58, followed by Vietnam with 2.44 and Ethiopia with 2.37. It is interesting to observe how optimistic respondents in these countries are about the quality of their local institutions, despite being internationally renowned for high corruption levels and often deficient institutions (WGI, 2014).

Control variables

Table 5.3 contains descriptive statistics for the control variables utilised. Following Strauss and Thomas's (2008) health model, these encompass the following four categories: *children's health inputs*, their *socio-demographic characteristics*, *parental and household characteristics* and *public health infrastructure*. In deciding on specific variables, existing analyses of children's health outcomes in the Young Lives data served as my inspiration (Galab *et al.*, 2006; Petrikova and Chadha, 2013). When using consumption levels as the dependent variables, the children's health-input and public health infrastructure variables were dropped and, following Chen *et al.* (2009), several household and community-level variables added. Finally, data on ethnic, religious and regional variables specific to each of the four countries were also used.

The first category, *children's health inputs*, contains each child's subjective birth size[5] and if the child was born prematurely. Children's *socio-demographic characteristics* include the age of the child in months and gender (male 1, female 0). *Parental and household characteristics* contain three variables that characterise the mother of the child in question – her age when the child was born, her highest level of education and her cognitive social capital[6] – and several household-level variables, including whether the household is female-headed, how many members it has and

Table 5.2 Descriptive statistics of project types and governance

Project types	Peru				Ethiopia				India				Vietnam			
	Mean	*StD*	*Min*	*Max*	*Mean*	*StD*	*Min*	*Max*	*Mean*	*StD*	*Min*	*Max*	*Mean*	*StD*	*Min*	*Max*
All	0.22	0.41	0	1	0.78	0.42	0	1	0.74	0.44	0	1	0.40	0.49	0	1
GO	0.20	0.40	0	1	0.54	0.05	0	1	0.73	0.44	0	1	0.32	0.47	0	1
NGO	0.05	0.23	0	1	0.28	0.43	0	1	0.03	0.18	0	1	0.12	0.33	0	1
CD					0.16	0.36	0	1	0.35	0.48	0	1				
NCD					0.57	0.49	0	1	0.39	0.49	0	1				
FA					0.21	0.40	0	1	0.03	0.16	0	1	0.20	0.40	0	1
NFA					0.56	0.50	0	1	0.72	0.45	0	1	0.19	0.40	0	1
HA					0.26	0.44	0	1	0.25	0.43	0	1	0.20	0.40	0	1
ST					0.41	0.49	0	1	0.58	0.49	0	1	0.14	0.34	0	1
LT					0.52	0.50	0	1	0.39	0.49	0	1	0.11	0.32	0	1
DIR					0.09	0.28	0	1	0.27	0.44	0	1	0.30	0.46	0	1
AGR					0.14	0.35	0	1	0.05	0.22	0	1	0.02	0.15	0	1
SOC					0.43	0.50	0	1	0.22	0.41	0	1	0.08	0.27	0	1
EC					0.32	0.47	0	1	0.43	0.50	0	1	0.00	0.04	0	1
Governance																
Quality of local governance					2.37	0.57	1.5	3	2.58	0.36	1.67	3	2.44	0.39	1.5	3
N of observations	1946				1853				1927				1935			

Source: Author's own calculations

Table 5.3 Descriptive statistics of control variables

Control variables	Peru				Ethiopia				India				Vietnam			
	Mean	StD	Min	Max	Mean	StD	Min	Max	Mean	StD	Min	Max	Mean	StD	Min	Max
Health inputs																
Birth size	2.89	0.99	1	5	2.99	1.02	1	5	3.07	0.91	1	5	2.93	0.68	1	5
Premature	0.27	0.44	0	1	0.09	0.29	0	1	0.09	0.29	0	1	0.12	0.33	0	1
Socio-demographic characteristics																
Child's gender (male)	0.50	0.50	0	1	0.53	0.48	0	1	0.54	0.50	0	1	0.51	0.50	0	1
Child's age (in months)					97.49	3.93	86.30	138.4	96.02	3.93	86.20	106.4	97.07	3.76	0.96	112.8
Parental/household characteristics																
Mother's age when child born	26.83	6.76	14	49	27.45	6.30	15	55	23.65	4.32	12	48	27.16	5.78	15	50
Mother's highest education	7.68	4.36	0	17	2.81	3.80	0	14	3.51	4.40	0	14	6.75	3.81	0	14
Cognitive social capital	1.49	0.61	0	2	1.87	0.36	0	2	1.92	0.27	0	2	1.90	0.3	0	2
Female-headed hh	0.12	0.33	0	1	0.14	0.35	0	1	0.08	0.28	0	1	0.16	0.36	0	1
hh size	5.71	2.33	2	18	6.19	1.92	2	14	5.43	2.37	2	22	4.90	1.84	2	14
Urban	0.66	0.48	0	1	0.37	0.48	0	1	0.24	0.43	0	1	0.21	0.41	0	1
Wealth index	0.54	0.21	0	0.93	0.33	0.17	0.01	0.86	0.51	0.18	0.01	0.95	0.59	0.2	0.79	1.00
Public health indicators																
Public health clinic in village	0.21	0.41	0	1	0.06	0.23	0	1	0.12	0.32	0	1	0.09	0.29	0	1
Additional consumption controls																
hh head primary education	0.94	0.25	0	1	0.27	0.44	0	1	0.41	0.49	0	1	0.68	0.47	0	1
Distance to closest town (in km)	13.65	15.48	0	67	26.62	41.33	0	180	75.00	39.4	14	200	13.41	11.78	1	40
Village accessible by road (month/year)					11.34	0.99	8	12								

	Mean	SD	Min	Max	Mean	SD	Min	Max	Mean	SD	Min	Max	Mean	SD	Min	Max
Village has an adult literacy course					0.47	0.50	0	1	0.92	0.27	0	1				
More than 20% land owned by one hh					0.17	0.37	0	1	0.15	0.35	0	1				
Country specifics																
Mestizo	0.92	0.26	0	1												
White	0.05	0.21	0	1												
Indigenous	0.03	0.17	0	1												
Oromo					0.21	0.41	0	1								
Amhara					0.29	0.45	0	1								
Tigrian					0.22	0.41	0	1								
Muslim					0.16	0.37	0	1								
Coastal Andhra Pradesh									0.35	0.48	0	1				
Rayalaseema									0.30	0.46	0	1				
Telangana									0.35	0.48	0	1				
Hindu									0.88	0.32	0	1				
Scheduled caste/tribe									0.33	0.47	0	1				
No religion													0.83	0.38	0	1
Red River Delta													0.20	0.40	0	1
Northern Uplands													0.20	0.40	0	1
Central Coastal													0.40	0.49	0	1
Mekong River Delta													0.20	0.40	0	1
N of observations	*1946*				*1853*				*1927*				*1935*			

Source: Author's own calculations

whether it resides in an urban area. Furthermore, it includes a household wealth index, which was constructed using principal component analysis from the following factors: housing quality (average number of rooms per person; floor, roof and wall type), ownership of consumer durables (fan, fridge, radio, TV, mobile phone, bike, motorcycle and car) and access to services (drinking water, electricity and toilet facilities). The resulting measure ranges from 0 to 1, with higher numbers signifying more wealth. The fourth category, *public health infrastructure*, enquires as to whether there is a public health centre or hospital in the village.

Additional income and consumption controls ask whether the head of household has a primary-level education, how far the community where the household resides is from the nearest district capital, how many months a year it is accessible by road, whether it has an adult literacy programme and whether more than 20 per cent of land within the community is owned by one household.

Finally, *country-specific variables* ask whether the respondent in Peru is of mestizo, indigenous, or white origin; whether the respondent in Ethiopia is of Oromo, Amhara, or Tigrian ethnicity and whether she is a Muslim; whether the respondent in India comes from Rayalaseema, Telangana or Coastal Andhra (regions within Andhra Pradesh[7]), whether she is a Hindu and whether she is from a scheduled caste/tribe; and whether the respondent in Vietnam is of no religious background and which Vietnamese region she comes from (Red River Delta, Northern Uplands, Central Coastal, or Mekong River Delta).

The descriptive statistics, displayed in Table 5.3, are interesting in their comparison across countries. The average subjective birth size in all four countries is approximately three (that is, medium size). Premature labour occurred in 9 per cent of births in India and Ethiopia, 12 per cent in Vietnam and 27(!) per cent in Peru. The result in the latter is actually so high that it raises concerns about the question's external validity. The youngest mothers are in India, with the average age at birth 23, followed by Peru, Vietnam and Ethiopia. The most educated mothers, in contrast, are in Peru, having finished more than seven years of schooling on average, followed by Vietnam with seven, India with three and a half and Ethiopia with fewer than three. Mothers in Peru, interestingly, have the lowest reported levels of cognitive social capital, followed by Ethiopia, Vietnam and India.

Female-headed households are most common in Vietnam (16 per cent) and least common in India (8 per cent). This is likely the result of women being relatively more empowered in Vietnam than in India to leave their husbands when dissatisfied. Household size is the highest in Ethiopia (more than six), followed by Peru, India and Vietnam (4.9). Sixty-six per cent of the sample in Peru lives in cities, 37 per cent in Ethiopia, 24 per cent in India and 21 per cent in Vietnam. Urbanisation rates for the whole countries are 77 per cent, 17 per cent, 31 per cent and 30 per cent, respectively, suggesting that the Young Lives data collection oversampled rural populations everywhere except for Ethiopia, where the rural population has been under-sampled (WDI, 2014). However, the diverging definitions about what constitutes an urban area can also be blamed for this discrepancy (Young Lives). The wealth index indicates that, on average, the most materially affluent families from the four countries reside in Vietnam and Peru, followed by India and Ethiopia.

Regarding the public health indicators, 21 per cent of respondents have access to a local public hospital in Peru, 12 per cent in India, 9 per cent in Vietnam and only 6 per cent in Ethiopia. However, the indicator does not speak about the quality of the public care provided, which is often more crucial to health outcomes than the time that it takes to reach the hospital. From the additional consumption controls, the only two that were available for all four countries were primary education of the head of household (a dummy) and the distance to the closest town. Ninety-four per cent of heads of households finished primary school in Peru, 68 per cent in Vietnam, 41 per cent in India and only 27 per cent in Ethiopia. Respondents in Peru and in Vietnam live, on average, 13 kilometres (km) from the nearest town; the equivalent figure is 27km in Peru and 75km in India.

Looking at the country-specific variables, in Peru 95 per cent of respondents are of mestizo origin, 3 per cent are white and 2 per cent are indigenous. The population in Ethiopia is split relatively equally into Amhara, Oromo, Tigrian and Muslims, with Amharans constituting the relatively most populous group. In India, about one third of respondents live in each of the three regions surveyed – Telangana, Rayalaseema and coastal Andhra, almost 90 per cent are Hindus and 33 per cent are of scheduled caste/tribe origin. Finally, more than 80 per cent of Vietnamese respondents have no religious background – undoubtedly thanks to the communist anti-religious party line – with 40 per cent residing in Central Coastal Vietnam and the rest equally distributed among the three remaining regions.

Empirical methods

Since the aid data utilised here are not continuous but binary (a survey respondent either received a certain type of assistance or not), my aim is to find the average treatment effect of each project type on the treated (ATET). The basic model can thus be expressed as the following:

$$FS_t^j = \alpha + \beta X_t^j + \gamma P_t^j + \vartheta^j + \varepsilon_t^j$$

where FS stands for the food security of household j for time t (FS is alternatively substituted with consumption levels), α is the constant, β is the coefficient of the control variables X, γ is the impact of the projects (P) on the treated and, finally, ϑ^j and ε_t^j are the time-invariant and time-variant components of the error term, respectively.

As for all evaluation researchers, my main challenge is to identify a counterfactual that most closely resembles the treated group had it not been treated. The best empirical method to do so, the double-difference approach, is not applicable here as the data for Peru, India and Vietnam are only cross-sectional. The Ethiopian data are panel but still do not contain baseline information. An approach frequently utilised in similar cases is propensity score matching (PSM), a quasi-experimental method based on the construction of a suitable control group to the treated one from untreated households on the basis of observable characteristics (e.g. Ravallion, 2001).

The two key assumptions of the model, expressed mathematically, are:

$$0 < P(X) < 1$$

where P(X) are the propensity scores calculated based on observable variables X, which implies that valid matches on P(X) can be found for all values of observable variables X and:

$$E(Y_{t0} \mid X, D = 1) = E(Y_{t0} \mid X, D = 0)$$

which presumes that, conditional on X, households that did not receive any aid have the same outcomes in the analysed variables as the households that did receive aid would have had they not received it. The PSM approach in its simple form is used to analyse data from Peru, India and Vietnam. For Ethiopia, I use a panel-data PSM approach described by Nguyen Viet (2012).

In order to elucidate this approach, let D_1 and D_2 denote the project intervention status within the first and the second time period in my dataset, respectively. Y_{1F} and Y_{0F} stand for outcomes with and without the intervention in the first period and Y_{1S} and Y_{0S} in the second time period. We are interested in the ATET in the second period, which can be expressed as the following:

$$ATT_X^S = E\left(Y_{1S} \mid X, D2 = 1\right) - E(Y_{0S} \mid X, D2 = 1) \tag{1}$$

Since the second term cannot be observed, the equation can be rewritten as following:

$$ATT_X^S = Pr\left(D_1 = 1 \mid X, D_2 = 1\right)\left[E\left(Y_{1S} \mid X, D_1 = 1, D_2 = 1\right) - E\left(Y_{0S} \mid X, D_1 = 1, D_2 = 1\right)\right] + \\ Pr\left(D_0 = 1 \mid X, D_2 = 1\right)\left[E\left(Y_{1S} \mid X, D_1 = 0, D_2 = 1\right) - E(Y_{0S} \mid X, D_1 = 0, D_2 = 1)\right] \tag{2}$$

Two additional assumptions added to this equation are that the difference in the non-intervention outcomes, conditional on X, between people who did not participate in the project in either period and those who participated only in the second period has remained constant over time. The second assumption is that the difference between the non-intervention outcomes in the first period has been the same for people who participated in the intervention in both periods and those who participated in the project in the first period but not in the second one. With the addition of these assumptions, equation 2 can be rewritten in the following manner:

$$ATT_X^S = Pr\left(D_1 = 1 \mid X, D_2 = 1\right)\left\{\left[E\left(Y_{1S} \mid X, D_1 = 1, D_2 = 1\right) - E\left(Y_{0S} \mid X, D_1 = 1, D_2 = 0\right)\right] - \left[E\left(Y_{1F} \mid X, \right.\right.\right. \\ \left. D_1 = 1, D_2 = 1\right) - E\left(Y_{1F} \mid X, D_1 = 1, D_2 = 0\right)\right]\right\} + Pr\left(D_1 = 0 \mid X, D_2 = 1\right)\left\{\left[E\left(Y_{1S} \mid X, D_1 = 0, D_2 = 1\right) - \right.\right. \tag{3} \\ \left. E\left(Y_{0S} \mid X, D_1 = 0, D_2 = 0\right)\right] - \left[E\left(Y_{0F} \mid X, D_1 = 0, D_2 = 1\right) - E\left(Y_{0F} \mid X, D_1 = 0, D_2 = 0\right)\right]\right\}$$

where all terms can now be observed. Matching is then performed between: 1) the people who were project recipients in both periods and those who were recipients only in the first period and 2) the people who were project recipients only in the second period and those who did not receive project benefits at all, in either time period.

The PSM approach is, first, applied to aid in general and, second, to each type of aid separately, controlling for the other types of projects within that categorisation since some households are receiving several types concurrently. In each equation, as a robustness check three different types of matching were used – the nearest-neighbour, the five-nearest-neighbours and the Kernel approach – but in order to minimise the amount of data presented to the reader only results of the Kernel matching are reported.

As another robustness test, and to assess the conditioning role of local governance, regular cross-section and panel regressions are employed. Their advantage is that they can fit all the different project variables within each category into one model.[8] The specific estimators used here are probit and OLS regressions with robust standard errors, with fixed effects for panel, which have the added benefit of eliminating any potential bias arising from time-invariant unobservable characteristics. The obvious downside of the non-PSM estimators used is that they do not belong among those standardly used in impact evaluation because they are believed to be biased.

Have aid projects improved food security on the ground?

This section discusses the results attained, first, regarding aid in general and, second, aid divided into different categories.

The general impact of projects on recipients' food security

Table 5.4 and Figure 5.1 display the results obtained when examining the impact of aid in general on household food security, first, without and, second, with conditioning on governance. The results are mostly insignificant, with some exceptions. In Peru, aid in general seems to have boosted the food-security index. In Ethiopia, while that variable appears unaffected, the prevalence of under-BMI children and the prevalence of underweight children were reduced through aid. In Vietnam, stunting was ameliorated through aid.

In India and in Vietnam, however, aid simultaneously appears to have an unintended negative impact. In India, it seems to have raised the percentage of stunted children while in Vietnam it raised people's food-insecurity index. The first finding is not robust – it does not appear in the PSM results and may be a fluke due to the inability of the Logit regression to control for all the relevant differences between the treatment and the control group. At the least it suggests, however, that project aid in Andhra Pradesh does not have a significant positive impact on recipients' food security across board.

The second finding regarding the negative impact of aid on the perception of food insecurity in Vietnam is more robust and hence more likely reflective of reality.

Table 5.4 The impact of project aid, conditioned on local governance, on recipients' food security

Peru

Model		Underweight	Stunted	Under-BMI	FSI	Cons
Project	PSM	0.03	0.02	0.00	**-0.08**	-7.77
		0.97	1.18	1.25	**1.68**	0.63
	OLS	0.13	0.13	0.14	**-0.09**	-1.99
		1.15	0.95	0.96	**2.53**	0.34
Matched treated				415		
Matched control				1531		

Ethiopia

Model		Underweight	Stunted	Under-BMI	FSI	Cons
Project	PSM	**-0.10**	0.15	**-0.09**	-0.12	-4.09
		1.88	1.26	**1.77**	1.20	0.22
	OLS	0.00	0.16	**-0.42**	-0.01	-0.13
		0.01	0.80	**1.85**	1.14	1.39
Project × gov		0.16	-0.09	**-0.46**	-0.04	0.09
		0.42	0.23	**1.68**	0.49	1.27
Matched treated				422		
Matched control				1431		

India

Model		Underweight	Stunted	Under-BMI	FSI	Cons
Project	PSM	0.10	0.08	0.01	-0.04	-25.12
		1.03	1.05	0.23	0.96	0.44
	OLS	0.18	**0.10**	0.01	-0.03	-10.98
		1.53	**2.14**	0.10	0.86	0.25
Project × gov		-0.23	-0.09	0.15	**-0.15**	-65.40
		0.94	0.32	0.61	**1.75**	0.83
Matched treated				402		
Matched control				1525		

Vietnam

Model		Underweight	Stunted	Under-BMI	FSI	Cons
Project	PSM	0.03	**-0.10**	0.00	**0.07**	-8.11
		0.83	**2.35**	0.06	**2.10**	0.32
	OLS	0.09	**-0.16**	0.04	**0.06**	-0.61
		1.17	**1.72**	0.50	**2.19**	0.04
Project × gov		0.09	**-0.20**	0.18	**-0.38**	**11.63**
		0.49	**1.75**	0.80	**2.21**	**3.06**
Matched treated				771		
Matched control				1164		

Note: The first statistic next to a variable is the ATET/coefficient, followed by the T Statistic/Z score below. Numbers in bold are significant at least at the 10% level. The PSM has been carried out using the Kernel approach

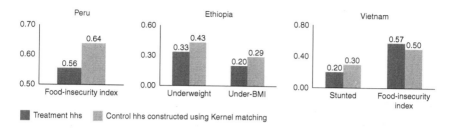

Figure 5.1 Visualising the significant impacts of aid projects on household food security.

It is also more surprising, since aid actually helps reduce child stunting. The underlying explanation could be that while aid in Vietnam does not actually make people less food secure, it makes them feel more vulnerable and worry more about their future food security, as aid receipts are generally volatile and unreliable. This ties in well with findings from the previous chapter, which concluded that aid volatility was higher in Vietnam than in any of the other countries examined, and hence most potentially worrisome. Looking at the country-level data on food security, which has dramatically improved in the last two decades, I presumed that aid volatility had likely no significant negative effect on food security in Vietnam. The micro data proved me wrong in this regard, however, by suggesting that although aid may have a positive impact on recipients' nutritional status, its volatile nature makes people more worried about future food security.

Turning to the conditioning role of local governance, in Ethiopia it apparently enhances the positive impact of aid on children's nutritional status. Similarly, in Vietnam it enhances the positive effect of aid on stunting and can counteract the negative impact of aid on the perception of food security and strengthen aid's positive effect on consumption levels. Even in India 'good' local governance improves the effect of aid on people's perceptions of food security.

From the un-displayed control variables, household wealth, mothers' education and cognitive social capital and children's birth size all have a positive effect on children's nutrition. Conversely, living in a rural area, in a more populous household, being younger and having been born prematurely are all associated with worse food security outcomes. Finally, in all four countries living in the capital district (in India, coastal Andhra Pradesh) had beneficial effects.

The impact of who gives aid on recipients' food security

Table 5.5 and Figure 5.2 contain results on the aid–food security relationship when aid is divided according to the type of donor executing it. In all four countries, implementing organisations were divided into GOs and NGOs. In Peru and in Ethiopia, both GOs and NGOs have a positive effect on the food-security index but the NGOs' effect is more consistent. In India, NGOs also appear to

Table 5.5 The impact of donor type, conditioned on local governance, on food security

Peru (left panel) and *India* (right panel)

Model		Underweight	Stunted	Under-BMI	FSI	Cons	Underweight	Stunted	Under-BMI	FSI	Cons
		Peru					*India*				
GO	PSM	0.03	0.05	0.01	0.00	-14.79	0.03	0.05	-0.02	-0.05	-1.55
		1.25	1.39	1.47	0.06	1.37	0.51	1.06	0.48	1.47	0.03
	OLS	0.22	0.10	0.35	-0.06	-0.39	0.79	0.39	-0.16	-0.54	34.26
		1.55	1.08	1.19	1.44	0.06	1.25	0.57	0.25	1.37	0.17
GO × gov							-0.25	-0.07	0.06	-0.14	-52.44
							1.04	0.26	0.24	1.53	0.68
NGO	PSM	0.03	0.03	0.03	**-0.13**	-6.25	-0.02	0.02	-0.02	**-0.07**	-130.45
		0.84	0.53	1.46	**1.79**	0.56	0.18	0.19	0.22	**1.73**	1.47
	OLS	0.17	0.11	0.62	**-0.14**	-0.28	0.15	0.26	-0.12	**-0.62**	-27.05
		0.35	0.45	0.85	**2.85**	0.03	0.91	1.57	0.69	**1.97**	0.58
NGO × gov							0.94	0.49	1.00	0.00	-69.90
							1.62	0.85	1.50	0.01	0.46

Ethiopia (left panel) and *Vietnam* (right panel)

Model		Underweight	Stunted	Under-BMI	FSI	Cons	Underweight	Stunted	Under-BMI	FSI	Cons
		Ethiopia					*Vietnam*				
GO	PSM	**-0.09**	-0.06	**-0.07**	0.03	-14.98	0.02	-0.04	-0.03	0.03	-41.76
		1.72	1.36	**1.76**	0.58	0.97	0.61	1.47	1.11	0.84	1.58
	OLS	-0.14	-0.40	-0.17	**-0.09**	-1.13	-0.17	0.51	-0.75	-0.23	-21.05
		0.78	0.03	1.01	**1.81**	1.33	0.36	1.01	1.34	1.59	1.25
GO × gov		-0.23	0.06	-0.42	**-0.09**	0.39	0.12	-0.24	0.33	**-0.16**	**73.90**
		0.70	0.17	1.36	**3.19**	1.32	0.60	1.16	1.40	**2.15**	**1.81**
NGO	PSM	0.01	0.01	0.04	**-0.10**	10.41	-0.02	**-0.06**	0.00	0.05	44.50
		0.19	0.31	1.45	**2.65**	1.29	0.43	**1.79**	0.00	1.04	1.50
	OLS	0.98	0.11	0.26	**-0.09**	-0.86	-0.48	**-2.27**	1.69	**-0.69**	-31.24
		1.19	0.56	1.56	**2.95**	0.53	0.50	**1.94**	1.60	**1.88**	1.12
NGO × gov		-0.30	**-0.95**	-0.29	-0.04	0.50	0.19	**-0.91**	-0.65	**-0.30**	**146.30**
		0.86	**2.64**	0.97	0.75	0.51	0.50	**2.00**	1.55	**2.09**	**2.46**

Note: The first statistic next to a variable is the ATET/coefficient, followed by the T Statistic/Z score below. Numbers in bold are significant at least at the 10% level. The PSM has been carried out using the Kernel approach

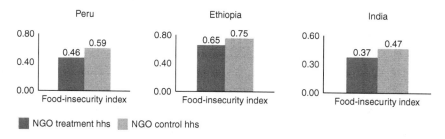

Figure 5.2 Visualising effects of *who* implements aid on household food security.

influence the food-security index more positively. In Vietnam, only NGOs strengthen recipients' food-security index and reduce stunting, but both GO and NGO aid is conditioned on the quality of governance. Higher-quality local governance in Ethiopia strengthens the positive effect of GO aid projects on the feelings of food security and of NGO aid projects on reducing children's stunting rates.

The results suggest that there is not a highly notable difference between the impacts that the aid implemented by governmental donors and by non-governmental donors has on recipients' food security. Yet, NGO aid appears to be a little more beneficial. This finding provides mild support to the second part of my second hypothesis (H2.2). However, there seems to be no significant difference between the way in which local governance conditions the effects of aid implemented by GOs and by NGOs.

The impact of how aid is provided on recipients' food security

Table 5.6 and Figure 5.3 display the results obtained when examining the different impact of credit and non-credit aid on recipients' food security. Since sufficient data were not obtained in Peru and Vietnam, the analysis considered only Ethiopia and India.

The table shows that, in Ethiopia, credit aid apparently contributed to an increase in the rate of under-BMI children and deterioration in aid recipients' food-security index. The underlying reason could be the over-indebtedness of households that received the credit. The negative impact seems to reverse in the presence of good-quality local governance however, indicating that in better-governed Ethiopian communities microcredit projects may have a positive effect on recipients. The results for India are similar. Credit aid without considering governance worsens the perceptions of food security; nevertheless, good local governance counteracts the negative effect. Non-credit aid, in contrast, not only strengthens participants' food-security index, but also reduces the rate of underweight and stunted children, regardless of the quality of local governance.

Table 5.6 The impact of credit vs non-credit aid, conditioned on local governance, on food security

Model		Ethiopia					India				
		Underweight	Stunted	Under-BMI	FSI	Cons	Underweight	Stunted	Under-BMI	FSI	Cons
CD	PSM	−0.02	−0.02	0.04	−0.03	3.39	0.10	0.06	0.07	−0.05	−91.36
		0.42	0.35	0.85	0.34	0.28	1.43	1.33	1.22	0.94	1.48
	OLS	−0.26	0.27	**2.15**	**0.37**	−1.48	0.42	0.03	0.13	**0.69**	−28.14
		0.23	0.23	2.25	2.15	0.69	0.63	0.04	0.19	2.65	0.13
CD × gov		0.17	−0.02	**−1.00**	**−0.16**	0.77	−0.11	0.06	−0.03	**−0.24**	−26.47
		0.34	0.05	2.41	2.10	0.61	0.44	0.21	0.12	2.48	0.33
NCD	PSM	−0.05	0.05	**−0.06**	−0.10	**−29.58**	0.10	**−0.13**	0.01	−0.04	−81.71
		1.08	1.15	1.71	1.31	2.18	1.54	2.53	0.12	0.96	1.17
	OLS	−0.04	0.14	−0.26	**−0.13**	−0.26	**−0.24**	**−0.41**	−0.05	**−0.12**	−11.85
		0.19	0.69	1.48	3.87	0.89	2.63	4.03	0.50	3.50	0.09
NCD × gov		0.17	−0.11	−0.26	−0.01	−0.07	−0.35	−0.23	0.36	−0.01	−117.85
		0.42	0.27	0.75	0.15	0.27	0.34	0.80	1.35	0.09	1.37

Note: The first statistic next to a variable is the ATET/coefficient, followed by the T Statistic/Z score below. Numbers in bold are significant at least at the 10% level. The PSM has been carried out using the Kernel approach

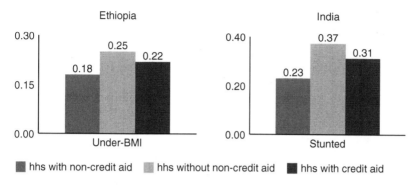

Figure 5.3 Visualisation of select significant findings on credit vs non-credit aid.

Table 5.7 shows the difference between the effects of food and non-food aid on food security. In all three countries, food aid lowered recipients' consumption levels. This seemingly counterintuitive finding can be explained by the fact that those who receive free food buy consequently less but at the same time do not report food aid when asked about consumption. On the one hand, in India and Ethiopia, food aid also increased the prevalence of stunting among children, although this effect was significant only in communities with relatively worse governance. On the other hand, food aid in Ethiopia also strengthens people's food-security index and in India reduces the prevalence of underweight children.

The impact of where aid goes on recipients' food security

Table 5.8 displays the results comparing the effects of aid to different sectors. In all three countries, agricultural aid has the most positive effect on food security. It uniformly strengthens recipients' food-security index; additionally, in Ethiopia agricultural aid reduced stunting and undernourishment among children. Social infrastructure aid is the second in line in its positive impact, reducing the rate of under-BMI children in Ethiopia, bolstering the food-security index in India and decreasing stunting in Vietnam. Direct transfer aid is very similar to food aid vis-à-vis its effects, with some short-term benefits but a slightly negative impact on stunting in Ethiopia and India. Finally, the impact of economic aid, constituted primarily by microfinance and business training activities, is largely insignificant, particularly when looking at the propensity matching results.

Turning to the discussion of the division of aid into humanitarian (emergency), short term and long term (Table 5.9), short-term and long-term aid appear to be similarly beneficial. In Ethiopia, both types strengthen the food-security index and reduce the prevalence of under-BMI children. In India, both types bolster the food-security index and short-term aid also lowers the rate of underweight children whereas long-term aid lowers the prevalence of under-BMI children.

Table 5.7 The impact of food vs non-food aid, conditioned on local governance, on food security

Ethiopia

Model		Underweight	Stunted	Under-BMI	FSI	Cons
FA	PSM	0.10	**0.07**	0.06	0.11	**-37.60**
		1.09	**1.67**	0.07	0.77	**2.05**
	OLS	0.39	**2.11**	0.92	**-0.48**	-0.82
		0.32	**2.00**	1.04	**3.07**	0.75
FA × gov		-0.08	**-0.95**	-0.37	**-0.20**	0.43
		0.18	**2.05**	0.98	**2.90**	0.59
NFA	PSM	-0.02	-0.05	0.00	**-0.09**	-15.53
		0.45	1.26	0.13	**1.80**	1.15
	OLS	-0.07	0.23	**-0.34**	**-0.12**	-0.19
		0.35	1.11	**1.91**	**3.67**	1.03
NFA × gov		0.31	0.34	-0.48	0.02	-0.07
		0.78	0.82	1.37	0.29	0.23

India

Model		Underweight	Stunted	Under-BMI	FSI	Cons
FA	PSM	0.22	**0.10**	-0.03	0.19	**-443.48**
		1.06	**1.93**	0.15	1.33	**1.76**
	OLS	**-0.42**	**0.40**	-0.06	0.29	**-116.78**
		2.02	**1.98**	0.27	3.77	**1.76**
FA × gov		**-1.52**	-1.01	-0.66	0.20	-175.33
		1.89	1.34	0.89	0.74	0.82
NFA	PSM	0.13	0.12	0.03	-0.04	-17.28
		2.63	2.92	0.70	0.94	0.30
	OLS	**-0.18**	**-0.29**	0.01	0.03	-10.64
		2.07	**3.12**	0.11	0.91	0.90
NFA × gov		-0.19	-0.06	0.16	0.12	-63.91
		0.79	0.23	0.66	1.31	0.81

Vietnam

Model		Underweight	Stunted	Under-BMI	FSI	Cons
FA	PSM	0.03	-0.01	0.04	**0.07**	**-68.65**
		0.85	0.34	1.22	**1.66**	**2.58**
	OLS	-0.10	-0.02	-0.08	0.02	**-25.62**
		1.15	0.16	0.75	0.72	**1.75**
FA × gov		0.21	-0.03	0.26	**-0.17**	24.62
		0.90	0.12	0.93	**1.87**	0.58
NFA	PSM	0.06	-0.01	**-0.05**	0.05	45.97
		1.45	0.35	**1.75**	1.12	1.45
	OLS	0.12	0.31	-0.23	**-0.36**	-14.21
		0.21	0.51	0.35	**1.68**	1.03
NFA × gov		-0.02	-0.17	0.10	**-0.19**	**195.64**
		0.10	0.70	0.35	**2.18**	**4.00**

Note: The first statistic next to a variable is the ATET/coefficient, followed by the T Statistic/Z score below. Numbers in bold are significant at least at the 10% level. The PSM has been carried out using the Kernel approach

Table 5.8 The impact of aid to different sectors, conditioned on local governance, on food security

Country		Ethiopia					India					Vietnam				
		Under-weight	Stunted	Under-BMI	FS	Cons	Under-weight	Stunted	Under-BMI	FS	Cons	Under-weight	Stunted	Under-BMI	FS	Cons
DIR	PSM	0.02	**0.13**	0.02	0.10	-12.35	0.06	**0.08**	0.00	-0.02	-5.51	**0.08**	0.00	**0.05**	0.06	-22.30
		0.40	**2.91**	0.64	1.16	1.05	1.39	**2.03**	0.05	0.48	0.15	**2.68**	0.05	**2.23**	1.59	0.83
	OLS	-0.56	1.97	-0.71	**-0.62**	1.16	0.15	**0.20**	0.06	-0.02	-42.30	-0.46	0.21	-0.44	**0.55**	-276.42
		0.49	1.73	0.67	**2.90**	1.23	1.11	**1.73**	0.86	0.85	1.90	0.90	0.39	0.72	**2.85**	2.74
DIR × gov		0.49	-0.58	0.24	**-0.23**	-0.49	0.01	0.02	-0.03	0.00	-37.47	0.22	-0.10	0.20	**-0.24**	**113.87**
		0.49	1.18	0.53	**2.73**	1.18	0.08	0.09	0.16	0.04	0.67	1.08	0.46	0.79	**3.13**	**2.65**
AGR	PSM	-0.06	**-0.06**	-0.01	**-0.08**	**13.88**	0.07	0.05	0.03	**-0.13**	-10.12	0.05	-0.11	0.05	**-0.12**	-8.30
		1.80	**1.71**	0.54	**1.75**	**2.30**	0.85	0.68	0.40	**2.28**	0.15	0.42	1.03	0.61	**1.81**	0.59
	OLS	-1.07	0.12	**-0.41**	**-0.06**	-0.29	-0.01	-0.04	0.09	**-0.18**	-29.41	0.02	-0.15	0.12	**-0.18**	**46.83**
		4.21	0.48	**1.77**	**1.57**	0.38	0.04	0.27	0.66	**3.37**	0.64	0.10	0.69	0.50	**2.25**	**1.95**
AGR × gov		0.47	-0.47	0.40	-0.08	0.28	-0.02	-0.02	-0.19	-0.01	57.14	-0.40	-0.53	**1.62**	0.12	65.25
		0.82	0.93	0.91	1.39	0.28	0.04	0.03	0.35	0.07	0.36	0.70	0.90	**2.30**	0.56	0.98
SOC	PSM	0.06	-0.07	**-0.07**	0.02	-4.65	0.11	0.10	0.05	**-0.08**	-9.64	-0.01	**-0.10**	-0.01	0.00	**120.38**
		1.53	1.32	**1.65**	0.86	1.02	1.48	0.96	0.96	**1.81**	0.19	0.11	**1.72**	0.15	0.10	**1.98**
	OLS	-0.60	-0.99	0.51	-0.11	0.24	0.81	0.85	-0.73	**-0.18**	41.14	0.33	0.15	0.80	-0.40	**139.90**
		0.71	1.15	0.70	0.96	0.26	1.08	1.10	1.24	**1.84**	1.46	0.38	0.18	0.68	1.31	**1.77**
SOC × gov		0.36	0.35	-0.35	**-0.11**	-0.24	**-0.61**	**-0.64**	0.35	-0.05	-18.19	-0.18	-0.10	-0.49	0.16	58.71
		0.84	0.98	1.14	**2.23**	0.44	**2.69**	**2.73**	1.56	0.54	0.76	0.47	0.25	0.89	1.19	0.69
EC	PSM	0.01	0.07	0.00	0.06	-20.09	0.07	0.01	0.07	**-0.13**	-15.85	-0.33	-0.33	0.00	0.07	125.78
		0.97	1.61	0.05	1.02	1.60	1.62	0.34	1.63	**3.48**	0.42	0.71	0.71	0.75	0.21	0.65
	OLS	1.49	-0.04	**1.76**	**0.48**	-0.30	0.11	**0.14**	0.09	**-0.10**	-25.91	160.95	5.82		15.16	-28.11
		1.91	0.05	**2.61**	**4.20**	1.03	1.61	**1.88**	1.22	**3.71**	1.21	0.04	0.34		1.24	0.38
EC × gov		0.33	0.08	**-0.76**	**-0.20**	0.25	-0.07	0.08	**-0.33**	**-0.15**	-14.41	-58.48	-2.01		-5.50	**103.09**
		1.53	0.25	**2.60**	**4.18**	0.64	0.38	0.41	**1.70**	**2.12**	0.26	0.04	0.33		1.23	**2.01**

Note: The first statistic next to a variable is the ATET/coefficient, with the T Statistic/Z score below. Numbers in bold are significant at least at the 10% level. The PSM has been carried out using the Kernel approach

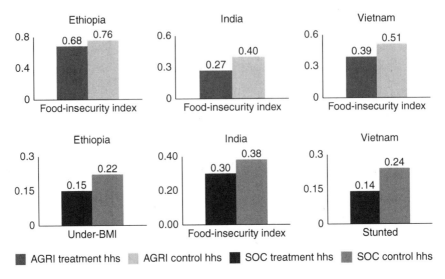

Figure 5.4 Visualising the positive effects of agricultural and social aid on food security.

In Vietnam, short-term aid reduces stunting while long-term aid reinforces people's feelings of food security. The one major difference, however, is that only long-term aid appears to be significantly conditioned on the quality of local governance. The results vis-à-vis humanitarian/emergency aid are similar to those on food aid.

Discussion of results and conclusion

The main purpose of this chapter has been to examine whether the relationships between aid in its different forms, food security and governance found to hold true on the country level can be detected also when examining the issue on the household level. On the one hand, many findings from the previous empirical chapters have indeed been confirmed here. On the other hand, the results have also revealed that, not unexpectedly, the effects of aid observable on the micro level are not identical to those on the macro level.

Regarding the effect of aid in general, it was found to have a mildly positive impact on food-security indicators in all the countries examined excepting India. In Ethiopia, India and Vietnam, the effect also appeared conditioned on the quality of governance. These findings fit well with those from the country-level studies and provide further support to the first hypothesis (H1) – with a few caveats.

First, albeit positive, the impact of aid on different measures of food security appeared less consistently significant here than in the quantitative cross-country study. In contrast, while the previous chapter could not conclude definitely that aid strengthened food security in Peru, the aid projects examined here do seem to

Table 5.9 The impact of emergency, short- and long-term aid, conditioned on governance, on food security

		Ethiopia					India					Vietnam				
Country		Under-weight	Stunted	Under-BMI	FS	Cons	Under-weight	Stunted	Under-BMI	FS	Cons	Under-weight	Stunted	Under-BMI	FS	Cons
EA	PSM	0.04	0.03	0.05	0.06	−2.52	0.05	0.02	−0.07	**0.10**	**−87.97**	0.04	0.03	0.01	**0.06**	−31.59
		1.45	0.88	1.45	1.20	1.10	1.11	0.45	1.58	**2.64**	**1.83**	0.89	0.75	0.33	**1.84**	1.33
	OLS	1.14	**1.48**	0.62	**−0.50**	0.08	0.09	**0.25**	0.09	**−0.07**	−19.07	0.08	0.01	0.07	0.00	**−33.03**
		1.50	**1.73**	0.93	**4.63**	0.16	0.98	**3.06**	1.05	**2.15**	0.78	0.95	0.10	0.69	0.06	**2.36**
EA × gov		−0.47	−0.48	−0.24	**−0.21**	−0.16	−0.09	**−0.32**	**−0.40**	0.01	43.50	0.24	0.01	0.23	−0.12	−20.25
		1.46	1.51	0.85	**4.69**	0.42	0.48	**1.69**	**2.06**	0.18	0.80	1.02	0.03	0.84	1.41	0.50
ST	PSM	−0.03	0.01	**−0.12**	**−0.10**	2.92	**−0.05**	0.05	−0.03	−0.02	−60.45	0.00	**−0.08**	0.01	−0.07	**61.49**
		0.99	0.48	**1.95**	**1.86**	0.48	**1.68**	1.52	0.86	1.30	1.54	0.08	**1.74**	0.33	1.56	**2.00**
	OLS	0.15	0.38	0.43	−0.07	−1.23	**−0.82**	−0.54	0.15	**−0.53**	**−278.38**	0.10	−0.05	0.05	−0.07	**56.17**
		0.19	0.48	0.64	0.61	1.36	**1.67**	1.08	0.29	**2.89**	**1.85**	0.97	0.48	0.40	0.83	**2.45**
ST × gov		−0.05	−0.12	−0.21	−0.03	0.51	−0.29	0.22	−0.07	0.18	79.91	0.12	0.02	0.19	0.10	24.35
		0.15	0.34	0.76	0.68	1.24	1.57	1.13	0.35	1.49	1.40	0.47	0.08	0.60	0.96	0.89
LT	PSM	0.05	0.07	**−0.07**	−0.02	−3.69	0.09	0.07	0.02	**−0.07**	−27.38	0.00	0.00	0.03	**−0.08**	−29.54
		0.98	0.94	**1.96**	1.31	1.20	1.06	0.93	0.59	**1.77**	0.71	0.09	0.09	0.26	**1.65**	0.58
	OLS	1.09	−0.11	**−1.38**	−0.02	0.80	0.09	0.09	**−1.14**	0.32	185.21	0.46	0.89	0.82	**−0.62**	−63.66
		1.43	0.14	**2.11**	1.05	0.55	0.99	1.01	**2.43**	1.59	1.37	0.61	1.14	0.82	**2.28**	0.41
LT × gov		−0.50	−0.01	**−0.60**	**−0.15**	−0.47	−0.23	−0.26	**−0.48**	**−0.13**	86.68	−0.19	−0.40	−0.47	**−0.24**	23.90
		1.57	0.04	**2.21**	**3.42**	0.55	1.31	1.41	**2.65**	**1.94**	1.48	0.57	1.14	1.02	**2.01**	0.33

Note: The first statistic next to a variable is the ATET/coefficient, with the T Statistic/Z score below. Numbers in bold are significant at least at the 10% level. The PSM has been carried out using the Kernel approach have had a positive effect. Thus, the conclusion vis-à-vis the macro–micro paradox of aid is not straightforward. Mosley (1986), noting that macro studies of aid effectiveness were less successful at finding a statistically significant impact of aid than micro studies of development projects, argued that the possible culprits, aside from data inaccuracies and biases, were aid fungibility and indirect negative effects of aid on the private sector. While any of the aforementioned factors might have played some role in Peru, a more honest explanation here is that, on the macro level, aid has come to constitute a very small part of Peru's budget and hence detection of a significant effect has become difficult.

Second, the discovery of the positive conditioning role of governance not only reinforces the validity of such findings from previous chapters, but also contains a novelty value, since governance here is measured on the local rather than on the national level. The results hence imply that it is not only national- or regional-level institutions and policies that enhance aid effectiveness – the quality of local institutions, including the police and the judge, can make a difference as well. The quality of the former and of the latter institutions is naturally related but even in countries with 'bad' national governance some communities are better managed, and vice versa.

Very little academic research to date has examined the role of local-governance quality in enhancing aid effectiveness, but within the policy world the situation has been different. The Accra Agenda for Action (OECD, 2008) and the Busan Partnership for Development Cooperation (OECD, 2011) both alluded to the importance of local government structures in improving the effectiveness of aid projects. Similarly, the United Cities and Local Governments (UCLG) and the Federation of Canadian Municipalities (FCM) posited that local governments play an important role in bringing together development stakeholders and in mobilising assets and resources to complement donor funds and hence improve the sustainability of project achievements (UCLG, 2009; FCM, 2010). My study, which found the quality of local governance to indeed contribute to more positive outcomes of development projects, is one of the first to provide empirical support to the argument extended by the above-cited policy agencies.

Looking to the heterogeneous effects of aid, many findings again aligned with those from the country-level studies. Results from the first categorisation, according to *who* implements aid, suggest that NGOs are more efficient project implementers than GOs but that the work of the latter is slightly more influenced by the quality of local governance (validating H2.2). Although this classification differs quite significantly from the one into multilateral and bilateral donors examined in the country-level studies, in some ways it conveys a similar message. NGOs, parallel to multilateral institutions, are less likely to be politically involved than GOs and can therefore provide aid in a more beneficial manner. Consequently, the quality of local governance has a larger conditioning potential in the effectiveness of the work of government agencies.

Analogous to the findings on the different effectiveness of loans and grants and of food aid and financial aid, in the categorisation of aid according to *how* it was disbursed non-credit and non-food aid were found to be more beneficial than their counterpart categories and credit and food aid to be more strongly conditioned on governance (validating H3.2 and H5). The division into food and non-food aid on the household level closely resembles such division on the country level and hence unsurprisingly the two sets of results are quite similar. Conversely, the division of aid into credit and non-credit is quite different from the division into concessional loans and grants, yet the reasons underlying the lower positive impact of credit aid are frequently similar to those culpable for the lower effectiveness of country loans – excessive debt, an improper use of the loans and a low quality of institutions. Surveys conducted in Andhra Pradesh in 2010 validated this view, showing that many poor families were simultaneously indebted to three or more microfinance institutions, taking out new loans just to repay interest on the old ones (Mader, 2013).[9] They also indicated that communities with better local administration were able to monitor the behaviour of microfinance institutions more closely, ensure that the correct procedures were followed and, in that way, improve the impact of many micro loans (ibid.).

This study's findings on aid classifications according to *where* it was provided differ the most from those in the country-level studies even though the divisions themselves are almost identical. First, vis-à-vis the sector division of aid, agricultural aid was found here to have the most consistently positive effect on household food security while its impact on the country level was not as beneficial. The qualitative country case study illustrated why that might have been the case, showing that while agricultural aid failed to strengthen food security in India, because of an inability to reach the most food-insecure and marginalised members of the society, it had a positive impact on food security in Vietnam. In this study, its impact appears even stronger, indicating that agricultural aid that actually manages to reach small-scale farmers – as are those surveyed by the Young Lives project – has a much more unambiguously positive impact on food security than agricultural aid in general. The impact of the recent scaling-up of private agricultural investment in Africa via an alliance with G8 countries and companies, which failed to involve in its design small farmers, on poverty reduction and food security of the countries involved can hence be viewed only with suspicion (FIAN, 2014).[10]

In a somewhat reverse fashion, social infrastructure aid, found to have the strongest impact on food security on the macro level, while still positive appears less consistently significant here. That is probably because some aid activities classified as social infrastructure aid (e.g. health extension services, drinking water provision and development, provision of sanitation facilities) can affect recipients' food security only some time after the beginning of their implementation. Findings by Petrikova (2014) substantiate this claim, showing that whereas the impact of social projects in Ethiopia on children's health was barely discernible during the projects' implementation, it appeared significant and strong several years later. The overall conclusion hence is that both agricultural aid and social aid strengthen household food security, which validates both my original and my amended eighth hypotheses (H8 and H8a).

Turning to the division of aid into emergency, short and long term, while the original hypothesis conjectured that short-term aid would appear to be most beneficial for food security, the previous two studies discovered long-term aid to have the largest positive impact. This study found both short- and long-term aid to be of value, thus providing some support to my original as well as to my amended seventh hypothesis (H7 and H7a). Consequently, the appropriate conclusion on this matter appears to be that both short-term and long-term aid have the potential to bolster food security, at least at the household level, as long as it is implemented through the right activities, inclusive of the most vulnerable households and individuals, and its impact is measured at the right time.

Two interesting country specificities also emerged in this study. First, in Vietnam, emergency aid, direct transfers and food aid impaired recipients' perception of food-security situation even when the aid simultaneously improved their children's nutritional outcomes. This effect was further exacerbated by poor local-governance quality. The most likely underlying explanation is that the Vietnamese people are afraid to rely on external help, particularly on the very short-term/emergency kind and, even though it might alleviate their physical suffering, due to the insecurity and volatility of its flows it actually undermines their confidence about the future. This finding fits well with the literature that found the unpredictable nature of aid to have negative effects on development outcomes on the macro as well as on the micro level (e.g. Lensink and Morrissey, 2000). However, the negative effect of aid on people's perception of food security did not emerge in the other three countries examined, only in Vietnam. One possible reason is that, out of the four countries, aid volatility is the highest in Vietnam (Chapter 4). Another reason could be a generally more worry-prone nature of the Vietnamese people, but cross-country comparisons of people's psychological predispositions in this regard failed to substantiate this conjecture (Ferrari *et al.*, 2013). More research in this direction would consequently be needed to be able to satisfactorily answer this question.

Second, aid in India appeared to have less of an overall impact on the recipients' food security than aid in the other three countries. Given India's persistently high levels of undernourishment, particularly among children, this finding is discouraging yet not unprecedented (e.g. Bosher, 2007). However, my data and their analysis from the three studies have thus far not offered a good explanation for this conundrum, aside from indicating that governance quality and deficient food utilisation due to sanitation problems are likely to play a role. This question, along with others, is explored in more detail in the next chapter.

Notes

1   More information can be found at younglives.org.uk
2   People might be ashamed to admit to suffer from food insecurity or, alternatively, might exaggerate their misery in hopes of receiving more support.
3   Both GOs and NGOs include foreign and domestic organisations.
4   The percentages in different classifications add up to generally higher numbers than the total amount of aid recipients, since many households examined receive more than one type of assistance at one time.
5   Birth size ranges from 1 for a very small to 5 for a very large baby.

6 Social capital ranges from 0 to 4, with 4 denoting the highest level.
7 In 2014, Telangana became a separate Indian state.
8 A VIF measure showed that there was no co-linearity present among the different project variables.
9 In 2010, the Andhra Pradesh government reacted to this unsustainable situation by placing strict regulations on all microfinance activity, which led to a significant decrease in the number of microfinance institutions in the state.
10 http://www.fian.org/fileadmin/media/publications/2014_G8NewAlliance_screen.pdf

References

Bosher, L. (2007). 'A case of inappropriately targeted vulnerability reduction initiatives in Andhra Pradesh, India?', *International Journal of Social Economics*, 34(10), pp. 754–71.
Chen, S., Mu, R., and Ravallion, M. (2009). 'Are there lasting impacts of aid to poor areas?', *Journal of Public Economics*, 93(3), pp. 512–528.
Clemens, M., Radelet, S., and Bhavnani, R. (2004). 'Counting chickens when they hatch: the short-term effect of aid on growth', *Center for Global Development Working Paper*, 44. New York: Center for Global Development.
FCM (2010). 'Enhancing aid effectiveness: the case for stronger local government involvement in development', *Commonwealth Journal of Local Governance*, 6(1), pp. 146–51.
Ferrari, A., Charlson, F., Norman, R., Patten, S., Freedman, G., Murray, C., Vos, T., and Whiteford, H. (2013). 'Burden of depressive disorders by country, sex, age, and year: findings from the global burden of disease study 2010', *PLoS Medicine*, 10(11), e1001547.
FIAN (2014). *G8 New Alliance for Food Security and Nutrition in Africa: A Critical Analysis from a Human Rights Perspective.* Available at: http://www.fian.org/fileadmin/media/publications/2014_G8NewAlliance_screen.pdf
Galab, S., Piush, A., Wilson, I., Jones, N., McCoy, A., Rama Raju, D., and Reddy, P. (2006). 'Exploring linkages between maternal social capital and children's nutritional status in Andhra Pradesh', *Young Lives Working Paper*, 32. Oxford: Young Lives.
Lensink, R., and Morrissey, O. (2000). 'Aid instability as a measure of uncertainty and the positive impact of aid on growth', *Journal of Development Studies*, 36(3), pp. 31–49.
Mader, P. (2013). 'Rise and fall of microfinance in India: the Andhra Pradesh crisis in perspective', *Strategic Change*, 22(1–2), pp. 47–66.
Mosley, P. (1986). 'Aid-effectiveness: the micro-macro paradox', *IDS Bulletin*, 17(2), pp. 22–7.
Moursi, M., Arimond, M., Dewey, K., Trèche, S., Ruel, M., and Delpeuch, F. (2008). 'Dietary diversity is a good predictor of the micronutrient density of the diet of 6- to 23-month-old children in Madagascar', *Journal of Nutrition*, 138(12), pp. 2448–53.
Nguyen Viet, C. (2012). 'A matching method with panel data', *Statistics in Medicine*, 32, pp. 577–88.
OECD (2008). *Accra Agenda for Action.* Paris: OECD.
OECD (2011). *Busan Partnership for Effective Development.* Paris: OECD.
Petrikova, I. (2014). 'The short- and long-term effects of development projects: evidence from Ethiopia', *Journal of International Development*, 26(8), pp. 1161–80.
Petrikova, I., and Chadha, D. (2013). 'The role of social capital in risk-sharing: lessons from Andhra Pradesh', *Journal of South Asian Development*, 8(3), pp. 359–83.

Ravallion, M. (2001). 'The mystery of the vanishing benefits: an introduction to impact evaluation', *World Bank Economic Review*, 15(1), pp. 115–40.

Strauss, J. and Thomas, D. (2008). 'Health over the life course', *Handbook of Development Economics*, 4(5), pp. 3375–474.

UCLG (2009). *UCLG Position Paper on Aid Effectiveness and Local Government: Understanding the Link between Governance and Development.* Barcelona: UCLG.

WDI (2014). Available at: http://data.worldbank.org/data-catalog/world-development-indicators

WGI (2014). Available at: http://info.worldbank.org/governance/wgi/index.aspx

WIIO (2014). *Global Database on Child Growth and Malnutrition.* Available at: http://www.who.int/nutgrowthdb/database/countries/en

6 Up close and personal in Uttar Pradesh, India

Introduction

This empirical chapter tightens the lens of observation even further and examines the impact of aid on food security using personally collected household and individual data. I conducted the field research in north-western India, close to the Nepali border. The choice to conduct the study in India was driven by my desire to study in more depth the 'South Asian enigma', in which India's food-insecurity levels have remained high despite rapid economic growth in the past few decades. The specific locality was selected in response to finding an aid organisation implementing a multi-sector development project that allowed me and my research assistant access to its project beneficiaries. The fact that this organisation works in Uttar Pradesh made the choice quite suitable for the purpose of my study, as Uttar Pradesh is one of India's most food-insecure states (IIPS, 2007).

Since small-scale field research is generally not good at providing answers to broad social-science questions, the primary purpose of this study is to offer greater insight into the processes underlying the influence of aid on recipients' food security. With this consideration in mind, quantitative analysis on the basis of survey-gathered data is used but it is heavily supplemented with qualitative analysis of information collected in longer interviews.

This chapter proceeds as follows. First, it briefly restates those hypotheses that can be plausibly tested in this study. Second, it talks about the chapter's conceptual and empirical approach, including the development initiatives examined, their Theory of Change strategies and the methods of data collection and analysis utilised. After that, it presents the results of the data analysis, discusses their significance and finishes with some concluding remarks.

Founding expectations

Relationships considered

As with the previous chapters, this one examines whether aid strengthens food security, whether governance conditions this relationship and whether the impact differs with the type of aid provided. Similar to the previous chapter and unlike the first two empirical ones, this one relies on micro-level data and hence considers as the main dependent variable household- and individual-level food security and as the main independent variable development assistance as reported by individual families.

The multi-sector development project, which I chose to examine, is run by the Indian branch of the international NGO Grameen Development Services (GDS) and aims to bolster recipients' food security through four separate initiatives – agricultural help, livestock help, credit assistance and water sanitation and hygiene (WASH) assistance. The different components are provided sometimes separately and at other times in compound to different recipients. The financing provided by the NGO to each component has been approximately equal, which has enabled me to compare the effectiveness of the different project components in strengthening food security (related to *where* aid goes), reminiscent of a natural experiment. Given that one of the project parts consists of credit provision, the credit portion of the aid provided with the non-credit portion (related to *how* aid is provided) can also be compared.

The data collection revealed that the people under study have not benefited from almost any other external assistance, with the main exception being the national government-operated Public Distribution System (PDS). Through this scheme, more than half of my survey respondents have acquired ration cards that enable them to purchase basic cereals (wheat and rice) at reduced prices. Thus, aside from considering the effect of the GDS project on beneficiaries' food security, this study also looks at the effect of the PDS and compares the NGO and government interventions to see how the aid provided by the government compares to the NGO-implemented aid (related to *who* provides/implements aid). Of course, given that the type of government aid considered here (direct transfer aid) does not overlap with the NGO aid, one has to be careful about drawing any firm conclusions with regard to the greater effectiveness of one implementer over the other.

Third, as with previous chapters, this one also examines if the quality of governance affects the aid–food security relationship. While national and district-level quality of governance might play a larger role here, their impact cannot be assessed directly as all the people considered in this study live in a cluster of villages located next to each other and thus there is no variation in their measures. Instead, a measure of village-level governance quality, explained in greater detail in the data section, is utilised here.

Hypotheses restated

First, this study examines whether the aid provided has had a positive impact on the food security of its recipients and whether this impact has been conditioned on the quality of local governance (H1). Then the study considers the different types of the aid provided and whether they affect the impact of aid on food security.

Regarding the question of *who* provides/implements the assistance under study, the GDS development project can be compared here with the governmental PDS scheme of ration cards. My initial hypothesis vis-à-vis this relationship (H2.2) was that aid projects implemented by NGOs were more effective than the ones implemented by government-related organisations due to their greater flexibility and fewer bureaucratic restrictions. The findings in the previous chapter lent some support to this hypothesis.

Turning attention to *how* aid is disbursed, this study allows me to once again examine whether credit aid is less effective and more conditioned on governance than non-credit aid (H3.2) and whether aid volatility has a negative effect on recipients' food security (H6). Both existing literature and my results from the previous chapters have substantiated these hypotheses.

Finally, this chapter compares the effectiveness of agricultural and livestock interventions as opposed to credit assistance, social infrastructure (WASH) help and the direct transfer aid provided by the government. My initial hypothesis was that agricultural aid would be the most impactful. In the course of the previous three studies, the hypothesis was expanded to expect to find also social infrastructural aid to be very beneficial in its effects on food security (H8a). Unlike in the previous chapters, this one further looks at the compound effects of the different aid initiatives. Authors such as Oxenham (2002) indicated that multi-component projects were in general more successful at strengthening food security and reducing poverty than projects focused on one activity only and I expect to discover something similar here.

Conceptual framework and methodology

Food security in India and Uttar Pradesh

The two preceding chapters described the serious situation of food insecurity in India, which has improved slightly in the last few decades but not nearly as much as one would have expected on the basis of India's recent high economic growth. Some researchers dubbed this phenomenon the 'South Asian enigma' and fierce debates ensued vis-à-vis its main cause. As a reminder, the most recent figures available from the WHO at the time of writing indicated that about 18.5 per cent of the Indian population was undernourished (lacked access to sufficient daily calories), 43 per cent of children under five were underweight and 48 per cent of children were stunted (WHO, 2014). India's National Family Health Survey (IIPS, 2007) helped complete the picture of India's food-insecurity state, suggesting that one third of all children in India were born with low weight (under 2,500 kg), one third of all adult women were undernourished (BMI below 18.5) and 56 per cent of adult women and 71 per cent of children under five were anaemic[1] (iron-deficient).

The situation in Uttar Pradesh is, in many respects, even worse than in India in general. While 'only' 42 per cent of children under five in Uttar Pradesh as opposed to 43 nationally were underweight, a whopping 57 per cent were stunted (48 nationally) (IIPS, 2007). Fifteen per cent of children were wasted (low weight for height) and 74 per cent anaemic. Furthermore, more than one third of all adults were considered too thin according to their BMI scores (ibid.).

Multi-component project in Uttar Pradesh

The project examined here is implemented among rural households in 20 villages in north-western Uttar Pradesh, in four districts: Siddharthnagar, Maharajganj, Gorakhpur and Sant Kabir Nagar. The communities lie in the basin of the Rapti river, a tributary of the Ghanghra, and are subject to major close-to-annual flooding. Land-based activities – agriculture and animal husbandry – have traditionally been the main source of livelihoods here. However, due to the heavy and increasing population pressure, the average size of landholdings is consistently on the decline, to the extent that for some farmers agriculture has become economically unviable. This perspective fits well with the opinion of some development scholars that small-scale agriculture in today's world constitutes an unsustainable way of life for many (e.g. Collier, 2008). Consequently, there is an emergent crisis of livelihoods along with serious food insecurity in the area.

Agricultural intervention

The main focus of this project component has been on strengthening the agricultural production and productivity of small and marginalised farmers through the introduction of new crops, techniques and technologies. Since the Maharajganj area is highly flood-prone, one of the main activities has been the distribution of 'pre-flood' rice-cultivation packages, which allow farmers to harvest their crop before the onset of floods. Similarly, the project workers tried to introduce farmers to more flood-tolerant rice varieties and less expensive practices of vegetable cultivation. In flood-less years, they encourage farmers to produce three crops in two seasons. They have also supported participating farmers in setting up small vegetable gardens for their own consumption and growing new types of vegetables.

According to the project's intended Theory of Change, the agricultural intervention should bolster recipients' food security via three pathways (Figure 6.1). First, by enabling farmers to produce more crops, the intervention should increase food availability in both farmer households and the community as a whole, since some of the extra produce may be sold in the local markets. Second, the

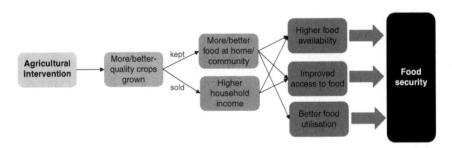

Figure 6.1 The envisioned effect of GDS agricultural intervention on recipients' food security.

Source: Author's own work

intervention ought to strengthen recipients' access to food, either to crops grown domestically or to foods purchased through income earned from selling the extra crops. Third, growing new crops could contribute to more nutritionally balanced meals among beneficiaries and hence improved food utilisation.

Livestock intervention

The aim of the livestock project component is to contribute to improving livestock breed, health and overall productivity. The main activity within the intervention has been training a troupe of local veterinarians ('para-vets'). These provide basic health care to domestic animals as well as artificial insemination services for breed improvement.

The intervention has aimed to promote participants' food security in four ways (Figure 6.2). First, by enabling farmers to have more healthy livestock it should contribute to a greater availability of milk and meat both in the farmers' households and in the communities. Second, by selling extra milk and meat farmers can achieve higher incomes, which strengthen access to food more generally. Third, more dairy and meat consumption could lead to better food utilisation – reducing, for example, high rates of anaemia (IIPS, 2007). Finally, since farmers in developing countries often regard livestock as a risk-insurance mechanism, which can be sold during lean times to ensure consumption smoothing, the livestock intervention can also strengthen participants' future certainty.

Credit intervention

Within this component, GDS has encouraged the establishment of self-help groups for microfinance. Unlike many NGOs, GDS has not created a microfinance institution itself but rather tried to promote and capacitate the Maharajganj community to manage their own saving and lending operations. The available

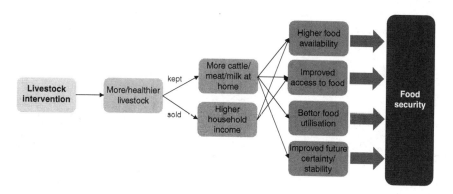

Figure 6.2 The envisioned effect of GDS livestock intervention on recipients' food security.

Source: Author's own work

Figure 6.3 The envisioned effect of GDS credit intervention on recipients' food security.

Source: Author's own work

credit should ideally be used to set up and grow micro-enterprises, including tea stalls, barber shops and shops with building materials.

According to the project's logic, the microcredit intervention should help increase recipients' food security by awarding them an easier access to loans, which could help them open or grow small businesses, thus facilitating them higher incomes and consequently improving their access to food (Figure 6.3). Similar to the agricultural component, the higher incomes are unlikely to boost people's perceptions of future food security due to the unpredictable nature of the business cycle.

Water sanitation and hygiene (WASH) intervention

The objective of this project component has been to improve hygiene, sanitation and nutrition practices and conditions among the Maharajganj communities. The main activities within this initiative have involved assistance with the construction of toilets in household premises and awareness-raising among participating households about the dangers of open defecation as well as about safe water drinking, sanitary handling of sewage, safe and sustainable waste-disposal management and nutritious, balanced meal planning.

The envisioned effects of the WASH intervention on recipients' food security, shown in Figure 6.4, have been through improved sanitation and hygiene as well

Figure 6.4 The envisioned effect of GDS WASH intervention on recipients' food security.

Source: Author's own work

as through improved nutritional knowledge. Better sanitation and hygiene and the consumption of more nutritious food should contribute to lower levels of diarrhoea and other health problems and thus to better food utilisation among participants. Eating more balanced meals strengthens food utilisation on its own as well. Furthermore, better health can bolster people's future food-security outlook, through reduced predicted spending on health care and greater expected ability to work.

Government scheme

Public Distribution System (PDS) and ration cards

The PDS is India's largest national programme aimed at improving food security. It dates back to the 1940s and has been managed jointly by the national and state governments (Masiero, 2015). Its basic premise is to allow poor people to purchase basic commodities such as wheat and rice but in some states also sugar and kerosene at subsidised prices.

Three different types of ration cards are available. The first is the Antyodaya Anna Yojana (AAY) card, which should be, in theory, provided to the 25 million poorest people across India, with the allocation decision left to local authorities. The Below Poverty Line (BPL) card is available to all the people living below the official poverty line (in 2013 set at 27 Indian rupees [IRS] a day for rural areas and 33 in urban areas) and the Above Poverty Line (APL) card to everyone else interested. In 2013, AAY card holders were entitled to purchase wheat for 2 IRS per kg and rice for 3 IRS per kg, BPL holders wheat for 4.15 and rice for 5.65 IRS per kg and APL holders wheat for 6.10 and rice for 8.30 IRS per kg, with the maximum purchase allowed usually set at 35 kg per month per household (DFPD, 2014).[2]

The Theory of Change, through which the PDS aims to bolster participants' food security, is displayed graphically in Figure 6.5. Under the first pathway, the ration cards allow their holders to purchase cereal grains at subsidised prices and hence improve their food access. The lower grain prices should also indirectly

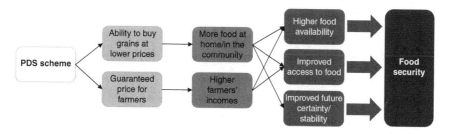

Figure 6.5 The envisioned effect of PDS cards on beneficiaries' food security.

Source: Author's own work

contribute to a larger amount of food available locally. Last, despite various changes to the scheme in the past decades, the PDS has been around in some form ever since the 1940s and, consequently, the ration cards can be expected to be viewed by their holders as a form of permanent safety net, contributing to a more positive outlook on future food security.

Data collection

I assess validity of the hypotheses and envisaged pathways to food security discussed above through quantitative and qualitative data, which I collected with the help of my research assistant, Vatsalya Sharma. The quantitative data were gathered using household surveys administered to 146 households that benefited from at least one of the GDS project's components and 23 households in villages that did not participate in the project at all (1,257 individuals overall). First, eight villages from the project-participating ones and three from the non-participating ones in close geographical proximity were selected at random to be examined. Second, from each village five to 15 households (depending on the size of the community) were randomly selected and surveyed. The survey data were collected between December 2012 and March 2013.

The surveys contained five main sections. The first one collected information about different project components – if any – that the households have benefited from and about the households' location. The second section gathered data on all household members, their age, education levels and religious affiliation. The third part attempted to gauge the households' wealth, based on both external observations about their dwelling and information about their income and asset ownership. The fourth section enquired whether the families under study were recipients of any other external assistance and the fifth one asked about their food security.

Qualitative data on the project were gathered between December 2013 and March 2014, through a series of longer interviews with household members from several project-participating and non-participating villages. The main objective of the second round of data collection was to uncover details about the processes underlying the effects of the different interventions, which could not be obtained or understood by simply looking at numbers. The households to be interviewed were selected also randomly and in total, ten people from project participants and five from non-participants were interviewed.

Empirical methods of analysis

The first approach used to estimate the effects of the different external interventions on their recipients' food security is propensity score matching (PSM), which allows for impact evaluation even in the absence of panel data, and was described in detail in the previous chapter. In estimating the effects of the GDS project and the PDS scheme in general, the households surveyed were divided into those that received that specific type of support (GDS or PDS) and those that did not receive it (control group). In assessing the impact of the different project and PDS components, the households were again divided into two groups, with one containing those who received that particular component and the second one those who did not, controlling for other project/PDS components in the case of their recipients.

In order to examine also the conditioning role of local governance in the aid–food security relationships along with assessing the robustness of the results obtained through the PSM, the second evaluative approach employs probit and ordered probit regressions with robust standard errors clustered by household ID, with food-security levels (nutritional status) as the dependent variable and the types of aid received as the main independent variables.

A primary method used for analysing the interview data gathered is simple content analysis, which is a detailed and systematic examination of text in an effort to identify patterns and themes and to discover procedural explanations (Berg and Lune, 2012).

Data and descriptive statistics

Food (in)security

Table 6.1 displays summary statistics of all the variables used in the quantitative part of the study. The main dependent variable is a food-security index, constructed on the basis of four questions, which asked about the adequacy of households' food consumption, food availability in the previous year, concerns about future food availability and the frequency of preference for consuming other foods.[3] The final index varies from 3 to 11 (high food insecurity), with the average individual reporting a score of 7.

Other food-security variables include the number of meals a person consumes per day (mean of 2.8) and the number of different food groups a person consumes per day (mean of 2.53).[4] Finally, variables assessing the number of times a person suffered from a bout of diarrhoea in the past month (on average between two and three times) and the number of times a person was ill in the past six months (three times on average) have constituted my attempt to include among food-security measurements also individual indicators of nutritional status.[5]

The final dependent variable, *financial situation*, is less concerned with food security and more with a subjective measurement of wellbeing as it enquires of surveyed households whether they are concerned about their financial situation in the coming year. The resultant values vary from 1 to 4 (high concern), with the average falling at 2.37.

Overall, the dependent variables paint a picture of moderate food insecurity in the villages surveyed, with people fairly worried about their future prospects. However, as the previous chapter implied, Indian households have the tendency to downplay the gravity of their suffering and the qualitative data gathered suggest that it is the case also here.

Assistance and governance variables

The first relevant variable here, *project*, enquired whether a respondent has been a beneficiary of any of the GDS project components. Out of the 1,257 people surveyed, 1,110 (89 per cent) received at least one of the components. The following four variables provide the same information vis-à-vis the four separate components – agricultural, livestock, credit and WASH. Table 6.1 shows that 81 per cent of respondents received the agricultural component, 69 per cent credit support, 46 per cent livestock help and 25 per cent support from WASH.

Table 6.1 Descriptive statistics of all variables used

	Mean	StD	Min	Max
Dependent variables				
Food insecurity	6.91	1.90	3	11
Food consumption	2.11	0.48	1	3
Future concern	2.20	0.74	1	4
Would prefer other foods	0.79	0.60	0	2
Food availability	1.21	0.41	1	2
No. of meals per day	2.80	0.28	2	3.5
No. of foods per day	2.53	0.19	2	3.5
Diarrhoea	2.69	1.35	0	7.5
Illness	3.05	0.92	1.5	7.5
Financial concern	2.37	0.77	1	4
Project and governance variables				
Project	0.88	0.32	0	1
Agricultural component	0.81	0.39	0	1
Livestock component	0.46	0.50	0	1
Credit component	0.69	0.46	0	1
Wash component	0.25	0.43	0	1
Ration card	0.62	0.49	0	1
AAY card	0.28	0.45	0	1
BPL card	0.31	0.46	0	1
APL card	0.03	0.18	0	1
Local-governance quality	6.59	1.62	4	9
Control variables				
Male	0.54	0.50	0	1
Age	26.24	19.22	0	90
Education (age>22y)	3.44	4.54	0	18
hh size	9.56	4.88	1	24
Female headed hh	0.13	0.34	0	1
Muslim	0.03	0.18	0	1
Scheduled caste/tribe	0.71	0.12	0	1
Pucca house	0.64	0.48	0	1
Wealth index	0.02	2.02	−4.01	14.69
Income per capita (USD)	86.74	45.95	26.20	392.93
N		1257		

Source: Author's own calculations

The four following variables in Table 6.1 provide information about the government's PDS scheme. The first one, *ration card*, shows that approximately 62 per cent individuals live in households holding some type of ration card. Twenty-eight per cent of households have the AAY card, 31 per cent the BPL card and 3 per cent the APL one. The graph in Figure 6.6 analyses the targeting of the three ration cards vis-à-vis income levels using concentration curves. These clearly demonstrate that while the BPL card has been targeted in a some-what pro-poor manner as the national strategy intended, the AAY card has actually been awarded in greater proportion to richer people in my sample. The APL card seems to be owned relatively equally by all income ventiles.

Turning attention back to Table 6.1, the final variable in this section, local governance quality, was obtained by asking three people deemed as community leaders in the area (GDS project worker and two project participants, one male and one female) to rate the 11 communities under study on a scale of 1 to 10 (good) based on the perceived quality of local institutions[6] and state of corruption. The three different measures were then averaged to obtain one indicator. Table 6.1 shows that the average community was ranked slightly above six, with no community scoring lower than four or higher than nine. These results would suggest that public affairs in the communities under study are being run rather well; however, interviews insinuated that corruption was an every-day presence in people's lives. An overly optimistic view of the state of local governance was also found in the Young Lives surveys discussed in Chapter 5. Nevertheless, given that what matters here most is the relative comparison of the communities to each other rather than the absolute ratings, this over-optimism should not significantly bias results.

Other factors

The control variables used here can be split into two groups. The first one is demographics, including gender, age, education, religion, household size and whether a household is female-headed. The second section gauges households' economic wellbeing, by enquiring about their annual income,[7] their type of dwelling ('pucca' or 'kachcha'[8]), and whether they own any valuable items (toilet, water pump, watch, pressure cooker, radio, fridge, TV, phone, sewing machine, fan, bicycle, motorcycle or a car).

Looking first at the demographics, 54 per cent of the sample is male, with the average age 26 years. The average education level of adults older than 22 years is 3.44, with a wide range from no education to 18 years of schooling. Thirteen per cent of respondents live in female-headed households and only 3 per cent are Muslim. The average household size is close to ten, indicating the co-habitation of several generations of families.

Turning attention to the economic indicators, 64 per cent of respondents live in pucca houses – that is, buildings constructed from firm materials (clay, bricks etc.). Kachcha houses are made of temporary materials, primarily mud and other organic matter. Data on the valuable items owned were used to create a wealth index, using

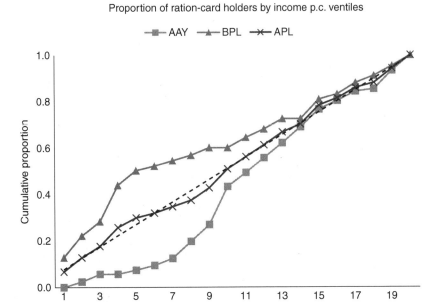

Figure 6.6 Relationship between PDS participation and income per capita.

Source: Author's own calculations

principal component analysis, with the resulting average somewhere around 0 on a scale from –4 to more than 14. Finally, the average per capita income in this sample is extremely low, less than 85 USD annually, deeply below the international poverty line of 1.25 USD per person per day. Nevertheless, these numbers cannot be taken at face value as all the households surveyed are agricultural and consume a lot of home-grown food, which is not reported as part of income.

Qualitative data

While the long interviews were conducted using mostly open-ended questions, a few statistics were collected on the respondents in order to compare them with the survey-respondent group. Due to the fact that Indian men generally see themselves as more competent at talking with strangers than women, 73 per cent (11 out of 15) of my interviewees were male. Unsurprisingly, then, the 15 interviewed people had a higher average level of finished education, 4.3 years of schooling[9] as opposed to the 3.4 years in the survey sample. The mean age of the interviewees was also higher than in the quantitative study, 42 as opposed to 26, due to older people regarding themselves more suitable to participate in interviews. The average household size and income per capita were similar, however, at nine members and 89 USD annually. Interviewed persons were also asked to rate their household financial situation on a scale of 1 (poor) to 3 (well-off) and their food security situation on a scale of 1 (bad) to 3 (good). An absolute majority of respondents replied 2 to both questions, suggesting living in a state of moderate food insecurity and mild poverty. Nevertheless, further questions indicated that most respondents' families were actually very poor, confirming yet again the suspicion about the tendency of poor families in India to downplay the true scale of their destitution.

Aid effectiveness and the heterogeneity of impact

Aid in general

The first part of Table 6.2 shows the impact of the GDS project on recipients' food security. Overall, the impact appears positive, with the most robust effects on increasing the number of meals consumed per day and reducing the frequency of diarrhoea in the past month. A less robust but still positive result appears regarding the project's impact on recipients' food-insecurity index. Paradoxically, it also seems that the project may have increased people's concern about future financial security, but that could be attributed to the inherently uncertain nature of project assistance. The quality of local governance strengthens the positive effects of the project, particularly in reducing the food-insecurity index and the frequency of diarrhoea and illnesses and in increasing dietary diversity.[10]

Information gathered through interviews generally confirmed these findings. Interviewees that were active beneficiaries of the project agreed that the assistance from GDS contributed to improving their food security. As an illustration, one of the project beneficiaries said that 'GDS has taught us so many ways to help ourselves in a better way using the same resources that we already have.' Another stated that 'ever since GDS started working here, we have more food in the house and eat better'. When asked about the effects of local governance, most respondents opined that although the local authorities did not interfere much with the NGO's work, in some instances the positive impacts of the project were dependent on the quality of the local bureaucracy, particularly on their willingness to cooperate and their likelihood to require bribes in exchange.

The PDS ration-card scheme appears much less effective than the project in the quantitative results. It might have slightly lowered the frequency with which survey respondents suffer with illnesses and diarrhoea but otherwise has had no impact on their food security. Thus, the logical pathway through which the PDS could have theoretically boosted recipients' food security by increasing their access to food and future certainty has not been realised by the scheme in general among the people surveyed. This finding of no PDS impact is not unprecedented, however (e.g. Kaushal and Muchomba, 2013).

The effect of the PDS has also not been conditioned on good local governance according to my calculations, a result that seems surprising in view of the information gathered from interviews, which suggested that some PDS shopkeepers were significantly more corrupt than others. For example, one woman said in the interviews:

> Often, when I go to the Fair Price Shop (FPS),[11] they tell me that they have run out of stock... but I know they have stock for their friends. Lalita [her friend] said that the FPS in Gram Mazgawa is better, they always sell her rice.

However, the ratings of local governance were not based on the quality of the Fair Price Shops, and thus there likely is a low if any level of correlation between 'good' local governance as measured here and the level of corruption among PDS administrators.

On the benefits of owning the ration cards, people in interviews reported that particularly the possession of the AAY cards was useful. In their words, 'having an AAY card is better than a BPL card... we are poor, we thought they would give it to us but they didn't... but at least we have the other one [BPL], some of our neighbours never got any'. At the same time, most interviewees expressed a wish that the cards covered more types of food than just wheat and rice.[12]

The heterogeneous impact of aid

First, looking at the aid implemented by GDS versus by the government, both the quantitative and qualitative data presented above suggest that NGO aid has been more effective at bolstering recipients' food security. When asked about the difference between NGO and government assistance, interviewees spoke about faster NGO delivery times, less bureaucracy and less corruption when compared to the PDS. One interviewee summed up this notion nicely, saying: 'Unlike the government, GDS gives its services without any hassle. There are lots of procedures involved in government services. And they always want some extra money.' This finding appears to validate my initial hypothesis (H2.2) on NGO versus government-implemented aid even more so than the findings from the previous chapter. However, the types of assistance provided here by the NGO differ in kind from those provided by the government, and hence it is not clear whether an agricultural extension service or microfinance provision run by the government would also be less successful than those of the NGO, examined here.

With a view to *how* aid is disbursed, the two categorisations assessed here are into credit and non-credit aid and according to aid volatility. Table 6.3 displays the results obtained vis-à-vis the different impacts of credit and non-credit aid and validates once again hypothesis 3.2, which argued that credit aid was likely to be less effective than non-credit aid but at the same time more conditioned on governance. While non-credit aid impacts positively almost all the food-security indicators examined, credit aid appears largely ineffective and, in addition, increases people's financial concerns.

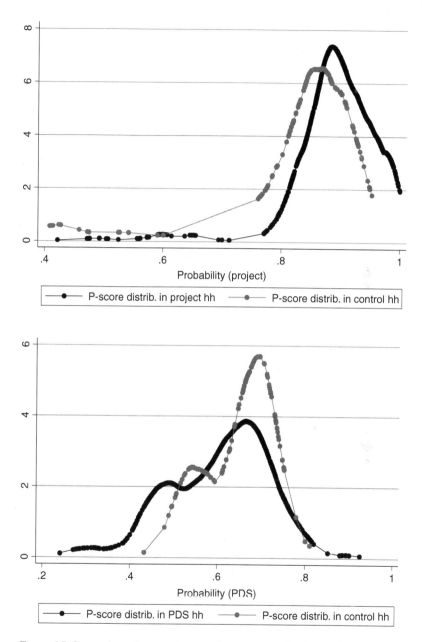

Figure 6.7 Comparison of propensity scores between treated and control matched households.

Source: Author's own figures

Table 6.2 The impact of aid on recipients' food security and the conditioning effect of governance

		Food insecurity	Meals per day	Foods per day	Diarrhoea	Illness	Financial concern
Project	PSM	−0.01	**0.23**	0.00	**−0.54**	−0.03	**0.23**
		0.05	**15.27**	0.34	**4.43**	1.44	**3.52**
	Ordered probit	−0.57	**1.30**	0.12	**−0.16**	−0.04	0.00
		−1.83	**5.23**	0.55	**1.78**	0.17	0.02
Governance		**−0.46**	**0.60**	**0.20**	−0.05	**−0.29**	0.09
		2.08	**4.49**	**1.84**	0.45	**2.87**	0.36
Project × gov		**−0.31**	**0.45**	0.17	**−0.30**	**−0.39**	0.13
		3.76	**2.68**	1.27	**2.28**	**3.29**	0.50
Matched treated					912		
Matched control					147		
Ration card	PSM	−0.23	−0.01	−0.02	−0.11	**−0.16**	0.01
		1.48	0.55	1.52	0.95	**1.82**	0.12
	Ordered probit	−0.04	0.12	−0.25	**−0.34**	−0.26	0.16
		0.18	0.51	1.01	**1.80**	1.32	0.67
Governance		**−0.25**	**−0.24**	−0.18	0.13	0.05	**−0.34**
		2.69	**1.92**	1.02	1.19	0.51	**2.38**
Ration card × gov		−0.11	0.09	0.21	0.11	0.01	−0.16
		0.88	0.80	1.13	0.93	0.12	0.96
Matched treated					741		
Matched control					479		

Note: The number next to each variable is the average treatment effect on the treated (ATET) in case of PSM regressions and a coefficient in case of the ordered probit regressions, the number below is the corresponding Z score. Results significant at least as the 90% level are in bold

The qualitative data confirmed these conclusions, suggesting that people in the Maharajganj area use the microcredit loans primarily to cover unexpected emergencies, to fund large weddings or funerals and to purchase material goods, and the high interest rates on the loans increase their worries for the future. One interviewed woman said:

> I got two loans, one to pay for my son's operation and one for my daughter's wedding. We are still paying off the second loan... and the payments are a burden. Last month I had to borrow from a neighbour to pay up on time.

Perhaps surprisingly, my data have suggested that very few people use the loans to start or support existing business and the few businesses that were started were, by and large, unsuccessful. Three people recollected the story of a woman who opened a cosmetics shop in one of the villages with the help of a micro loan but unfortunately went out of business shortly after the opening.

Regarding aid volatility, no relevant quantitative data were collected, but, in the interviews, people did not appear to be seriously harmed by it in the context of the GDS project as it has provided assistance continuously for more than

Table 6.3 The impact of credit vs non-credit aid on recipients' food security

		Food insecurity	Meals per day	Foods per day	Diarrhoea	Illness	Financial concern
Credit	*PSM*	0.25	0.00	−0.01	0.00	**−0.64**	0.37
		1.26	0.17	0.26	0.01	**7.28**	1.45
	Ordered	0.32	0.27	−0.42	−0.20	−0.31	**0.51**
	probit	0.19	0.97	1.35	0.65	1.32	**1.89**
Non−credit	*PSM*	−1.39	**0.22**	0.00	**−0.45**	−0.13	−0.02
		1.72	**13.03**	0.41	**3.56**	1.57	0.43
	Ordered	**−3.08**	**3.43**	3.03	**−1.28**	−1.49	**−2.35**
	probit	**1.81**	**2.15**	1.64	**2.13**	0.93	**1.90**
Governance	*Ordered*	**−0.48**	0.07	−0.15	0.03	−0.26	0.04
	probit	**2.44**	1.22	1.28	0.18	2.20	0.16
Credit × gov	*Ordered*	**−0.27**	0.11	**0.92**	0.05	0.23	**−0.21**
	probit	**2.13**	0.52	**2.88**	0.29	1.08	**1.97**
Non-credit ×	*Ordered*	−0.38	0.25	−0.05	0.28	0.24	0.34
gov	*probit*	1.64	1.12	0.89	1.13	1.00	0.96

Note: The number next to each variable is the average treatment effect on the treated (ATET) in case of PSM regressions and a coefficient in case of the ordered probit regressions, the number below is the corresponding Z score. Results significant at least as the 90% level are in bold

seven years, with no plans to discontinue thus far. Nevertheless, some people did express a mild worry that things would deteriorate again once GDS left the area. Looking to the PDS scheme, while the households that have a ration card generally have it for life, the availability of the subsidised grains for purchase varies over time and food-insecure families cannot consequently fully rely on the cards. Particularly in times of droughts or floods when the harvest is bad and people are in most need of subsidised food, Fair Price Shops tend to run out of stock. As one interviewed man said: 'The [ration] card is good but often when we want to use it, our FPS has nothing to sell.' Moreover, since 2012 there has been a push in Uttar Pradesh to replace all the existing plastic ration cards with digitised ones, in an effort to curb corruption.[13] As of 2014, this process had not been completed but it added an extra element of insecurity into the scheme. Hence, overall, the data clearly provide support to my original sixth hypothesis (H6).

Finally, the data gathered can be used to examine the heterogeneous impact of aid on food security on the basis of *where* the aid specifically goes. Looking at the different effects of the four project components, displayed in Table 6.4, agricultural and livestock help appear most beneficial, followed by WASH.

The agricultural intervention bolstered most robustly the number of meals a person consumes per day along with the number of different food groups consumed. This result, the interviewees explained, arose thanks to the project workers introducing them to new types of crops (primarily vegetables) as well as to the use of drip irrigation. For several farmers the intervention backfired one year, however, as they grew only one new, hybrid rice variety and proceeded to

Table 6.4 The heterogeneous impact of the various GDS components on food security

		Food insecurity	Meals per day	Foods per day	Diarrhoea	Illness	Financial concern
Agriculture	PSM	−0.47	**0.12**	**0.04**	**−0.99**	**−0.64**	−0.20
		1.69	**2.80**	**5.98**	**2.85**	**3.39**	1.39
	Ordered	−0.26	**0.50**	**0.35**	−0.20	0.29	−0.18
	probit	0.90	**2.02**	1.67	0.84	1.24	0.65
Livestock	PSM	**−0.61**	**0.09**	**0.03**	−0.02	0.16	**−0.46**
		2.99	**3.12**	**2.16**	0.12	1.60	**5.93**
	Ordered	**−0.19**	0.46	0.32	−0.21	**−0.48**	−0.26
	probit	**1.72**	1.60	0.89	1.49	**1.97**	1.27
Credit	PSM	0.25	0.00	−0.01	0.00	**−0.64**	0.37
		1.26	0.17	0.26	0.01	**7.28**	1.45
	Ordered	0.32	0.27	−0.42	−0.20	−0.31	**0.51**
	probit	0.19	0.97	1.35	0.65	1.32	**1.89**
WASH	PSM	**−0.46**	0.17	0.10	**−0.63**	−0.11	**−0.59**
		2.57	0.87	1.16	**5.37**	1.15	**8.45**
	Ordered	**−0.22**	0.45	0.47	**−0.90**	0.30	**−0.73**
	probit	**1.68**	1.56	1.19	**4.01**	1.08	**2.63**
Governance	Ordered	**−0.27**	**0.31**	**0.39**	−0.12	−0.10	−0.02
	probit	**1.92**	**2.11**	**2.76**	1.16	0.80	0.11
Agri × gov	Ordered	−0.26	0.10	**0.66**	−0.06	0.03	0.13
	probit	1.61	0.45	**2.77**	0.40	0.17	0.77
Livestock × gov	Ordered	−0.14	0.32	**0.44**	−0.26	0.08	0.05
	probit	0.95	1.63	**2.02**	**1.90**	0.43	0.76
Credit × gov	Ordered	**−0.27**	0.11	**0.92**	0.05	0.23	**−0.21**
	probit	**2.13**	0.52	**2.88**	0.29	1.08	**1.97**
WASH × gov	Ordered	−0.06	0.15	**0.96**	**−0.35**	0.29	0.17
	probit	0.59	1.15	**3.88**	**2.30**	1.27	1.04

Note: The number next to each variable is the average treatment effect on the treated (ATET) in case of PSM regressions and a coefficient in case of the ordered probit regressions, the number below is the corresponding Z score. Results significant at least as the 90% level are in bold

lose their whole harvest in a flood. In one farmer's words: 'It was very bad that year. We lost almost the whole harvest. We had very little to eat the whole winter. My brother [who works in Delhi] sent us some money – I don't know how we would have managed otherwise.'

Other positive but less robust effects of the agricultural component have been reduction in participants' perception of food insecurity along with the frequency with which they suffer from diarrhoea and other illnesses. In interviews, beneficiaries described this effect as a result of consuming food of better quality and variety, which has contributed to their overall improved food security. Thus, the evidence suggests that the agricultural project component indeed bolstered food security via the mechanisms laid out in Figure 6.1.

The livestock project component appears to have improved the recipients' food-security index even more. The intervention has also augmented the number of meals participants consume per day, lowered the frequency with which they suffer from diseases and lessened their financial concerns about the future. The last effect, according to the interviews conducted, is related to the increase in the size of the recipients' herds thanks to GDS's help with livestock breeding and health care, confirming my earlier conjecture about livestock being seen by the villagers as a form of insurance. When asked, one farmer said: 'We have two cows now. We have more milk than before... I feel better because even if one cow dies, we'll still have the other one.' At the same time, as the farmer also indicated, owning more animals has enabled their owners to drink more milk and eat more butter, cheese (paneer) and meat than before, resulting in a greater number of daily meals and types of food consumed. My data hence confirm that the livestock intervention indeed bolstered food security via all four its components: by increasing food availability in the project communities, expanding recipients' access to food, improving their food utilisation through an augmented consumption of animal protein and, finally, enhancing their future food-security outlook thanks to domestic animals being perceived as insurance.

The credit part of the project performed the worst from the viewpoint of the recipients' food security. As Table 6.4 reveals, its effect on most outcome variables has been insignificant. Only one PSM result suggests that those with access to microcredit suffer less often from illnesses. However, an ordered probit result insinuates that the microloans heightened people's financial concerns. This finding can logically be attributed to people's fears that they will be unable to repay the loans. The four interviewed women who borrowed from the GDS-supported self-help groups all used the money to cover consumption rather than production costs (medical costs, weddings etc.) and the repayment of the loans has strained their already-tight household budgets. Nevertheless, people who have taken loans from the credit groups would have perhaps borrowed money even in their absence, from local money lenders, and thus it is not clear whether the negative effect discovered can fully be attributed to the GDS project's credit component. More straightforward is the conclusion that the credit intervention failed to bolster recipients' food security via the pathway displayed in Figure 6.3, as it did not significantly raise household incomes and thus did not translate into improved access to food.

The WASH project component has had a robust positive effect on people's food-insecurity index, comparable in size and consistency to the positive effect of the livestock component. It has also reduced the frequency of recipients' diarrhoea. This finding, as explained in interviews, is mainly thanks to the WASH beneficiaries gaining access to in-household toilets and to more knowledge about safe water- and food-handling practices, which contributes to lowering the occurrence of digestive health problems. One interviewee said:

> One of the greatest services which GDS has given us are the toilets. Earlier, there were lots of flies and insects. Kids used to get lots of diseases. Ladies had to clean all the places around the house. Kids used to run around the house with stained legs. Now that we have the toilet, things are better.

The WASH intervention thus contributed to better food utilisation. The other pathway to food security displayed in Figure 6.4, via higher future certainty, has also manifested itself, as demonstrated by the intervention's alleviation of recipients' financial concerns. This likely happened due to a realisation that improved sanitary standards would render household members healthier and hence less needy of emergency credit assistance.

The quality of local governance reinforced the positive effects of all four project components. This conditioning effect has been the strongest in the case of the credit intervention. Interviewed credit recipients suggested that communities with better local authorities (less corruption, more efficient) provided some support to those organised in microfinance self-help groups, ranging from arranging additional business training courses to providing locations where the groups could meet. Interviewees also highlighted the importance of governance in strengthening the impact of the WASH component, as the physical toilets themselves were supposed to be provided through the local government (with GDS only assuring their proper installation) and in some communities, their delivery was much more efficient than in others.

The effectiveness of the three different PDS ration cards is also compared (Table 6.5), even though they all constitute a form of direct transfer aid and hence their comparison does not add much to the assessment of my hypotheses. The results show that while holding an AAY card unequivocally helps people improve their food security, it is not so in the case of the other two cards, with the BPL card actually appearing harmful in its effect on several of the food-insecurity indicators examined. There are two reasons for the AAY's apparently larger impact. First, by design the AAY card confers more benefits on its holders, as they are entitled to buy wheat and rice at lower prices than BPL and APL holders. Second, according to some interviewees, when stocks of subsidised food are low, only AAY card holders are often allowed to purchase. One man said:

> The AAY card is better than the BPL. The rice and cereal are cheaper and the FPS often gives preference to the AAY [holders]. Me [BPL holder], they shoo away, saying they have nothing left. But I know they have some.

The BPL and APL cards are hence considered to be an inferior possession to the AAY cards, which explains why particularly the distribution of AAY cards is so income-regressive (Figure 6.6). Since the AAY cards render more significant positive effects, people with more money for bribes and better connections are more interested in obtaining them.

Unlike in Table 6.2, however, governance quality here appears to condition positively the impact of AAY and BPL cards on the number of food groups recipients consume per day. Information from interviews indicated that, in some better-governed communities, Fair Price Shops ran out of supplies less frequently and hence even BPL cards might have had a positive impact on recipients' food security.

Table 6.5 The heterogeneous impact of ration cards on food security

		Food insecurity	Meals per day	Foods per day	Diarrhoea	Illness	Financial concern
AAY	PSM	**−0.42**	**0.06**	**0.03**	−0.18	−0.13	**−0.22**
		3.24	**3.28**	**2.82**	1.76	**2.08**	**4.30**
	Ordered	**−0.16**	**0.27**	**0.32**	−0.45	**−0.27**	**−0.21**
	probit	**1.89**	**3.37**	**2.71**	1.75	**3.43**	**2.25**
BPL	PSM	0.63	0.13	−0.05	−0.54	**0.35**	**0.62**
		1.48	1.58	1.13	1.28	**2.05**	**3.80**
	Ordered	0.04	0.05	**−0.87**	−0.28	−0.23	**0.47**
	probit	0.16	0.55	**2.69**	1.43	0.98	**2.00**
APL	PSM	−0.08	−0.07	0.01	0.05	−0.16	−0.14
		0.21	1.20	1.05	0.20	1.51	1.56
	Ordered	0.16	−0.38	−0.04	0.08	**−0.52**	0.21
	probit	0.32	1.53	0.12	0.19	**1.90**	1.10
Governance	Ordered	**−0.15**	**0.23**	0.22	**−0.22**	0.03	**−0.18**
	probit	**1.90**	**2.21**	1.68	**3.24**	0.41	**2.09**
AAY × gov	Ordered	0.02	0.15	**0.50**	0.00	0.11	0.05
	probit	0.15	1.47	**3.19**	0.01	0.97	0.34
BPL × gov	Ordered probit	0.02	−0.03	**0.18**	−0.01	−0.04	0.01
		0.65	0.67	**3.30**	0.17	0.91	0.55
APL × gov	Ordered	0.00	−0.01	0.03	−0.02	−0.06	0.00
	probit	0.05	0.17	0.50	0.40	1.59	0.00

Note: The number next to each variable is the average treatment effect on the treated (ATET) in case of PSM regressions and a coefficient in case of the ordered probit regressions, the number below is the corresponding Z score. Results significant at least as the 90% level are in bold

In order to find out whether the positive effects of the different aid initiatives increase when more than one is implemented simultaneously, an impact evaluation of the compound effects of the different GDS and PDS components on household food-insecurity index was conducted. Table 6.6 shows that the livestock component in combination with WASH and with the agricultural initiative has the most sizeable effect on food security. Interestingly, the size of the impact is larger than the sum of the positive effects of the three individual components, highlighting the existence of synergy among the three interventions. One interviewee explained this finding:

> Through the agricultural intervention I started growing vegetables; the livestock component helped me buy a second cow. And I got the toilet. So now my kids eat more food, drink more milk and they are ill less often. And they are doing well. So yes, I think it is good to receive help from several sides.

Livestock help joined with WASH and AAY also has a positive influence on food security but not as large in size as the agricultural component combined with the

Table 6.6 The impact of two/three aid initiatives combined on recipients' food security

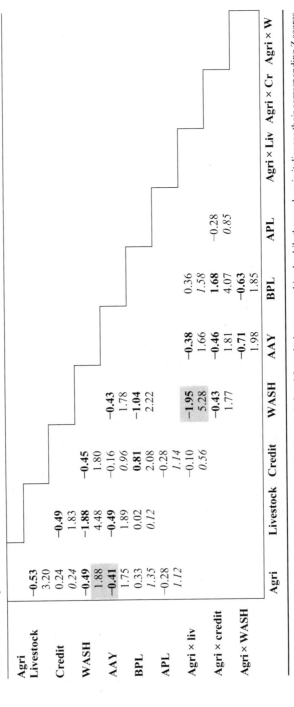

	Agri	Livestock	Credit	WASH	AAY	BPL	APL	Agri × Liv	Agri × Cr	Agri × W
Agri Livestock	**-0.53**									
	3.20									
Credit	0.24	**-0.49**								
	0.24	*1.83*								
WASH	**-0.49**	**-1.88**	**-0.45**							
	1.88	*4.48*	*1.80*							
AAY	**-0.41**	**-0.49**	-0.16	**-0.43**						
	1.75	*1.89*	*0.96*	*1.78*						
BPL	0.33	0.02	**0.81**	**-1.04**						
	1.35	*0.12*	*2.08*	*2.22*						
APL	-0.28		-0.28							
	1.12		*1.14*							
Agri × liv			-0.10	**-1.95**	**-0.38**	0.36				
			0.56	*5.28*	*1.66*	*1.58*				
Agri × credit				**-0.43**	**-0.46**	**1.68**	-0.28			
				1.77	*1.81*	*4.07*	*0.85*			
Agri × WASH					**-0.71**	**-0.63**				
					1.98	*1.85*				

Note: Numbers not in italics are the ATET of variables from the left and from the bottom combined, while the numbers in italics are their corresponding Z scores. Results significant at least at the 90% level are in bold livestock one and WASH, suggesting that those in receipt of productive help from GDS no longer rely to the same extent on subsidised food from the government. Since the effects were estimated using PSM only, the conditioning role of governance could not be assessed here.

Discussion of results and conclusion

Have NGO and government schemes improved food security in Uttar Pradesh?

This study, similar to the preceding ones, found that aid has a small but significant positive impact on recipients' food security, which is at least to some extent positively conditioned on the quality of governance, in this case of the local kind. This finding validates my first hypothesis (H1) once again and in combination with results from the previous chapter shows that not only the quality of governance at the national level, but also at the local levels matters in ensuring aid effectiveness. Accordingly, local authorities possess a notable ability to either enhance or hinder the impact of aid projects implemented within their jurisdictions.

Regarding heterogeneity of aid impact, this study confirmed several of my other initial hypotheses. Non-governmental aid was again found to be more effective than governmental aid, thanks to being faster, less bureaucratic and less corrupt (H2.2). Credit aid was significantly less effective than non-credit aid and positive at all only in communities deemed to be well governed locally (H3.2). Credit recipients elucidated the lack of effectiveness by pointing out that most people took out loans to cover consumption rather than production expenses and found it hard to subsequently repay them. They also pointed out that many people obtained loans from the self-help groups to repay other loans, from banks, microfinance institutions and money lenders, which often led them into a vicious cycle of over-indebtedness. The inconsistency in the availability of subsidised food rations (that is, aid volatility) was reported as one of the crucial problems undermining the effectiveness of the PDS (H6).

Vis-à-vis the effectiveness of different aid activities, agricultural aid – to crops and livestock – and social infrastructure aid (water, sanitation and hygiene activities) appeared to be most effective at boosting recipients food security, validating hypothesis eight (H8/H8a) in its original as well as amended form. Analysis of the initiatives' compound impact moreover suggested that receiving agricultural (crop and livestock) and social infrastructure aid at the same time has the most positive impact on food security. The positive effect of aid to crops and livestock appears to come primarily from the greater amount and variety of foods produced as a result. Some beneficiaries were also able to sell their surplus produce, improving their financial situation and, in turn, their ability to purchase more/different types of food if needed. The sanitation and hygiene project component bolstered recipients' food security primarily by improving the sanitary handling of food and water and consequently reducing the frequency of digestive illnesses.

The direct transfer aid supplied by the national government did not have a significantly positive impact overall but its most beneficial card, the AAY, was found to be, on its own, highly effective at reducing food insecurity.[14] The data available, however, did not allow me to examine whether this positive impact would hold also in the long run and, more importantly, the targeting of the initiative to the richer people in the communities surveyed suggested that many of the most food-insecure people were left out of the initiative.

The 'South Asian enigma'

This study certainly did not resolve the 'South Asian enigma', but hopefully contributed to its greater understanding. The term, coined by Ramalingaswami *et al.* (1997), refers to the fact that the rate of South Asian (and particularly Indian) child undernourishment is disproportionately high in view of the region's economic development. Bhagwati and Panagariya (2013) argued that the rates of child undernourishment were not actually higher in India than elsewhere, but that the international reference standards used were inapplicable to India – that Indian children were genetically shorter and lighter than children elsewhere. Nevertheless, a multi-reference growth study by the WHO (2009) showed that children living in affluent Indian neighbourhoods in New Delhi were not significantly different in their height or weight from their peers in the US or Norway. Alternative explanations for the enigma have focused on discrimination against girls and higher-order children within Indian households, with parents providing relatively more resources to boys and first-born children (Jayachandran and Pande, 2012), and on the negative effects of low hygiene, which might instigate undernourishment even among economically better-off households (Spears, 2013).

My study did not collect specific nutritional data and hence could not examine child undernourishment precisely. What the surveys and interviews carried out suggested, however, is that parents in general desired male offspring more than female and consequently invested less in girls, also in terms of their feeding. When asked who went hungry first within the household in the case of food scarcity, all survey respondents without exception responded that it was women and girls. Interviewees confirmed this view, admitting that men and boys were always fed with priority. These findings hence provide some support to the hypothesis that the high rates of child undernourishment in India might be at least partially driven by the intra-familiar discrimination of girls.

More of a contributing factor in my study, however, seems to be the lack of good hygiene and sanitary practices. Out of the 1,257 survey respondents, only 31 per cent had access to a toilet within household premises and out of the remaining 69 per cent, most practised open defecation. The results of both my quantitative and qualitative data analysis suggest that the WASH project component, focused on the installation of in-household toilets and provision of sanitary and nutritional education, significantly contributed to better food security among recipients and that this relationship was further strengthened by the presence of 'good' local governance. Hence, my case study supports conclusions by Spears (ibid.) and Haddad *et al.* (2014) that one of the best ways to tackle food insecurity and child undernourishment in India is by increasing investment in sanitation and hygiene programmes and raising awareness about the issues to achieve a greater involvement of both national and local governments. Moreover, it shows that even small-scale initiatives can have a meaningful positive effect on strengthening food security, implying that more well-designed pro-poor social and economic initiatives would likely reduce undernourishment and poverty faster than higher but less socially aware economic growth (as argued by Drèze and Sen, 2013, as opposed to Bhagwati and Panagariya, 2013).

However, as the failure of a large-scale toilet-construction project in Odisha to improve food security showed (Chapter 4, Box 4.3), the supportive services in the WASH interventions might be equally (if not more) important as the physical provision of toilets and, as with all development initiatives, this is not, single-handedly, a panacea to India's food insecurity (Clasen *et al.*, 2014). Rather, as results of the compound-effect analysis imply, strengthening food security via different pathways simultaneously is likely the most beneficial approach. The pledge of the current Indian Prime Minister Narendra Modi to build 600 million toilets by 2019 thus might not translate into as dramatic improvement in food security as some might envision (Pasricha, 2014).

Notes

1 Anaemia leads to increased morbidity from infectious diseases and in children also to impaired cognitive performance, motor development and lower scholastic achievement (IIPS, 2007).
2 In November 2013, the Government of India promulgated the National Food Security Act (NFSA). The main mechanism, through which the NFSA is to be implemented, is an expanded PDS. The implementation has begun only recently, however, and it is not yet clear what the impact of the law will be.
3 I adapted my survey's food-security module from the Young Lives' and the World Bank's Living Standard Measurement Studies surveys.
4 Dietary diversity, as measured by the number of food groups usually consumed, has been increasingly praised for its accuracy as a food-security indicator (e.g. Headey and Ecker, 2013).
5 Initially, I aimed to obtain weight and height measurements from household members as well, but due to logistical difficulties I had to eventually abandon the idea.
6 Particularly the municipal workers, the police and the judge (if any).
7 Income, however, is not used in matching due to its endogenous relationship with the project variables.
8 Permanent versus makeshift housing.
9 The average level for adults over 22 who are male in the whole sample is 5.1.
10 From the un-displayed control variables, the most significant were the ones capturing household wealth, namely the wealth index and whether a household lives in a permanent 'pucca' house. Female-headed households also appear to be more vulnerable to food insecurity than male-headed ones.
11 Fair Price Shops are where the PDS grains can be purchased.
12 In some states/communities, sugar and kerosene are also sold for subsidised prices at the FPS, but not in the villages surveyed.

13 This effort is related to the aadhaar scheme, which is an effort by the Indian government to afford each Indian citizen a unique biometric identifier, which could eventually be linked to social welfare schemes in order to reduce diversion, leakage and other types of corruption (e.g. Zelazny, 2012).

14 These findings align with those from a decade ago by Dev (2003).

References

Berg, B., and Lune, H. (2012). *Qualitative Research Methods*, 8th edn. London: Allyn and Bacon.

Bhagwati, J., and Panagariya, A. (2013). *Why Growth Matters: How Economic Growth in India Reduced Poverty and the Lessons for Other Developing Countries*. New York: Public Affairs.

Clasen, T., Boisson, S., Routray, P., Torondel, B., Bell, M., Cumming, O., Ensink, J., Freeman, M., Jenkins, M., Odagiri, M., Ray, S., Sinha, A., Suar, M., and Schmidt, W. P. (2014). 'Effectiveness of a rural sanitation programme on diarrhoea, soil-transmitted helminth infection, and child malnutrition in Odisha, India: a cluster-randomised trial', *The Lancet Global Health*, 2(11), pp. 645–53.

Collier, P. (2008). 'The politics of hunger: how illusion and greed fan the food crisis', *Foreign Affairs*, 87(6), pp. 67–79.

Dev, S. (2003). *Right to Food in India*. Hyderabad: Centre for Economic and Social Studies.

DFPD (2014). September. Available at: http://dfpd.nic.in/?q=node/999

Drèze, J., and Sen, A. (2013). *An Uncertain Glory: India and Its Contradictions*. Princeton, NJ: Princeton University Press.

Haddad, L., Nisbett, N., Barnett, I., and Valli, E. (2014). 'Maharashtra's child stunting declines: what is driving them? Findings of a multidisciplinary analysis', *IDS Working Paper*. Sussex: IDS.

Headey, D., and Ecker, O. (2013). 'Rethinking the measurement of food security: from first principles to best practice', *Food Security*, 5(3), pp. 327–43.

IIPS (2007). *National Family Health Survey (NFHS-3), 2005–06, India: Key Findings*. Mumbai: IIPS. Available at: http://dhsprogram.com/pubs/pdf/FRIND3/FRIND3-Vol1andVol2.pdf

Jayachandran, S., and Pande, R. (2012). The puzzle of high child malnutrition in South Asia. *Presentation Slides, International Growth Centre*. London: International Growth Centre.

Kaushal, N., and Muchomba, F. (2013). *How Consumer Price Subsidies Affect Nutrition* (No. w19404). New York: NBER.

Masiero, S. (2015). 'Redesigning the Indian food security system through e-governance: the case of Kerala', *World Development*, 67, pp. 126–37.

Oxenham, J. (2002). *Skills and Literacy Training for Better Livelihoods: A Review of Approaches and Experiences*. Washington, DC: The World Bank Group.

Pasricha, A. (2014). 'On World Toilet Day, India focuses on pledge to build toilets for all', *Voice of America*, 19 November. Available at: http://www.voanews.com/content/on-world-toilet-day-india-focuses-on-pledge-to-build-toilets-for-all/2526262.html

Ramalingaswami, V., Jonsson, U., and Rohde, J. (1997). 'Malnutrition: a South Asian enigma', in *Malnutrition in South Asia: A Regional Profile*. Kathmandu: UNICEF.

Spears, D. (2013). 'The nutritional value of toilets: how much international variation in child height can sanitation explain?', *RICE Working Paper*. Delhi: Research Institute for Compassionate Economics.

WHO (2009). *WHO Child Growth Standards and the Identification of Severe and Acute Malnutrition in Infants and Children*. Available at: http://apps.who.int/iris/bitstream/10665/44129/1/9789241598163_eng.pdf

WHO (2014). *Global Database on Child Growth and Malnutrition*. Available at: http://www.who.int/nutgrowthdb/database/countries/en

Zelazny, F. (2012). *The Evolution of India's UID Program*. New York: Center for Global Development.

7 Does *who* gives aid *where* and *how* affect food security?

This last chapter initially summarises the main findings, which emerged in the course of the previous empirical chapters. Second, it mentions the limitations of my research and how they could be remedied in the future. Third, it briefly considers some issues that are important either within the field of food security or development aid but have not been addressed thus far. Fourth, on the basis of conclusions drawn in the three preceding sections, the chapter discusses the relevance of its discoveries for the 'real world' and offers some concrete policy recommendations.

Summary of overall findings

The overarching theme of this book has been the question whether development aid strengthens the food security of recipients. Existing literature has examined this relationship very scarcely; yet, given that food insecurity remains an ongoing global problem and that development aid is an important tool used to address existing global inequality, the question deserves more attention than it has received thus far. In order to render the answer in as nuanced a way as possible, in addition to considering the general impact of aid on food security the book examined the heterogeneous effects of different types of aid and the conditioning role of governance. Moreover, it investigated the query on two different levels – country (macro) and household/individual (micro) – and utilised a variety of quantitative and qualitative methods of analysis, in order to strengthen the validity of results.

The impact of aid in general

All four empirical studies in this book found aid to have a small but mostly significant and positive impact on food security. At first sight, this finding may seem tautological. After all, development aid is provided to poor countries with the official aim to stimulate development and hence discovering that it, indeed, strengthens a key development indicator, food security, can seem anything but surprising. Nevertheless, many authors and organisations dispute that development aid has any positive effect on countries' development, partially due to its political nature and partially due to the lack of knowledge vis-à-vis the truly helpful interventions. From this perspective then, my finding carries some importance and, given the number of different studies and methods utilised to reach it, it would be hard to discredit its validity.

On the macro level, the quantitative cross-country study indicated that doubling the amount of aid per GDP would reduce undernourishment prevalence by around 1 percentage point and the rate of underweight and stunted children by 0.5 to 3 percentage points (Chapter 3). The qualitative four-country case study suggested that aid bolstered food security in Ethiopia and Vietnam but could not conclusively draw a similar link in India and Peru (Chapter 4). The second finding does not annul the first but expands on it, as it was expected that the positive effect of aid varies by country as well as by the time period examined. In addition, it highlights the greater importance of aid to food security in countries with higher proportion of budgets constituted by aid. Also, importantly, the impact of aid on food security did not appear to be significantly negative in any country examined.

On the one hand, at the micro level, the quantitative four-country household study found aid projects to reduce the prevalence of child undernourishment among recipient families by an average of 10 percentage points in three of the four countries examined – in Peru, Ethiopia and Vietnam (Chapter 5). Looking at other food-security indicators than nutritional status, the field study in Uttar Pradesh concluded that the aid project analysed lowered recipients' feelings of food insecurity and the frequency with which they suffered from diarrhoea, and increased the number of meals and types of food groups consumed. The government food-security scheme, on the other hand, had no significant impact overall (Chapter 6).

In view of the 'macro–micro paradox' of aid effectiveness (Mosley, 1986), I expected to find aid in the country studies less significant than in the household ones. However, my results have provided very limited support for this hypothesis when looking at aid in general. Whereas the four-country case study could not conclude that between 1990 and 2010 aid strengthened food security in Peru as a whole, aid projects within that period seem to have done so at the household level (Chapter 6). Authors have cited various possible reasons for such discrepancies, including data inaccuracies and biases, aid fungibility, aid-induced institutional deterioration and aid's high transaction costs (ibid.). Nevertheless, in my particular case the problem seems to lie primarily[1] in the small size of aid flows relative to the size of Peruvian economy, which made the detection of a significant national impact very difficult. The finding that such an impact *is* notable on the household level suggests that even in Peru aid can still improve the lives of the poor and the marginalised.

However, when looking at the different indicators used to measure food insecurity, the macro results have appeared to be actually more consistent in their significance than the micro ones, where aid was often found to improve only one or two of the several indicators considered. The most likely explanation is that the country-level studies examined the effect of aid on food security over two decades, while the micro studies only looked at one or two years in that time frame. Since the effects of aid on food security, as on many other development indicators, are cumulative, more significant effects would likely be uncovered if the household-level data were gathered annually, as the country data were. The second explanation might be related to rising global inequality. While development aid strengthens food security in developing countries in general, the positive effects may sometimes accrue in greater degree to the richer sections of the population than to the poorer ones, examined in the micro-level studies, which could also contribute to rendering the micro-level results less consistently significant than the macro ones (e.g. Pathak and Singh, 2011).

The conditioning role of governance on the effect of aid in general

All four empirical studies found the quality of governance to reinforce the effect of aid on food security. The intensity of the conditioning effect varied, based on the type of aid, but even when looking at the impact of aid in general, the quality of governance seems important. Results from the quantitative cross-country study suggest that an increase in the quality of national governance as measured by the worldwide governance indicators (WGI) by one point on the scale of five bolsters the positive impact of aid on food security by an average of 10 per cent (Chapter 3). Moreover, disaggregation of the index into its six separate components intimated that particularly political stability and the absence of violence, regulatory quality and control of corruption are crucial to aid effectiveness. The following country case studies provided anecdotal support for the importance of political stability, along with relatively low corruption in programme/project implementation and the ability of national governments to cooperate with donors in the design of poverty-reduction strategies, in strengthening the positive effect of aid on food security.

The two micro-level studies furthermore demonstrated that lower-than-national levels of governance matter in aid effectiveness as well. Chapter 5 considered the influence of community-level institutional quality, as rated by community leaders, on aid's effect on household food security and discovered a positive conditioning impact with regard to several food-security indicators examined. Chapter 6 scrutinised the role of village-level governance and found a positive link, with the underlying explanation that villages with better local authorities and institutions had better operating public programmes and were more willing, as well as capable of supporting the implementation of assistance initiatives. These findings provide unprecedented empirical support to the rising voices within the policy world that call for paying more attention to the role that local government structures play in aid effectiveness, as evidenced by allusions to their importance by the Accra Agenda for Action (OECD, 2008) and the Busan Partnership for Effective Development Cooperation (OECD, 2011).

The impact of different aid types

This book uses a simple aid classification: according to *who* provides and/or implements aid, *how* aid is provided and *where* it is provided. As Figure 1.2 showed graphically, aid according to *who* provides it was divided into multilateral and bilateral,[2] with bilateral divided further into DAC and non-DAC aid, and according to *who* implements it into governmental and non-governmental aid. The second dimension, of *how* aid is provided, looked at the different effects of concessional loans versus grants – or, on the micro level, of credit versus non-credit aid, of budget support versus programme and project aid, of aid channelled through public–private partnerships versus otherwise, of food versus financial aid and of varying degrees of aid volatility. Finally, the dimension of *where* aid goes classified aid first into long term, short term and humanitarian (following Clemens *et al.*, 2004) and second into agricultural, social, economic and 'other' aid (in the macro studies represented primarily by aid to tourism, finance and transport; in the micro studies constituted by direct transfers of cash or food).

Who *provides aid*

On the basis of theoretical considerations and existing findings, I expected multi-lateral aid to be more supportive of food security on the country level than bilateral aid and, within that, DAC aid to be more effective than non-DAC aid. Looking to the implementing side of aid provision, NGOs were foreseen to be more successful than governmental agencies. Aid provided by donors bilaterally as compared to aid from multinational organisations has largely been portrayed as more political and burdened with economic strings attached, which can dampen its ability to achieve desired development objectives. In a similar vein, NGOs are generally seen as more effective and efficient than government organisations thanks to lower administrative costs, greater operational efficiency and fewer opportunities for corruption; therefore, it could be anticipated that NGO-implemented aid projects would strengthen food security more than those implemented by government agencies.

My research found some support for both hypotheses. Multilateral aid indeed appears to strengthen food security more than bilateral aid but the difference is small. DAC aid was also found to be somewhat more beneficial for food security than non-DAC aid, although in reality the difference may be larger (or smaller) given the paucity of publicly available data on non-DAC aid flows. However, bilateral aid appears to be significantly more conditioned on the quality of governance than multilateral aid. This finding can likely be ascribed to its more political nature (Chapters 3 and 4).

Looking at *who* implements aid programmes and projects, NGO-executed projects were found to bolster household food security more consistently than government-run ones (Chapters 5 and 6). The difference was particularly notable in the Indian field study, where I compared a multi-component NGO project with a government-operated food-transfer scheme, and found the latter to be riddled with corruption at all stages of implementation and, as a result, largely ineffective. The quality of local governance was found to play a positive reinforcing role in both NGO- and GO-implemented aid, however, since local authorities can facilitate or hinder the work of private institutions as well, through cooperation or non-cooperation.

How *aid is provided*

Findings with regard to whether the aid provided needs to be repaid have been one of the strongest and most consistent throughout the four different studies in this book. My original expectation was that loan/credit aid would appear to have a less positive effect on food security than grant/non-credit aid, but that the former would be more susceptible to the influence of governance. The results have confirmed this hypothesis. In country-level studies, loans had a less consistently positive impact than grants but were more positively reinforced by good governance. In household-level studies, credit aid had no or even negative effect on food security, but, again, its influence was positively conditioned on governance. We can thus conclude that concessional loans constitute the right tool for strengthening food security only in countries with above-average quality of institutions. Furthermore, microcredit projects should apparently not be used as a primary means of combating food insecurity and, in order to have a positive development impact at all, should only be utilised in communities with local governance structures willing to engage constructively with the interventions. Qualitative information from the Indian field study also showed that credit used for productive purposes could achieve more beneficial outcomes than credit utilised for consumption – a finding repeatedly restated in existing literature on microfinance (e.g. Imai and Azam, 2012).

The budget support – programme/project aid division could only be explored at the macro level, due to the nature of budget support, which is provided as a sum of money to the recipient government to be used for whatever development purpose it sees fit.[3] I hypothesised that programme/project aid would be more effective at bolstering food security than budget support unless used in countries with above-average quality of governance. My findings confirmed that hypothesis only partially. They did not reveal, in fact, budget support to have a statistically different effect on food security indicators from programme and project aid on its own. This result can be seen as encouraging or discouraging, depending on one's point of view, as it suggests that the effects of budget support on food security are not statistically different from those of programme and project aid.

However, they did show budget support to be influenced more strongly by the quality of governance, which is logical given that this aid modality leaves more room for the recipient government to decide how the aid is to be used. In the absence of appropriate institutions and corruption controls, the money provided to the government may never reach the recipients intended. With this view in mind, it was sad to discover in the four-country qualitative case study that Ethiopia, a country with a very poor governance record, received more aid in budget support than any of the other three countries examined. The most likely explanation is political: Ethiopia is currently an important Western ally in the 'War on Terror' in the Horn of Africa, which has granted the Ethiopian government an important advantage in negotiations with donors (e.g. Hackenesch, 2013). That is probably also why, despite well-publicised findings of serious human-rights abuses against its own people, Ethiopia continues to receive ever growing amounts of aid (e.g. HRW, 2012; Oakland Institute, 2013).

The popularity of aid channelled through public–private partnerships (PPPs) has increased in recent decades but still remains proportionally miniscule when compared to aid channelled through more conventional routes (Chapter 3 and 4). Discovering whether it has a more or less positive effect than other aid or whether it is more or less conditioned on the quality of governance has been consequently difficult. The cross-country analysis suggested that aid channelled through PPPs may actually worsen recipients' food security, although that finding was not very robust. The four countries studied in greater detailed have thus far received little aid through PPPs – and none in the projects examined on the household level – even though it has been suggested by some researchers that partnering with private actors in agriculture could bring in more finance into Ethiopia (Chapters 4 and 5).

Results on the heterogeneous impacts of commodity (food) aid and non-commodity aid were, in contrast, quite consistent with my hypotheses. At first sight, food aid could seem the most natural method of improving food security – after all, what fills people's stomachs if not food? Nevertheless, controversy abounds in literature regarding the side-effects that food shipments might have on recipient countries/ localities, not least the pricing out of local producers and reductions in domestic agricultural production in the long run. My initial hypothesis was that non-food aid would be more directly supportive of food security than food aid, except for cases of famine or other emergencies. Indeed, both the macro and micro studies found food aid to be less effective at strengthening food security than financial aid. The qualitative case study also suggested that agricultural production in Ethiopia, one of the countries that currently receive the highest amount of food-aid shipments in the world, suffers from the continuous influx of free food and the country has consequently remained reliant on food aid even in non-drought years (Chapter 5). Further, it discovered some, originally not expected, evidence that food aid may be more conditioned on the quality of governance than financial aid. This was evident particularly in the Indian field study, where leakages, diversion and national- and local-level corruption rendered its national food-transfer scheme, the Public Distribution System, quite ineffective (Chapter 6, also Kaushal and Muchomba, 2013).

Finally, aid volatility turned out to have a negative effect on food security just as was expected. The country-level studies confirmed the hypothesis, first, quantitatively and, then, suggested that the effect was particularly bad in Vietnam, where a swarm of donors was continuously entering and exiting the aid market (Chapters 3 and 4). However, the deleterious impact of aid volatility on Vietnam's food security was becoming ameliorated as governance improved. Nevertheless, the results from Chapter 5 suggested that Vietnamese people were still worried by the unpredictability of aid even if its physical effects were no longer significantly notable.

Where *aid goes*

Based on the existing literature and my own theoretical considerations vis-à-vis *where* aid goes, short-term and agricultural aid were expected to be most effective at boosting food security. Clemens *et al.* (2004), who were the first to use the classification of aid into humanitarian, short term and long term, found only short-term aid to have a discernibly positive impact on growth. However, in this research only long-term aid has consistently appeared to strengthen food security. Results on the heterogeneous effects of aid to various sectors elucidated why. In the quantitative cross-country study, social infrastructure aid had the most significant positive impact on food security while agricultural aid had, surprisingly, no significant effect (Chapter 3). Since social infrastructure aid falls fully under long-term aid and agricultural aid mostly under short-term aid, this finding explains why long-term aid appeared more beneficial to food security than short-term aid. Moreover, the finding led me to modify the hypothesis vis-à-vis the effects of aid to various sectors to include social infrastructure aid alongside agricultural aid as the kinds that strengthen food security the most.

The following studies confirmed both the original and the modified hypothesis. The four-country case study again suggested that social-infrastructure aid, particularly to public health, nutritional education and water and sanitation, was one of the most helpful to food security but also showed that agricultural aid could be equally helpful if combined with better quality of certain types of governance (primarily political stability and control of corruption) and with effective pro-poor policies, as was the case in Vietnam (Chapter 4). In India, conversely, much of agricultural aid was diverted to larger farmers, without ever reaching the poorest and most marginalised, and, as a result, its impact on national-level food security was not notable. The household-level studies illustrated this point further, showing that, when provided to the poorest farmers, agricultural aid indeed had a strong positive effect on food security (Chapter 5). The specifics of the project matter as well, however; for example, the Indian field study demonstrated how encouraging an overt reliance on higher-yielding hybrid crops at the expense of traditional crop varieties and multi-cropping could, in the case of floods, contribute to greater harvest losses and consequently deepen food insecurity (Chapter 6).

The household-level studies also showed that social infrastructure aid – to water, sanitation, health and education – had a positive and often very cost-effective impact on recipients' food security, but that its evidence took longer to become apparent than the evidence of agricultural or other short-term aid (Chapter 5; Petrikova, 2014). Finally, analysis of data from the field study in India (Chapter 6) confirmed that combining agricultural interventions with social infrastructure ones was very helpful to achieving food security – more beneficial, in fact, than the sum of the interventions' effects on their own. Accordingly, this study adds its voice to findings by IYCN (2011) and Walingo (2006), who highlighted the importance of multi-component projects in achieving sustainable development outcomes among participants.

With regard to the conditioning role of governance, on the country level, on the one hand, it appears to matter most in ensuring the effectiveness of agricultural aid (Chapter 3) – likely because, without proper institutions and policies in place, it can easily be siphoned off by corrupt channels or directed to middle-class farmers, who are generally not the most food insecure. This happened during India's

'Green Revolution', which consequently failed to significantly reduce poverty in rural areas, and continues to occur in India's procurement arm of the PDS (Chapter 6). On the other hand, the household-level studies, particularly the Indian field study, showed that the quality of governance matters in aid to all sectors, particularly if implementation of that aid type relies on cooperative action from national or local authorities (Chapter 6). If aid does not rely on such cooperation, in the short term it can affect food security positively even in the presence of low-quality governance; nevertheless, the long-term sustainability and effects of such development projects on countries' institutions and development are questionable, as discussed in more detail further in this chapter.

Macro–micro paradox within different aid modalities

When comparing the effects of the different aid modalities on the macro with those on the micro level, one type of aid stands out because of the discrepancy – agricultural aid. In the cross-country quantitative study, aid to agriculture did not appear to significantly strengthen countries' food security; the household-level studies, in contrast, found agricultural aid to be highly supportive of recipients' food security. One explanation, for which this study offers some evidence, is that agricultural aid to countries may fail to achieve its desired results in the absence of pro-poor policies in place, as appears to have been the case in India and to some extent also in Ethiopia as opposed to Vietnam. The fact that the quantitative cross-country study found agricultural aid to be highly conditioned on the quality of governance further corroborates this conjecture. Undoubtedly other factors underlying the macro–micro paradox may come into play here as well – for example, the non-aggregation of positive micro results to a positive macro result due to aid fungibility. Regardless, however, the results highlight the need to carefully consider the type of aid suitable for strengthening countries' food security and considering other types of aid, particularly aid to social sectors, as potentially more useful in some cases than agricultural aid (Demeke *et al.*, 2014).

Recapitulation of hypotheses

The four preceding empirical studies tested, modified and tested again the nine hypotheses, which I formulated on the basis of theoretical deliberations and existing empirical findings in Chapter 1. Figure 7.1 summarises my findings on the different questions graphically and displays clearly which hypotheses were validated and which were not. In fact, the table shows that none of the original hypotheses were refuted in full; however, hypotheses 2.1, 4, 5, 6, 7, 8 and 9, as the preceding discussion also illuminated, were expanded or confirmed only partially.

Research limitations

The research presented in this book has several limitations: among the most significant are the choice of case-study countries, the amount of data analysis carried out,

			Impact on food security		Validating hypotheses
	Actual effects		*Levels*		
			Macro	**Micro**	
	Aid in general		↑ G	↑ G	**H1** √
***Who* gives/ implements aid?**	Multilateral agencies		↑	–	**H2.1** √?
	Bilateral donors	DAC	↑ G	–	
		Non-DAC	? G	–	
	Governmental organisations (GOs)		–	↑ G	**H2.2** √
	Non-governmental organisations (NGOs)		–	↑ G	
***How* is aid disbursed?**	Concessional loans/credit aid		↑ G	↑ G	**H3.1** √, **H3.2** √
	Grants/non-credit aid		↑ G	↑ G	
	General budget support		? G	–	**H4** √?
	Programme aid		↑ G	–	
	Project aid		↑ G	–	
	Public–private partnerships		??	–	**H5** √?
	Other aid		↑ G	–	
	Commodity/food aid		↑ G	↑ G	**H6** √?
	Financial aid		↑ G	↑ G	
	Aid volatility		↓ G	↓ G	**H7** √?
***Where* does aid go?**	Humanitarian aid		? G	↑ G	**H8** √?
	Short-term aid		? G	↑ G	
	Long-term aid		↑ G	↑ G	
	Agriculture		? G	↑ G	**H9** √?
	Social infrastructure		↑ G	↑ G	
	Economic infrastructure		? G	? G	
	Other sectors/direct transfers		?	↑ G	

Note: ↑ positive effect, ↓ negative effect, ? mixed effect, – no effect; • most, •less, •least; G conditioned on governance

Figure 7.1 Graphic summary of the discovered effects of different types of aid on food security.

choosing breadth over depth and, finally, leaving out of the discussion some important issues. First, the choice of the four countries to be examined, as discussed in Chapters 2 and 4, was driven by the availability of appropriate household-level data on food security and development aid. This introduced a slight bias into the study, complicating the generalisability of results.[4]

To turn to the second main limitation, the quantitative sections of the book contain the results of more than 500 regressions, amounting to at least 5,000 data points.

With addition of the results of the qualitative studies, this constitutes a great amount of research information generated by one person – hence, it is statistically unlikely that all of it is correct. The desire to remain removed from the research matter has also likely not fully prevented my personal opinions and preferences influencing my findings. In awareness of this possibility, a number of robustness tests were carried out in each study, separately as well as overall, with each subsequent chapter to some extent testing the results from the previous one.

Third, the book has often chosen breadth over depth. This is particularly evident in Chapter 4, where a whole book could have been devoted to each country's history of aid receipts, food security and their various links. The choice of breadth over depth stems from the research questions posed initially, which endeavoured to provide a comprehensive, even if reasonably nuanced, answer to whether and how aid could strengthen recipients' food security. In view of the to-date unexplored nature of the question, I still believe that my approach was warranted, but now it leaves room for further research to explore the various findings and propositions, which emerged throughout the book's studies, in more depth.

Some issues with regard to development aid and food security deserve to be mentioned even in a largely technical study as this one, however, to which the next section is devoted. In particular, the section discusses the negative effects of food waste, climate change, water scarcity and conflict on food security in developing countries, and ponders whether aid can play a positive role in resolving these issues as well. Then it discusses the view of food security as a human-rights issue, its application in practice and its connection with aid. Finally, it touches on the possibly imperialistic and de-politicising nature of aid and, by extension, on the question whether aid should be provided at all.

Issues not discussed

Development finance other than aid

One important issue that this book has not discussed in detail is the effect of development finance other than aid on food security. In the past few decades, the importance of development aid as a mechanism of development finance has proportionally declined while other mechanisms – particularly foreign direct investment (FDI) and remittances – have gained in prominence. By 2010, remittances constituted a flow approximately equal in amount to aid, whereas FDI was three times higher (WDI, 2016). Are these new mechanisms in a better position to address food insecurity in developing countries?

Remittances, as discussed in Chapter 1, have, theoretically, good potential to do so as they are sent directly to households. Among recipients, they have been shown to bolster at least some aspects of food security (Chapter 3; as well as Abadi *et al.*, 2013; United Nations Somalia, 2013; Regmi *et al.*, 2014). However, these have not always translated into long-term nutritional improvements; they have reached proportionally more urban and well-off households than poorer and rural ones, and because most households receive remittances from just one person, they have remained a relatively unstable source of income (ibid.).

Thus far, FDI has been analysed only rarely for its effect on food security. Similar to aid, FDI constitutes a highly diverse flow of funds and, hence, its impact likely varies by its modality. Mihalache-O'Keef and Li (2011) examined the different effects of FDI for primary sectors, manufacturing and services, and found that only FDI to manufacturing strengthened recipient countries' food security. FDI to primary sectors (e.g. agriculture) was actually discovered to reduce food security, which is not surprising in view of the preliminary estimates by Davis *et al.* (2014) that the recent increase in agricultural FDI in developing countries (i.e. 'land grabs') has thus far led to the loss of livelihoods – and consequently weakened food security – among approximately 12 million people.

Food waste

Another important subject related to food security, but not yet addressed, has been the issue of food waste. As pointed out in the Introduction, global food production exceeds global food consumption, yet a large number of people lack access to sufficient food – much of the extra food is wasted. The amount of food waste is estimated to constitute between 30 and 40 per cent of overall production (Godfray *et al.*, 2010). Developed and developing countries do not differ significantly in this regard but the reasons underlying their waste are different. In developed countries, most food losses occur at the retail and post-retail stages. Due to stringent use-by dates, a lot of food sold in stores ends up in landfill. For the same reason, consumers throw away large amounts of the food they buy (Tielens and Candel, 2014). In contrast, most food losses in developing countries take place prior to the retail stage, due to post-harvest losses and deficient storage technologies. For example, in Vietnam 25 per cent and in India 40 per cent of fresh produce are lost because retail outlets lack refrigeration (Parfitt *et al.*, 2010).

Would food security be strengthened if food waste were reduced? Research suggests that the answer is positive, but primarily with regard to reducing food waste in food-insecure countries, especially among small-holding farmers (Tielens and Candel, 2014). Their reduction in post-harvest losses can translate directly into improved household food security. The link between reduction in food prices driven by lower global food waste and greater access to food among the food insecure is also possible, but more tenuous. Even if not strengthening food security directly, however, the reduction of food waste and thus a more efficient use of natural resources in food production would translate into a lower environmental and climate impact of food production, which – as the next section discusses in more detail – would be beneficial for global food security in the long run. Cutting the global food waste by half would also reduce the need to increase global food production by 2050 by 22 per cent (ibid.).

In theory, aid can contribute to bolstering food security by helping to reduce food losses. The FAO has undertaken many such initiatives, most notably the

Action Programme for the Prevention of Food Loss, in which the FAO implemented more than 250 projects aimed at reducing post-harvest losses in developing countries (FAO, 2011). As the FAO itself cautions, however, food-waste reduction projects can be expensive and thus may increase the price of food production and, in turn, weaken food security in the short run.

Climate change

Climate change has been mentioned already, but only briefly, as one of several important control variables that affect food security. However, since climate change has risen in recent years to the top of global concerns and the great magnitude of its potential negative impact on global food security has become ever clearer, no discussion of food security can be complete without discussing the issue in more detail.

To date, researchers have routinely assessed, primarily, the effects of climate change on food availability. While they do not agree on the precise estimations, they concur that the impact is likely to be negative overall (e.g. Funk and Brown, 2009; Lobell *et al.*, 2008; Schmidhuber and Tubiello, 2007). The effects will vary significantly for different regions, however, with Central Asia and Russia expected to be the greatest net beneficiaries thanks to rising temperatures in regions currently too cold for agriculture. In contrast, sub-Saharan Africa and South Asia, which already suffer from food insecurity the most, are predicted to be the greatest net losers in food production as a result of climate change-induced decrease in rainfall and increase in temperatures (ibid.).

The negative effect of declining food availability on global food security is going to be further compounded by the negative effects of climate change on the stability aspect of food security, due to greater climate and food-price volatility, as well as on the utilisation aspect, due to an anticipated increase in the occurrence of water-borne and tropical infectious diseases (Schmidhuber and Tubiello, 2007). The impact of climate change on people's access to food is harder to estimate, but it is not likely to be positive.

Can aid play a positive role in ameliorating the destructive effects of climate change and thus strengthen food security in developing countries? It has certainly tried to achieve the first goal. Hicks *et al.* (2008), in their book *Greening Aid?*, showed that between the 1970s and 2000s donors increased the amount of aid aimed at improving the environment, with the largest relative increase in aid targeted at efforts to curb climate change and to improve water supply. In 2000, 'environmental' aid constituted, according to the authors, approximately 10 per cent of all aid provided globally. However, little if any research has measured whether this type of aid has had any actually positive impact on the environment.

Related to the second goal, even if aid could ameliorate climate change and hence contribute to better food security in developing countries in the longer run, in the short run 'environmental' or 'green' aid can have perhaps unintended but certainly negative side-effects on people's food security (Davies, 1992). For example, helping to enforce stricter regulation on deforestation through aid projects that enclose certain parts of the forest can perhaps reduce the emission of greenhouse gases through the preservation of a larger forest cover, but, at the same time, it may exacerbate food insecurity among those who rely on forests for their livelihoods. Dercon (2012) extends this idea to 'green' economic efforts more generally, arguing that 'green' growth and pro-poor growth are not necessarily synonymous and that the poor should not be made to pay the price for greening the planet.

Water scarcity

Related to climate change and environmental damage more generally, water scarcity has been rising on the food-security agenda as another major impeding factor. Water is a key element in agricultural production and hence its shortage can adversely impact food production and, in turn, food availability and access to food. Deterioration in the quality of water used can undermine the food-utilisation aspect of food security.

Global demand for water has tripled since the 1950s whereas the supply of fresh water has decreased (Gleick, 2003). Consequently, by 2025 more than 3 billion people are predicted to live in water-stressed or water-scarce countries (Molden *et al.*, 2010). By 2050, demand for water by 9 billion people is expected to surpass the available supply by 3,300 km^3/year (Hanjra and Qureshi, 2010). Agriculture, as the largest user of water in the world – accounting for 70 to 90 per cent of global water consumption (FAO, 2008; Molden *et al.*, 2010) – is the first sector likely to lose out under these conditions, eclipsing global food production and fuelling food insecurity. The challenges of water scarcity will be further amplified in this regard by the rising cost of developing new water resources, irrigation-induced land degradation and groundwater depletion (Hanjra and Qureshi, 2010). Rising water pollution will, in turn, drive up the incidence of water-borne and diarrhoeal diseases, negatively affecting food utilisation, particularly among the poorest and most marginalised social groups (Prüss *et al.*, 2002; Tilman *et al.*, 2002). Ensuing tensions over the use of water can also lead to conflicts, both national and international (Giordano *et al.*, 2005).

Could aid help with water scarcity? As my study showed, well-implemented aid initiatives in water and sanitation can enhance the quality of drinking water and sanitation and thus improve recipients' food security via the food-utilisation route. From this perspective it is encouraging, then, that amount of aid disbursed for development programmes and projects in water and sanitation quadrupled between 2003 and 2013 (CRS, 2015). Development aid could, theoretically, help increase also the efficiency of water usage, by, for example, redirecting farmers from flood to drip or spray irrigation. In the past, however, the trend has been the opposite, with aid financing large hydrological and irrigation projects, which have encouraged unsustainable water management. More importantly, aid cannot create new water sources nor speed up the refill of depleted water aquifers; instead, people need to learn to live within the physical constraints of the planet Earth more modestly and/or efficiently.

Genetically modified organisms (GMOs)

Some researchers see GMOs as one potential tool to reduce the ecological footprint of agriculture in the face of climate change and water scarcity while simultaneously increasing production (Buiatti et al., 2013). Imbuing seeds with better genetic traits is argued to improve their yield, hence facilitating greater food availability. If the imbued traits are pest- or weed-resistance, the modified crops would consequently need also less chemical treatment, which could ameliorate the negative impact of agricultural production on the environment (James, 2010). However, opponents of GMO cultivation raise concerns about the possibility of the transferred genes escaping the crops and cross-pollinating surrounding vegetation. Regarding food security specifically, they argue that GMO cultivation favours large farmers and brings profit primarily to the multinational companies who designed the modified seeds (e.g. Monsanto, Syngenta) while driving small farmers, effectively, out of the market and threatening their food security (Altieri and Rosset, 1999).

The debate on GMOs is very heated and even research published in top scientific journals has been accused of subjectively taking sides in the argument (Buiatti et al., 2013). For this reason, development aid has generally steered clear of the issue, with the exception of food aid. In a controversial move, the United States provided genetically modified food aid to sub-Saharan African countries, arguably in order to enlarge the market for its biotech food production (Zerbe, 2004). Hence, whether GMOs are a mechanism through which aid can strengthen food security in developing countries remains unresolved, but existing evidence certainly points to the need to be cautious not to marginalise in production the very same food-insecure people whom aid is trying to help the most.

Conflict

Like climate change and water scarcity, conflicts can and do have a negative effect on countries' and people's food security; as with climate change, although the country-level studies briefly discussed the role of conflict in food security, they did not analyse it in detail. Yet, the harm that conflicts inflict on global food security can be dramatic. At the time of writing (August 2014), the World Food Programme was providing food aid to eight global hunger hotspots – Iraq, Syria, South Sudan, Central African Republic, Cameroon, West Africa and Somalia – all of which could be directly or indirectly connected to ongoing or past conflicts in the regions.

The primary pathway through which conflicts exacerbate food insecurity is the use of food as a weapon (Cohen and Pinstrup-Andersen, 1999). Armed sides in conflicts often aim to subjugate each other through starvation, which they hope to impose through the destruction of agricultural production. That is achieved by a variety of methods, ranging from physically destroying crops to preventing local populations from cultivating fields to blocking the entry of food imports to the affected areas. Even if not coerced, however, rural populations often flee conflict-ridden areas and agricultural production inevitably falls (Seddon and Adhikari, 2003). The resulting state of escalating food shortages and hunger can then, in turn, further fuel the conflicts (Barnett and Adger, 2007; Cohen and Pinstrup-Andersen, 1999).

From aid, primarily food aid is frequently deployed to conflict situations to preclude starvation but accessing the most vulnerable and food insecure is often highly problematic as the armed sides frequently discover ways to siphon it off for themselves and those whom they wish to reward. However, if aid does manage to reach its intended targets, it can serve if not as a boost to long-term security at least to ward off acute malnutrition and unnecessary depletion of populations' asset base. Moreover, aid can also play a valuable role in reconstruction efforts, including the recovery of agricultural production and other measures that would strengthen food security in the long run. Of course, some donors play a role in the instigation of the conflicts in the first place; however, that issue usually is too complex to be given justice by discussing it only briefly here.

Rural–urban divide

Food insecurity has traditionally been portrayed as a predominantly rural issue. However, in 2008, when for the first time more than half the world's population lived in cities, this divide began to change (Lerner and Eakin, 2011). Even before that, most research concluded that the determinants of food security were very similar in both locations, with income and maternal education the most important strengthening factors (Garrett and Ruel, 1999; Smith *et al.*, 2005). In urban areas, these were traditionally much higher than in rural areas. Nevertheless, with urbanisation rates increasing dramatically in developing countries at the end of the twentieth and beginning of twenty-first century, driven not by pull factors from cities but rather by push factors from rural areas, differences in income and maternal education, as well as public-health conditions, between rural and urban areas became generally less pronounced (Fotso, 2007). Consequently, the rates of undernourishment in rural versus urban areas became more balanced and the rates of stunting among the poorest quintiles of population in rural and urban areas equalised (Menon *et al.*, 2000). Similarly, countries' urbanisation rates and urban areas appeared significant in reducing some food-insecurity measures in my study, but only marginally (Chapters 3 and 5).

Gender

As with climate change, conflict and urbanisation rates, gender plays a crucial role in food security. Women in the developing world have been predominantly those responsible for preparing food and, in many countries, also for obtaining it, whether through own cultivation or purchase (Quisumbing *et al.*, 1995). However, they have traditionally faced many constraints in doing so, ranging from weak land rights and limited access to common resources through a lack of equipment and technology and limited contact with agricultural extension to lower education as compared to men and a lack of access to credit (ibid.). Simultaneously, women constitute the population group that tends to be the most calorically and nutritionally deprived, as many traditional cultures dictate that women eat last, after men and children, despite their greater nutritional requirements during pregnancy and breastfeeding (Van Esterik, 1999). This discrimination begins at birth, with male infants often breastfed longer than female ones and fed more nutritious food (Quisumbing *et al.*, 1995).

I did not find evidence for this practice in my household-level study, with mothers reporting to have breastfed girl and boy infants for approximately the same amount of time in Peru, Ethiopia and India, as well as in Vietnam (Young Lives data). Girls were not found to suffer from greater rates of undernourishment than boys either; in fact, the opposite appeared to be true in India and in Vietnam, where boys were significantly more stunted and underweight than girls (Chapter 5). Nevertheless, the studies also suggested that this initial difference might reverse in older age, with girls and women attaining significantly lower levels of education than boys and men and reporting that they are always the last to eat in Indian households (Chapters 5 and 6).

Aid donors, particularly those grouped in the DAC, have committed to 'mainstreaming' gender in their aid programmes and projects, meaning that they would strive to promote gender equality in all their aid activities. As a result, and recognising that women spend a significantly larger share of their incomes on feeding and clothing children than men, for example, microcredit programmes all over the world have targeted predominantly female borrowers. In some instances, microfinance may have thus had a positive impact on female empowerment (MacIsaac and Branch, 1997). Nevertheless, discrimination against women is deeply ingrained in most societies and attempting to combat it through aid is often problematic. For example, Rao (2006) explains how in India better women's land rights, a goal promoted by many donors, failed to strengthen women's food security. Instead, the new land legislation led to the devaluation of agriculture as a livelihood strategy: men began to perceive it more as women's work and, as a result, women's work burden increased without much change in their status or decision-making authority. Similarly, DFID's deference to cultural rights in Muslim countries, where it is customary, for example, that women are not allowed to walk alone after dark, might be further reinforcing gender inequity (Elliott, 2010).

Human rights

This point brings me to the question of human rights and their connection with food security. The human-rights issue does not constitute another element affecting food security like climate change, conflict or gender, but rather a different lens through which one can view food (in)security. In human-rights language, food security is referred to as a 'right to food'. Even though the two concepts are defined in a similar fashion (Khoo, 2010), the crucial difference lies in the perception of the 'right to food' not merely as a means to achieve food security, but also as a wider objective, part and parcel of human dignity (Mechlem, 2004).

Both international and national laws have enshrined this right. Article 25 of the Universal Declaration of Human Rights states that 'everyone has the right to a standard of living adequate for the health and well-being of [one]self and [one's] family, including food'. Article 11 of the International Covenant on Economic, Social and Cultural Rights (ICESCR) is more specific with regard to the right's guarantor, recognising the fundamental right of everyone to be free from hunger that should be ensured either through national institutions and policies or through international cooperation. These international rights are often not enforceable on the national level; however, 20 developing countries, including Peru, Ethiopia and India, also mention the right to food in their constitutions. Even so, legal recourses to ensure that one's right to food is guaranteed are generally unavailable, with the notable exception of India.

In 2013, the Indian Parliament passed the National Food Security Act (NFSA), also called the Right to Food Act, which promises to provide 5 kg of grains (wheat, rice, or coarse grains) at very low prices to 50 per cent of the poorest urban and 75 per cent of the poorest rural families every month. Thanks to this bill, the right to food is 'legally justiciable'; that is, people have the theoretical possibility to seek accountability and remedies if their right to food is violated (Khoo, 2010). However, thus far not much has changed since the passing of the act – the extra grains are supposed to be distributed through the Public Distribution System, discussed herein at various points, which has, throughout its history, been shown to be highly corrupt and quite inefficient. Moreover, the BJP government that took power in 2014 to date has not raised the portion of the budget assigned to the PDS, hence effectively preventing a full implementation of the NFSA. Even if it were realised in full, however, it would still not guarantee beneficiaries food security due to the caloric insufficiency of 5 kg of grains per month, the nutritional insufficiency of the foods included (only grains), the non-consideration of health and hygiene aspects of food security and many other reasons. That is not to condemn the human-rights approach to food security in general, nor India's effort to legalise it more specifically, but to point to the importance of the quality of institutions even in this area.

Can aid play any role either in directly ensuring the right to food of people in developing countries or indirectly in encouraging developing countries to ensure it for their citizens? In relation to the first point, as was examined and shown in this book, the international community has not guaranteed the food security of people in developing countries, but it has, at least, strengthened it. However, it has generally not portrayed its actions as acts of obligation or duty but rather as acts of charity, which is quite contrary to the view of food security as every person's inalienable human right that can be enforceable through the international community, as stated by the ICESCR. In relation to the second point, donors sometimes try to encourage their development partners to fulfil their citizens' human rights as well. However, such behaviour has often been criticised by academics from both developed and developing countries, which brings me to the next point.

The imperialist and de-politicising nature of aid

Research on the effects of aid on human-rights NGOs and other civil-society actors in developing countries often found the impact to be negative. Henderson (2002) used a Russian case study to examine to what degree Western countries could 'purchase' civic engagement and participation, and concluded that aid actually obstructed collective action towards building a vibrant civil society by encouraging domestic NGOs to focus on the short-term goal of obtaining international funding at the expense of the long-term goals of development. In a parallel fashion, Bano (2008) investigated the behaviour of NGOs in Pakistan and found that receipts of aid were positively correlated with the material aspirations of NGO leaders, which undermined their performance and led to a decline in overall NGO membership. Berkovitch and Gordon (2008) darkened this picture further, positing that donors formulated support for human-rights NGOs under the influence of the aid-receiving states, as a result of which NGOs obtained funding only for activities that were not in opposition to their states' plans. As an illustration, they argued that under the current global neo-liberal regime, most states and, in turn, most donors were prone to prefer the advocacy of civil and political rights rather than economic and social rights. The absence of such critique can then be interpreted as the lack of any wrong in that dimension (of social and economic rights), which serves to both legitimise neo-liberal regimes and to strengthen the states. This is particularly concerning for the promotion of the right to food, which falls squarely under the realm of economic and social human rights.

In addition to being used to silence domestic human-rights NGOs through the provision of funding, aid has been described as imperialist and de-politicising also because it has offered piecemeal solutions to social problems in developing countries that might have diverted attention from more systemic solutions. Petras (1997), discussing the behaviour of NGOs in Latin America in the 1980s and 1990s, accused the organisations of complicity with the dictatorial regimes in the region for not denouncing the support rendered to the regimes by the US and European countries and for organising 'soup kitchens' to help victims of the dictatorships' austerity policies instead of criticising the policies in the first place. Harrigan (2011) described donors as propping up repressive autocratic regimes in Northern Africa, including Mubarak's regime in Egypt and Ben Ali's regime in Tunisia. In line with these and similar criticisms, some researchers have depicted all foreign aid as designed to 'fragment, subjugate, silence, or erase the local' while hiding the political through 'technical discourse that naturalises poverty, objectifies the poor, and depoliticises development' (Ferguson, 1994; also Easterly, 2014; Escobar, 2000; Mosse, 2004). If these claims are true, should aid not stop being provided altogether?

Ferguson (1994) appears to believe in such a solution, arguing that the agencies that plan and implement development projects are not social actors likely to truly advance the empowerment of the poor and, consequently, the best form of action for Western people wishing to bring about change in developing countries is to participate politically in their own countries to combat their imperialist policies (p. 181). However, that is not a pragmatic proposition. As Riddell (2014) realistically points out, foreign aid is simply not going to disappear anytime soon.

> The political and moral drivers that have created and preserve the official aid system and the compassion and sense of injustice which drives individuals to support NGO and CSO projects and programmes means that aid as a form of 'helping' will be with us for… many decades to come. (p. 17)

The correct question then is not *whether* aid should be provided – it clearly will be – but *how* can its provision be improved?

Recommendations and conclusion

Recommendations

My largely technical analysis of the aid–food security relationships can contribute to answering this question. My first main conclusion – that aid has a small positive effect on recipients' food security – in light of the discussion above, cannot be translated into a practical recommendation. As previously suggested, aid will be provided regardless of whether researchers conclude that its overall effects are positive or negative. It can, however, at least assuage our conscience to know that this aid might, as a side-effect, also bolster recipients' food security, at least in the relatively short term. However, since this book has not used simulation studies to analyse how countries' food security would be affected if aid were to be significantly scaled up, it cannot make any suggestions in that regard.[5]

The second main conclusion, that aid is conditioned on 'good governance' in its positive effect on food security, can give rise to more substantial recommendations. This book has treated the quality of governance as largely exogenous to aid, but that depiction has simplified reality, given that aid influences governance both directly and indirectly. Aside from the already mentioned inadvertent and often negative effects that aid can have on recipients' governance structures (e.g. Knack, 2001; Prasad *et al.*, 2007; Abouharb and Cingranelli, 2006), aid engages with recipient governance also purposefully. This engagement usually takes the form of political conditionality or positive support (Uvin, 2004).

Political conditionality involves full or partial suspension of aid in case of 'bad governance', in hopes of fomenting the improvement of governance quality, and has mostly turned out to be ineffective (Morrissey, 2004; Uvin, 2004). 'Positive support' involves the provision of aid specifically in support of strengthening institutions and improving governance quality. Generally, it has been considered superior to conditionality and increasingly utilised by donors as it fits both with the emerging development–security nexus and with the renewed interest of the development community in recipients' politics and policies (Carothers and de Gramont, 2013; QWIDS, 2015). Surprisingly little analysis on the effectiveness of 'positive support' aid has been conducted thus far; however, the existing evidence has been rather disappointing (e.g. Carothers and Barndt, 1999; Uvin, 2004). This is, perhaps, not surprising since the building of quality institutions is a non-linear, unpredictable and hard-to-replicate process and it is rare for donors to possess sufficient knowledge, expertise and long-term commitment to be able to positively contribute to (let alone instigate) such a process (Uvin, 2004, p. 96).

Returning, then, to the formulation of policy recommendations on the basis of this book's findings vis-à-vis aid in general and governance, since the empirical studies did not find a dramatic difference between aid effectiveness in countries with better and with worse governance quality, and countries/localities with worse governance are simultaneously those most adversely affected by food insecurity, political conditionality should be used sparsely and preferably only with aid modalities that are most susceptible to the quality of governance in their effects on food security. Aid specifically directed at building better institutions and formulating better policies should be provided only by donors with deep knowledge of the local context and willingness to build on what is already there, rather than from scratch (Grindle, 2004). Finally, a recommendation regarding the quality of local governance quality can also be extended here: that is for donors to engage more with community- and village-level government institutions, as they can often tip the scales of project results towards success.

Turning to the possibility of selective conditioning, particularly bilateral aid, concessional loans and credit aid, budget support and food aid appeared to be influenced in their impact on food security by the quality of governance. With regard to concessional loans and budget support, the appropriate recommendation seems to be that donors provide these types of aid in greater amount only to countries with institutions that are able to shoulder the burdens of interest rates and can successfully design and implement national poverty-reduction strategies. In countries with lower quality of institutions, grants and programme and project aid appear to be better instruments of strengthening food security, despite their potentially subversive side-effects on recipients' administrative capacities and fiscal discipline. Looking at aid provision at the household level, in the disbursement of credit aid the quality of local governance and the planned use of the credit (whether for production or for consumption) should be seriously taken into account, since credit aid provided under the wrong conditions not only does not strengthen recipients' food security, but actually might undermine it.

Bilateral and food aid bolster food security more in the presence of better governance as well, but formulating recommendations on the basis of such findings is more complicated. First, bilateral aid is conditioned on governance more than multilateral aid because it is provided for more political reasons than compassionate ones. However, advising countries to stop providing aid for political reasons is naturally not realistic; political considerations are often the main reason underpinning the choice of development-aid recipients. Second, in relation with food aid, even though this type of aid works better in countries and localities with better governance, it is often provided in emergency situations where concerns about the quality of governance cannot supersede the need to quickly intervene. The finding can, however, serve to encourage donors to keep the quality of governance in mind when providing food aid and to try to overcome institutional deficiencies (corruption, nepotism, violence) to reach those in most need of assistance. However, the case of Ethiopia, which has become essentially 'addicted' to food aid at the expense of developing its agricultural sector, should serve as a cautionary tale against using food aid for too long or outside emergency situations.

From the perspective of *where* aid should go, my findings suggest that donors aiming to strengthen food security should focus on providing primarily agricultural and social infrastructure aid, with a few qualifications, however. Agricultural aid is also heavily influenced in its impact on food security by countries' quality of governance and hence, when disbursing it to countries deficient in that regard, donors should do their best to ensure that the aid manages to reach the most marginalised sections of society that are generally the most food insecure. In order to do so, the aid should either support the adoption of innovative low-cost solutions rather than practices requiring pricy inputs that only larger farmers can afford (as happened during India's 'Green Revolution', for example) or, alternatively, should ensure the support of the government for enabling access to such inputs also to small farmers through universal or targeted subsidies (for evaluations of such programmes in Sierra Leone, see, e.g., Spenser, 2012).

Social-infrastructure aid is not susceptible to the quality of governance to the same extent as agricultural aid and particularly its public-health, water-and-sanitation and nutritional-education components appear to be very beneficial to food security. The caveat here has more to do with the timing of the aid. As a study related to this book showed (Petrikova, 2014), the positive effects of social-infrastructure aid become evident later than the effects of agricultural aid and hence examining the impact of this type of aid too early could fail to notice the positive results. Nevertheless, the positive effects of social-infrastructure aid also appear to be often long-lasting and hence more sustainable. Combining that with their relatively low costs, social-infrastructure initiatives such as the construction of toilets or safe-water access points and provision of hygiene and nutritional education can constitute a very cost-effective manner of bolstering food security. Additionally, their positive effect is compounded further when implemented in combination with agricultural initiatives (Chapter 6).

The final two findings that could give rise to policy recommendations are that NGO-implemented projects have a stronger positive effect on food security than projects implemented by governmental agencies and that aid volatility is harmful to food security. Accordingly, NGOs – despite their many shortcomings – should be preferred to governmental agencies in the implementation of projects aimed at improving food security because they are, on average, less corrupt and more cost-effective in implementation and, in turn, more likely to instil real benefits through their work. Countries and households would also likely be more food secure if aid were planned on a longer-term basis so that they could better prepare for the future. Improving aid predictability belongs among donors' chief commitments in the Paris Declaration on Aid Effectiveness (2005) and hence one can hope that the corresponding recommendation to decrease aid volatility will also materialise.

In view of the other issues discussed in this chapter as influential in the aid–food security relationship – other types of development finance, climate change, water scarcity, GMOs, conflict, rural–urban divide, gender, human rights, de-politicising nature of aid – in order to improve the effect of aid on food security, donors should keep the issues in mind in both the design and implementation of all their projects, programmes and other aid initiatives. Many DAC donors are already committed to respecting these issues verbally, but the execution of the commitments in reality is often lacking.

Directions for further research

As mentioned in the limitations section, this study often chose breadth over depth and hence many of the issues examined here could be explored deeper. The links between different types of aid and food security in individual countries could be investigated further using more primary data obtained through surveys and interviews with key informants. The complexities of the aid–governance–food security relationship could be traced in more detail through larger and longer field studies. The classification of aid into different types could be taken a step further as well, by comparing, for example, the effectiveness of grants and loans to social infrastructure or bilateral versus multilateral budget support.

Other issues – less directly related to the topics of aid, food security and governance, yet still interesting – that emerged in this study and were not explored sufficiently include, among others, the following questions. Why are countries with larger populations more food secure than countries with smaller populations, *ceteris paribus*? Why is the rate of premature births in Peru so much higher than the global average? Why are Vietnamese people more disturbed by the unpredictable nature of aid than people in Peru, India and Ethiopia? Why do Indian people report to be much more food secure than objective data indicate? Why are Indian and Vietnamese boys more often stunted and underweight than girls? Has the pattern of nutritional discrimination against girls now reversed?

Notes

1 That is not to claim that aid to Peru certainly does not undermine institutional quality or the private sector – but as aid constitutes a progressively smaller portion of Peru's budget and these results are particularly notable in highly aid-dependent countries, it is increasingly unlikely.
2 I considered including here also private aid, but so far insufficient data on this aid flow are available.
3 This is naturally a simplified portrayal – in reality, many donors put various restrictions/requirements on how budget support can or should be used.
4 Generalising results from small-N case studies is fraught with difficulties regardless of case selection strategy, however.
5 Issues such as countries' absorptive capacity of aid would also have to be considered.

References

Abadi, N., Techane, A., Tesfay, G., Maxwel, D., and Vaitla, B. (2013). *The Impact of Remittances on Household Food Security: A Micro Perspective from Tigray, Ethiopia.* Available at: https://editorialexpress.com/cgi-bin/conference/download.cgi?db_name=CSAE2014&paper_id=258

Abouharb, M., and Cingranelli, D. (2006). 'The human rights effects of World Bank structural adjustment, 1981–2000', *International Studies Quarterly*, 50(2), pp. 233–62.

Altieri, M., and Rosset, P. (1999). 'Ten reasons why biotechnology will not help the developing world', *AgBioForum*, 2(3–4), pp. 155–62.

Bano, M. (2008). 'Dangerous correlations: aid's impact on NGOs' performance and ability to mobilize members in Pakistan', *World Development*, 36(11), pp. 2297–313.

Barnett, J., and Adger, W. (2007). 'Climate change, human security, and violent conflict', *Political Geography*, 26(6), pp. 639–55.

Berkovitch, N., and Gordon, N. (2008). 'The political economy of transnational regimes: the case of human rights', *International Studies Quarterly*, 52(4), pp. 881–904.

Buiatti, M., Christou, P., and Pastore, G. (2013). 'The application of GMOs in agriculture and in food production for a better nutrition: two different scientific points of view', *Genes and Nutrition*, 8(3), pp. 255–70.

Carothers, T., and Barndt, W. (1999). 'Civil society', *Foreign Policy*, 117, pp. 18–29.

Carothers, T., and De Gramont, D. (2013). *Development Aid Confronts Politics: The Almost Revolution.* Washington, DC: Carnegie Endowment for International Peace.

Clemens, M., Radelet, S., and Bhavnani, R. (2004). 'Counting chickens when they hatch: the short-term effect of aid on growth', *Center for Global Development Working Paper*, 44. New York: Center for Global Development.

Cohen, M. J., and Pinstrup-Andersen, P. (1999). 'Food security and conflict', *Social Research*, 66(1), pp. 375–416.

CRS (2015). Available at: https://stats.oecd.org/Index.aspx?DataSetCode=CRS1

Davies, S. (1992). 'Green conditionality and food security: winners and losers from the greening of aid', *Journal of International Development*, 4(2), pp. 151–65.

Davis, K., D'Odorico, P., and Rulli, M. (2014). 'Land grabbing: a preliminary quantification of economic impacts on rural livelihoods', *Population and Environment*, 36(2), pp. 180–92.

Demeke, M., Spinelli, A., Croce, S., Pernechele, V., Stefanelli, E., Jafari, A., Pangrazio, G., Carrasco, G., Lanos, B., and Roux, C. (2014). *Food and Agriculture Policy Decisions: Trends, Emerging Issues and Policy Alignments since the 2007/08 Food Security Crisis.* Rome: FAO.

Dercon, S. (2012). 'Is green growth good for the poor?', *World Bank Policy Research Working Paper*, 6231. Washington, DC: The World Bank Group.

Easterly, W. (2014). *The Tyranny of Experts.* New York: Basic Civitas.

Elliott, C. (2010). 'Power, knowledge, and technology: scratching over confused and entangled parchments using NVivo', *SPP Seminar Paper*. London: UCL.

Escobar, A. (2000). 'Beyond the search for a paradigm? Post-development and beyond', *Development*, 43(4), pp. 11–14.

Ferguson, J. (1994). *The Anti-Politics Machine: Development, De-politicisation, and Bureaucratic Power in Lesotho.* Minneapolis: University of Minnesota Press.

FAO (2008). *Coping with Water Scarcity: An Action Framework for Agriculture and Food Security.* Rome: FAO.

FAO (2011). *Global Food Losses and Food Waste.* Rome: FAO.

Fotso, J. (2007). 'Urban–rural differentials in child malnutrition: trends and socioeconomic correlates in sub-Saharan Africa', *Health and Place*, 13(1), pp. 205–23.

Funk, C. C., and Brown, M. E. (2009). 'Declining global per capita agricultural production and warming oceans threaten food security', *Food Security*, 1(3), pp. 271–89.

Garrett, J., and Ruel, M. (1999). 'Are determinants of rural and urban food security and nutritional status different? Some insights from Mozambique', *World Development*, 27(11), pp. 1955–75.

Giordano, M., Giordano, M., and Wolf, A. (2005). 'International resource conflict and mitigation', *Journal of Peace Research*, 42(1), pp. 47–65.

Gleick, P. (2003). 'Global freshwater resources: soft-path solutions for the 21st century', *Science*, 302(28), pp. 1524–8.

Godfray, H., Beddington, J., Crute, I., Haddad, L., Lawrence, D., Muir, J., Pretty, J., Robinson, S., Thomas, S., and Toulmin, C. (2010). 'Food security: the challenge of feeding 9 billion people', *Science*, 327(5967), pp. 812–18.

Grindle, M. (2004). 'Good enough governance: poverty reduction and reform in developing countries', *Governance*, 17(4), pp. 525–48.

Hackenesch, C. (2013). 'Aid donor meets strategic partner? The European Union's and China's relations with Ethiopia', *Journal of Current Chinese Affairs*, 42(1), pp. 7–36.

Hanjra, M., and Qureshi, M. (2010). 'Global water crisis and future food security in an era of climate change', *Food Policy*, 35(5), pp. 365–77.

Harrigan, J. (2011). 'The political economy of aid flows to North Africa', *World Institute for Development Economics Research Working Paper*, 72.

Henderson, S. (2002). 'Selling civil society western aid and the nongovernmental organization sector in Russia', *Comparative Political Studies*, 35(2), pp. 139–67.

Hicks, R., Parks, B., Roberts, J., and Tierney, M. (2008). *Greening Aid? Understanding the Environmental Impact of Development Assistance*. Oxford: Oxford University Press.

HRW (2012). *'Waiting Here for Death': Displacement and 'Villagisation' in Ethiopia's Gambella Region*. Available at: http://www.hrw.org/sites/default/files/reports/ethiopia0112webwcover_0.pdf

Imai, K. S. and Azam, M. S. (2012). 'Does microfinance reduce poverty in Bangladesh? New evidence from household panel data', *Journal of Development Studies*, 48(5), pp. 633–53.

Imai, K., Gaiha, R., and Kang, W. (2011). 'Poverty, inequality and ethnic minorities in Vietnam', *International Review of Applied Economics*, 25(3), pp. 249–82.

IYCN (2011). *Nutrition and Food Security Impacts of Agriculture Projects*. Washington, DC: IYCN.

James, C. (2010). 'A global overview of biotech (GM) crops: adoption, impact and future prospects', *GM Crops*, 1(1), pp. 8–12.

Kaushal, N., and Muchomba, F. (2013). *How Consumer Price Subsidies Affect Nutrition*. New York: National Bureau of Economic Research.

Khoo, S. (2010). 'The right to food: legal, political, and human implications for a food security agenda', *Trocaire Development Review*, pp. 33–50.

Knack, S. (2001). 'Trust, associational life, and economic performance', *MPRA Working Paper*, 27247. University Library of Munich, Germany.

Lerner, A., and Eakin, H. (2011). 'An obsolete dichotomy? Rethinking the rural–urban interface in terms of food security and production in the global south', *The Geographical Journal*, 177(4), pp. 311–20.

Lobell, D., Burke, M., Tebaldi, C., Mastrandrea, M., Falcon, W., and Naylor, R. (2008). 'Prioritizing climate change adaptation needs for food security in 2030', *Science*, 319(5863), pp. 607–10.

MacIsaac, N., and Branch, A. (1997). 'The role of microcredit in poverty reduction and promoting gender equity', *CIDA Discussion Paper*. Ottawa: CIDA.

Mechlem, K. (2004). 'Food security and the right to food in the discourse of the United Nations', *European Law Journal*, 10(5), pp. 631–48.

Menon, P., Ruel, M., and Morris, S. (2000). 'Socio-economic differentials in child stunting are consistently larger in urban than in rural areas', *Food and Nutrition Bulletin*, 21(3), pp. 282–9.

Mihalache-O'Keef, A., and Li, Q. (2011). 'Modernisation vs dependency revisited: effects of foreign direct investment on food security in less developed countries', *International Studies Quarterly*, 55(1), pp. 71–93.

Molden, D., Oweis, T., Steduto, P., Bindraban, P., Hanjra, M., and Kijne, J. (2010). 'Improving agricultural water productivity: between optimism and caution', *Agricultural Water Management, Comprehensive Assessment of Water Management in Agriculture*, 97(4), pp. 528–35.

Morrissey, O. (2004). 'Conditionality and aid effectiveness re-evaluated', *World Economy*, 27(2), pp. 153–71.

Mosley, P. (1986). 'Aid-effectiveness: the micro-macro paradox', *IDS Bulletin*, 17(2), pp. 22–7.

Mosse, D. (2004). 'Is good policy unimplementable? Reflections on the ethnography of aid policy and practice', *Development and Change*, 35(4), pp. 639–71.

Oakland Institute (2013). *Development Aid to Ethiopia: Overlooking Violence, Marginalisation, and Political Repression*. Oakland, CA: Oakland Institute.

OECD (2008). *Accra Agenda for Action*. Paris: OECD.

OECD (2011). *Busan Partnership for Effective Development Cooperation*. Paris: OECD.

Parfitt, J., Barthel, M., and Macnaughton, S. (2010). 'Food waste within food supply chains: quantification and potential for change to 2050', *Philosophical Transactions of the Royal Society B: Biological Sciences*, 365(1554), pp. 3065–81.

Pathak, P., and Singh, A. (2011). 'Trends in malnutrition among children in India: growing inequalities across different economic groups', *Social Science and Medicine*, 73(4), pp. 576–85.

Petras, J. (1997). 'Imperialism and NGOs in Latin America', *Monthly Review*, 49(7), pp. 10–27.

Petrikova, I. (2014). 'The short- and long-term effects of development projects: evidence from Ethiopia', *Journal of International Development*, 26(8), pp. 1161–80.

Prasad, E., Rajan, R., and Subramanian, A. (2007). 'Foreign capital and economic growth', *National Bureau of Economic Research Paper*, 13619. New York: NBER.

Prüss, A., Kay, D., Fewtrell, L., and Bartram, J. (2002). 'Estimating the burden of disease from water, sanitation, and hygiene at a global level', *Environmental Health Perspectives*, 110(5), pp. 537–42.

Quisumbing, A., Brown, L., Feldstein, H., Haddad, L., and Peña, C. (1995). 'Women: the key to food security', *Food Policy Report*. Washington, DC: IFPRI.

QWIDS (2015). Available at: https://stats.oecd.org/qwids

Rao, N. (2006). 'Land rights, gender equality, and household food security: exploring the conceptual links in the case of India', *Food Policy*, 31(2), pp. 180–93.

Regmi, M., Paudel, K, and Williams, D. (2014). *Migration and Remittance and Their Impact on Food Security in Nepal*. Available at: https://www.researchgate.net/publication/261027749_Migration_and_Remittance_and_Their_Impacts_on_Food_Security_in_Nepal

Riddell, R. (2014). *Does Foreign Aid Really Work?* Keynote address to the Australasian Aid and International Development Workshop, Canberra, Australia. Available at: http://devpolicy.org/2014-Australasian-Aid-and-International-Development-Policy-Workshop/Roger-Riddell-Keynote-Address.pdf

Schmidhuber, J., and Tubiello, F. (2007). 'Global food security under climate change', *Proceedings of the National Academy of Sciences*, 104(50), pp. 19703–8.

Seddon, D., and Adhikari, J. (2003). 'Conflict and food security in Nepal: a preliminary analysis', *RN Report Series.* Kathmandu: Rural Reconstruction Nepal.

Smith, L. C., Ruel, M. T., and Ndiaye, A. (2005). 'Why is child malnutrition lower in urban than in rural areas? Evidence from 36 developing countries', *World Development*, 33(8), pp. 1285–305.

Spenser, D. (2012). 'Issues in food security and cash crop production in Sierra Leone', *Enterprise Development Services for the World Bank.* Available at: http://www.eds-sl.com/docs/IssuesInFoodSecurityInSierraLeone.pdf

Tielens, J., and Candel, J. (2014). *Reducing Food Wastage, Improving Food Security?* The Hague: Food and Business Knowledge Platform.

Tilman, D., Cassman, K., Matson, P., Naylor, R., and Polasky, S. (2002). 'Agricultural sustainability and intensive production practices', *Nature*, 418 (6898), pp. 671–7.

United Nations Somalia (2013). *Family Ties: Remittances and Livelihoods Support in Puntland and Somaliland.* Nairobi: UN.

Uvin, P. (2004). *Human Rights and Development.* Sterling, VA: Kumarian Press.

Van Esterik, P. (1999). 'Right to food; right to feed; right to be fed. The intersection of women's rights and the right to food', *Agriculture and Human Values*, 16(2), pp. 225–32.

Walingo, M. (2006). 'The role of education in agricultural projects for food security and poverty reduction in Kenya', *International Review of Education*, 52(3–4), pp. 287–304.

WDI (2016). Available at: http://data.worldbank.org/data-catalog/world-development-indicators

Zerbe, N. (2004). 'Feeding the famine? American food aid and the GMO debate in Southern Africa', *Food Policy*, 29(6), pp. 593–608.

Conclusion

Despite achievements in reducing hunger on the global scale, more than 800 million people in the world remain food insecure. Even mild food insecurity leads to a host of negative psychosocial consequences, including feelings of exclusion, powerlessness, desperation, fear, stress, disrupted household dynamics, deviant behaviour and revolts. More serious food insecurity can contribute to the depletion of economic bases, distress migration of masses, conflicts, famines and death. In view of climate change-induced rise in global temperatures and unpredictability of weather patterns, the unrelenting growth in human population and stagnating cereal yields, global food insecurity is almost certain to intensify in the following decades. While development aid constitutes a relatively small portion of global finance flows, with larger amounts exchanged in trade or investment, it still constitutes a financial flow called upon to help tackle food insecurity in developing countries as a means of redistributing global wealth. To date, however, very little research has examined the link between this flow and food security.

This book has contributed to filling this void: by examining if aid in general strengthens food security, whether this effect differs based on the type of aid provided, and if it is influenced by the quality of governance in the receiving country or locality. The book investigated this question through four related studies – a quantitative cross-country study of data intended to uncover global patterns of aid–food security relationships; a qualitative case study of Peru, Ethiopia, India and Vietnam; a quantitative household-level study from the same countries; and a mixed-method field study from northern India. Across the board, aid appeared to have a small but positive effect on food security, strengthened by both national and local good governance. However, the influence of governance was found to matter more in some aid modalities than others, specifically in bilateral aid, concessional loans, budget support, food aid, agricultural aid and microfinance aid.

Do these findings suggest that development aid is the right tool for strengthening food security in developing countries? Yes and no. Development aid has clearly many negative aspects, as the previous chapter discussed at some length. However, development aid, among others, will continue being provided due to donors' political and economic interests in developing countries (Riddel, 2014). Relying solely on their own financial resources would condemn the poorest developing countries to decades of deplorably low human development or alternatively to mortgaging their natural resources in dubious deals (Manning, 2012, p. 3). Aid thus constitutes a second-best solution that *can* become more effective at achieving some of its alleged development goals. It will never be capable of resolving food insecurity either globally or in individual countries on its own. However, with enough political and policy will, if provided more in line with the recommendations extended in this book, development aid could help strengthen food security in developing countries to a significantly greater extent than it has managed to do thus far.

References

Manning, R. (2012). 'Aid as a second-best solution: seven problems of effectiveness and how to tackle them', *WIDER Working Paper*, 24. Available at: https://www.econstor.eu/dspace/bitstream/10419/80994/1/688040675.pdf

Riddell, R. (2014). *Does Foreign Aid Really Work?* Keynote address to the Australasian Aid and International Development Workshop, Canberra, Australia. Available at: http://devpolicy.org/2014-Australasian-Aid-and-International-Development-Policy-Workshop/Roger-Riddell-Keynote-Address.pdf

Index

access to food 7, 15–17, 31–3, 87, 89, 155; *see also* food security, pillars
age 32, 126–30, 156, 159–60, 191
agricultural policies xv, 27, **30**, 32, 34, *82*; in Ethiopia 86–7; in India 88–9, in Vietnam 87–8
Arellano, M. 59–60
Arndt, C. 16, 48, 56

Barrett, C. 7, 10, 25
Berti, P. 13, 18, 27
Bond, S. 59–60
budget support *see* development aid
Burnside, C. 16, 19, 21, 35n10, 48

caste 33, 89, 130–1, **158**
cereal yield 32, 34, 56, 65, 103–4, 182, 189
changing diets xiii–xiv, 27
Chen, S. 28, 126
Cingranelli, D. 56, 194
Clasen, T. 111, 173
Clemens, M. 11, 14, 20, 26, 55, 59, 71, 75, 125, 179, 182
climate change xiv, 87, 187–8, 202
CO2 emissions xiv, 188
Cohen, M. J. 27, 32, 189–90
Collier, P. 18, 152
concessional loans *see* development aid
conflict 31, 33, 56, 59, 65, 105–6, 189–90
Creditor Reporting System (CRS) 47, 54–5, 82, 188

debt 22–3, 56, 80, 94, 110, 137, 145
Del Ninno, C. 25, 32
democracy 15, 100
depoliticising effect of aid 193–4
Devarajan, S. 24
development aid: agricultural 27–8, **57**, 71–3, 75–6, 109–10, 114–15, 139, 145,

152–3, 165–8, 171, 182–3; bilateral 21–2, **57**, 67–9, 74–5, 112–13, 179; as budget support 23–4, **57**, 69–11, 75, 113–14, 180–1; classification 11–13, 83, 125, 150–1; in concessional loans 22, **57**, 69–71, 75, 180; as credit aid 23, 137, 144–5, 153–4, 162–4, 171, 182–3; data 47–9, 55, 82, 113–14, 122, 125–6, 158–9; definition of 10–11; as direct-transfer 139, 145, 155–6, 165–8, 171–2, 182–3; economic 27–8, **57**, 71–3, 75–6, 114–15, 139, 145, 165–8, 171, 182–3; emergency 26–7, **57**, 71–3, 75–6, 114–15, 139, 142, 145, 171, 182–3; in food 25, **57**, 69–71, 107–9, 113–14, 139, 144–5, 181; global xv, 177; in grants 22, **57**, 69–71, 75, 113–14, 180; long-term 26–7, **57**, 71–3, 75–6, 114–15, 139, 142, 145; multilateral 21–2, **57**, 67–9, 74–5, 112–13, 179; NGO-implemented 135–7, 144, 162, 171, 179; politics of 32, 34, 107–8, 193–4, project-level 125–6, 133–5, 161–2, 171, 177; in Public-Private Partnerships (PPPs) 24, **57**, 69–71, 75, 113–14; recommendations 194–7; short-term 26–7, **57**, 71–3, 75–6, 114–15, 139, 142, 145, 171, 182–3; social-infrastructure 27–8, **57**, 71–3, 75–6, 111, 114–15, 139, 145, 154–5, 165–8, 171, 182–3; volatility of 25–6, **57**, 69–71, 75, 113–14, 164–5, 171, 181
development assistance *see* development aid
Devereux, S. 34, 87
dietary diversity 173n4
disasters 31, 33, 60, 76n6, 88, 105–6
Dollar, D. 16, 19, 21, 31, 35n10, 48
donors: Development Assistance Committee (DAC) 10–11, 21–2, 35n11,

67–8, 74–5, 91–2, 179; non-
Development Assistance Committee
(non-DAC) 10–11, 21–2, 67–9, 74–5,
91–2, 113, 179; private 10–11
Doucouliagos, H. 16
Dreher, A. 17, 22, 28, 59
Drèze, J. 20, 85, 89, 104, 111, 173
droughts 87, 100, 105, 108; *see also*
disasters and water scarcity

Easterly, W. 35n10, 193
education 32, 86, 105, 130–1, 159–60;
maternal 126, 135, 190; nutritional 17, 28
employment 8, 17, 33; in agriculture 88,
103–4
environmental factors xiii, 8, 30–3, 81–2,
105–7, 110; environmental aid 187–8
Ethiopia: agricultural aid to **95**, 96–8, 104,
108; child undernourishment **85**, 86–7,
108; development aid to 89–91, 96–8;
EPRDF 86, 97, 102, 108, 113; food
aid to 80, 86–7, **93**, 98, 104–5, 107–9,
114, 126; food security in 83–4, 86–7,
108; governance quality 100–2, 108,
113; relationship with donors 97; social
safety nets 98; 'villagisation' 104, 108

Fafchamps, M. 32
famine xiv, 25, 77n14, 87, 97, 107, 114
female-headed household 88, 126, 130,
159, 173n10
floods 94, 100, 105, 152, 165–6, 182;
see also disasters
food aid *see* development aid, in food
Food and Agriculture Organisation (FAO)
xiii-xiv, 32, 109, 186–7; statistics 47,
54, 56, 73, 82–3, *84*
food availability xiii-xiv, 7, 47, 87–9,
152–5, 157–8, 187, 189; *see also* food
security, pillars
food crisis xiii
food insecurity *see* food security
food prices 17–18, 31–3, 65, 98, 186
food production 25–6, 32, 56, 64–5, 82,
103–5, 186–7; *see also* food availability
food safety 8, **9**, 17
food security: causes of 8–10, *9*;
consequences of 10; definition 7–8;
global xiii-xiv, 202–3; index 122–4,
157; measurement 47–9, 54, 59, 82–3,
120, 122–5, 157; relationship with
aid in general 15–20, 53, 62, 73, *80,*
81–2, 107–12, 133–5, 142–4, 161–2,
171–2, 176–8; pillars 7–8, *9*, 15–18;

see also Ethiopia, India, Peru and
Vietnam
food transportation 8, 87, 107
food utilisation 8, 17, 87, 89, 125, 146, 153,
167–8; *see also* food security, pillars
food waste 186–7
foreign aid *see* development aid
Foreign Direct Investment (FDI) 31, 185–6
Frongillo, E. A. 16, 33

Gelan, A. 25, 98, 105, 108
gender 32–3, 86, 130, 151, 159–60, 172,
190–1
governance: definition 13–14, 100; 'good'
13–14; intervening effect of in aid
effectiveness 19–20, 178; importance
in effectiveness of aid in country-level
food security 62–4, 74–6, 110–15,
178–83; importance in effectiveness
of aid in household-level food security
135, 161–2, 171, 178–83; local 15,
121, 125–6, 133, 135, 144, 171; quality
measurement 14, 47–9, 55–6, 125–6,
158–9
green aid *see* environmental aid
'Green Revolution' 80, 99–100, 104,
109–10, 114, 183, 196
Grindle, M. S. 13, 195
Gross Domestic Product (GDP) xv; growth
8, 18–19, 31, 85–9, 102–3; per capita 8,
31, 64–5, 73, 85–9, 102–13

Haddad, L. 33–4, 173, 186, 190–1
health 27–8, 33–4, 55, 71, 87, 105,
155, 167, 192; public 7–8, 17, 89,
126, 131, 182
Hoque, B. 18, 28
Hudson, D. 13, 20, 47, 94
Human Development Index (HDI) 16
human rights 32, 191–2; in Ethiopia 104,
107, 181
Human Rights Watch (HRW) 107–8, 181
humanitarian aid *see* development aid,
emergency
hunger 7, 10, 189–90; as a weapon 31,
189–90; depth of 47, 54, 56, 73

impact evaluation: of projects 51, 131–3;
Propensity Score Matching (PSM) 51,
131–3, 156, 171
income: household 27, 31–3, 88, 130,
159–61, 190; rural-urban divide in 86
India: agricultural aid to **95**, 98–9, 104;
Andhra Pradesh 99, 124, 130–1, 145,

147; child undernourishment **85**, 89, 111, **123**, 124, 151; development aid to 89–91; food security in 83–4, 88–9, 111, 122–5, 151; governance quality 100–2, 111, 113–14, 126, 159, 173; hygiene and sanitation in 89, 111, 146, 172–3; National Food Security Act (NFSA) 173n2, 192; Public Distribution System (PDS) 150–1, 155–6, *160*, 161–2, 165, 168, 171, 173n2, 192; relationship with donors 98–9; Uttar Pradesh 149, 151–2, 165

inequality xv, 80, 82, 86, 88, 178

institutions *see* governance

International Food Policy Research Institute (IFPRI) 83, 85–9

International Fund for Agricultural Development (IFAD) 32, 86–9

Kaufmann, D. 14, 48, 55, 74

Knack, S. 16, 64, 74, 100, 194

Kraay, A. 14, 31, 48, 55, 74

land grabs xiv, xvin1, 15, 108, 186

Least Developed Countries (LDCs) 56, **58**, 65

Lensink, R. 16, 19, 26, 35n10, 146

macro-micro paradox 19, 46, 144, 177, 183

Maputo Declaration xv, 13

Masud, N. 16, 22

Maxwell, S. 7, 16, 33

methods *see* research methods

Michaelowa, K. 17, 59

migration 10, 202

minority 33, 80, 86, 88

Morrissey, O. 14, 16, 20, 26, 102, 146, 194

Mosley, P. 16, 19, 26, 144, 177

National Food Security Act (NFSA) *see* India

Nguyen Viet, C. 132

Nunnenhamp, P. 17, 22, 28, 59

Organisation for Economic Co-operation and Development (OECD) 10, 13–14, 109; data 11, 47, 54

Oxenham, J. 28, 151

Paldam, M. 16

Peru: child undernourishment 85–6, 122–5; development aid to 89–91,

94–6; food security in 83–6, 112, 122–5; governance quality 100–2, 112–13; mining in 112; relationship with donors 94–6

Petrikova, I. 21–2, 30, 47, 55, 65, 126, 182, 196

Pinstrup-Andersen, P. 7, 27, 189

population growth xiii, 30–1, 105–6; in Ethiopia 87

poverty 16–17, 33; in Ethiopia 86–7; in India 88–9, 160–1; in Peru 85–6; in Vietnam 87–8; relationship with economic growth 173

principal component analysis 130, 160

Public-Private Partnerships (PPPs) 24, **57**, 69, 92, 181; *see also* development aid

race 33

Rajan, R. 59, 67, 194

Ramalingaswami, V. 88, 172

Ravallion, M. 28, 126, 131

remittances 31, 34, 65–6, 185–6

research methods: mixed 46, 176; qualitative 44, 50–1, 81–3, 156–7; quantitative 44, 50–1, 59–60, 131–3, 156–7

right to food 191–3

Rodrik, D. 50, 56, 81

Roodman, D. 16, 60

Ruel, M. 33, 122, 190

rural-urban divide 33, 80, 86, 190

Sen, A. 85, 89, 104, 111, 173

social capital 8, 34; cognitive 126, 130, 135

'South Asian' enigma 88, 124, 151, 172–3

South-South Cooperation *see* donors, non-DAC

Strauss, J. 33–4, 126

stunting 47, 51n2, 54, 73; *see also* undernourishment and hunger

Subramanian, A. 59, 67, 194

Swaroop, V. 24, 98

Tarp, F. 16, 35n10, 59

Thomas, D. 33–4, 126

trade 31, 56, 65, **103**

undernourishment 7, 10, 47, 54, 56, 73; *see also* Ethiopia, India, Peru and Vietnam

underweight 47, 51n2, 54, 73; *see also* undernourishment and hunger

United Nations Development Programme (UNDP) 13–14

urbanisation 33, 86, 130, 190

Uvin, P. 25, 194–5

Vietnam: agricultural aid to **95**, 99–100, 104–5, 109, 122–5; child undernourishment **85**, 87–8, 109; development aid to 89–91, 99–100; 'doi moi' 87, 115n3; food security in 83–4, 87–8, 109, 122–5; governance quality 100–2, 109, 113; relationship with donors 99–100; social safety nets 109–10
volatility *see* development aid
Von Braun, J. 13, 27, 33, 87, 107

water scarcity 87, 106, 188
Water, Sanitation, and Hygiene (WASH) 150, 154–5, 167–8, 172–3

Weber, A. 17, 59
World Bank (WB) 13, 24, 88, 98
World Development Indicators (WDI) 56, 80, 85–8, 109, 130, 182
World Food Programme (WFP) 83, 86
World Health Organisation (WHO) 7, 47, 54, 80, 82, 109, 111, 122, 124, 151, 172

Yontcheva, B. 16, 22
Young Lives 45, 80, 121–2, 124–6, 130, 145, 173n3

Zerbe, N. 25, 189